D0203707

Contemplative Practices in Action

Contemplative Practices in Action

Spirituality, Meditation, and Health

THOMAS G. PLANTE, PhD, EDITOR

Foreword by Huston Smith, PhD

 PRAEGER

AN IMPRINT OF ABC-CLIO, LLC
Santa Barbara, California • Denver, Colorado • Oxford, England

Library of Congress Cataloging-in-Publication Data

Contemplative practices in action : spirituality, meditation, and health / edited by Thomas G. Plante ; foreword by Huston Smith.
    p. ; cm.
  Includes bibliographical references and index.
  ISBN 978–0–313–38256–7 (hard copy : alk. paper) — ISBN 978–0–313–38257–4 (ebook)
1. Meditation—Health aspects. 2. Medicine—Religious aspects. I. Plante, Thomas G.
  [DNLM: 1. Mind-Body Relations (Metaphysics) 2. Religion and Medicine.
3. Spirituality. WB 880 C761 2010]
BL65.M4C587   2010
204′.35—dc22   2010006509

ISBN: 978–0–313–38256–7
EISBN: 978–0–313–38257–4

14 13 12 11 10   1 2 3 4 5

This book is also available on the World Wide Web as an eBook.
Visit www.abc-clio.com for details.

Praeger
An Imprint of ABC-CLIO, LLC

ABC-CLIO, LLC
130 Cremona Drive, P.O. Box 1911
Santa Barbara, California 93116-1911

This book is printed on acid-free paper ∞

Manufactured in the United States of America

Contents

Foreword

If I ask myself why it is I who has been asked to write the Foreword to this important book, I suspect that it is because it is in line with my own book, *The World's Religions*, which is, like this one, ecumenically inclusive. In its 14 chapters, *Contemplative Practices in Action* introduces a broad array of contemplative practices drawn from Hinduism, Buddhism, Christianity, Islam, and Judaism. No faith or religion is accorded privileged status above others.

However, towering above the virtue (which I consider it to be) of ecumenism, is this book's persuasive conviction that the world's religions house inexhaustible resources for transforming and augmenting the human spirit, a conviction with which I concur.

There is another and somewhat more personal connection, however, which has to do with the fact that the Eight-Point Program of Passage Meditation developed by the late Eknath Easwaran figures importantly in several chapters of *Contemplative Practices in Action*. Easwaran was a professor of English from Kerala, in South India, who came to this country on a Fulbright fellowship in 1959 and became a widely read and deeply respected teacher of meditation who lived out his days in an ashram in Northern California. I had the privilege of meeting him more than once and held him in high regard.

On several occasions, friends drove me to Easwaran's ashram to participate in the evening gatherings of the community that sprang up around him. After supper, residents would join their teacher to listen to his short homilies, ask questions about their spiritual practice, or simply sit quietly in the community's soothing, collective peace. Those evenings made me think of Mahatma Gandhi's ashram, where, after their simple suppers, villagers would gather around their leader for brief prayer meetings. Gandhi always made sure those services included prayers and scriptural readings from all the great religious traditions, and so did Easwaran.

That is half of the story, and the book in hand tells the other half. Contemplative evenings with a great spiritual teacher are not ends in themselves. It would not be amiss to think of them as times when communicants recharge their batteries for the next day's work. The title of this book, *Contemplative Practices in Action*, splices the two halves together. Like Gandhi, like the Buddha, like all great spiritual teachers, Easwaran had no use for beliefs unless they generated actions. Doing, not saying, is what counts.

Welcome to this book, which ought not to leave any serious reader unchanged.

Huston Smith
Berkeley, California
January 2010

Preface

There has been a remarkable amount of interest in the relationship between science, faith, and contemplative practices such as meditation for centuries and perhaps especially in most recent years as new scientifically based research and clinical findings have appeared in the professional and popular press. In addition to the publication of high-quality scholarly articles and books, the popular news weeklies such as *Time* and *Newsweek* have published cover stories on this topic on multiple occasions in recent months and years. The professional, medical, and psychological community has responded with numerous conferences, articles, and scholarly activities that have greatly helped move this area of research and practice forward. In fact, our Spirituality and Health Institute (SHI) group here at Santa Clara University recently published an edited book on spirituality and health entitled *Spirit, Science, and Health: How the Spiritual Mind Fuels Physical Wellness* (2007, Greenwood). In this book, we examined a broad range of topics that highlight both research and practice in spirituality and health integration. In this book project, we would like to focus our attention on contemplative practices such as meditation among the various religious and spiritual traditions in efforts to improve health and well-being. Contemplative practices such as mindfulness meditation have become very popular both in the general population as well as among health care professionals. However, mindfulness is just one of many contemplative practices that have been successfully used in various professional and nonprofessional health care outlets that also have adequate research support for their use in improving both psychological and physical health. Other contemplative approaches generally have not entered the public or professional imagination. Our book project seeks to help to educate a wide audience in the various forms of contemplative practices used within a wider range of spiritual and religious traditions in achieving well-being, wisdom, and healing, most especially in these stressful times.

This book seeks to provide a scholarly and multidisciplinary approach on the topic of contemplative practices for the development of well-being, wisdom, healing, and stress management that includes state-of-the-art science, practice, and applications of contemplative practices in the professional workplace, educational settings, pastoral care, and medical, psychological, or other health care interventions. The chapters articulate current findings and practice in contemplative practices from a wide range of religious and spiritual traditions and from experts in the integration of contemplative practices and psychology, nursing, pastoral care, business, and so forth in order to achieve well-being.

In order to avoid some of the disadvantages of edited books, which sometimes feel fragmented, and to increase the flow between chapters, almost all of the contributors participated in a conference at Santa Clara University during October 2009 to present their research to each other and to the local professional health care community. The conference was cosponsored by Santa Clara University Center for Professional Development, the Ignatian Center, and generously funded by a Bannan grant and SHI. Furthermore, many of the contributors are members of SHI who meet regularly to discuss multidisciplinary research and practice in the area of spirituality and health. We hope that the conference and ongoing research institute activities have resulted in a more cohesive and seamless book.

Acknowledgments

Numerous people other than the author or editor assist in the development and completion of a book project. Some provide help in a direct and concrete manner while others provide help in less direct and more supportive ways. We would like to acknowledge the assistance of the many people who have helped in both ways and have contributed to the development of this project.

First, I would like to thank the many wonderful people at ABC-CLIO who have enthusiastically worked to publish this book (most especially my editor, Deborah Carvalko, for her interest in the project and her high level of professionalism). I would also like to thank the production staff as well.

Second, I would like to thank the Santa Clara University Ignatian Center for Jesuit Education (Fr. Kevin Quinn, SJ, Director, and Paul Woolley, Assistant Director) for funding and supporting our research institute and activities on campus, including this project and the associated October 2009 conference.

Third, special thanks to Professor Doug Oman at UC Berkeley, who provided thoughtful and detailed commentary on many of the chapters and supplied the prefaces to the three main parts of the book.

Finally, I would like to thank my wife, Lori, and son, Zach, for being who they are.

CHAPTER 1

Introduction: Contemplative Practices in Action

Thomas G. Plante, Adi Raz, and Doug Oman

Several decades ago in his book *The Meditative Mind*,[1] Daniel Goleman reviewed more than a dozen major Eastern and Western methods of contemplative practice, ranging from Christian hesychasm and Jewish Kaballah to Transcendental Meditation and Tibetan Buddhism. He reported that two major approaches or strategies to meditation were incorporated: One recurrent approach was concentration, that is, focused attention on a single object, such as the breath, a mantram, or a prayer. The other recurrent approach was mindfulness (the detached observation of one's thinking process). Sometimes concentration and mindfulness were used separately, and sometimes they were combined in various ways. Goleman argued that both mindfulness and concentrative meditation have been directed to a single objective, the retraining of attention, a skill that he believed "amplifies the effectiveness of any kind of activity" (p. 168). Goleman also reported that "the need for the meditator to retrain his attention, whether through concentration or mindfulness, is the single invariant ingredient in the recipe for altering consciousness of every meditation system" (p. 107). Nearly a century earlier, William James, one of the founders of modern psychology, had argued that "the faculty of voluntarily bringing back a wandering attention, over and over again, is the very root of judgment, character, and will. . . . An education which should improve this faculty would be *the* education *par excellence*" (p. 424).[2]

In modern health promotion, psychotherapy, and other human service interventions, these contemplative practices have largely been taken out of their religious and spiritual contexts and then secularized and repackaged.[3,4] For example, the health and mental health care community has incorporated mindfulness meditation in recent years with numerous books, workshops, conferences, and trainings being offered. Yoga studios can be found in many strip malls, and meditation workshops are offered by human resource departments in many diverse companies.[5]

The currently popular mindfulness meditation approach stems from Zen Buddhism and Hindu yogic practices, and it is a common misconception that only by borrowing from these Eastern traditions can one secure any benefits from contemplative practices. Many Christians and Jews, for example, who identify and engage with their religious tradition, are often not aware of the long history of contemplative practices within their own faith tradition. As many in our culture have become more familiar and comfortable with the Eastern contemplative practices, the Western practices have been largely ignored, even though they also often offer contemplative approaches that can provide effective stress management, well-being, and healing.[6,7]

All of the major religious and spiritual traditions have developed specific principles and techniques to help their members assimilate contemplative perspectives and behaviors aimed at fostering a fuller experience of wisdom, wholeness, and enlightenment.[1,7,8] Research studies have reported many physical and mental health benefits from regular contemplative practices, as well as confirming their stress management functions.[4,5,9,10] Benson,[11] for example, has documented that meditation helps to promote a "relaxation response." He argues that when meditation is associated with one's religious or spiritual convictions, it further enhances relaxation, leading to greater psychological and physical health benefits. Recent well-controlled research studies have further supported Benson's arguments, reporting advantages for spiritually based meditation over otherwise nearly identical secular forms of meditation.[12,13]

There are a number of books available on contemplative practices. However, almost all focus on one particular religious or spiritual tradition and most are practice oriented without solid research grounding. Usually, they highlight the Eastern traditions and overlook the Western ones. This is especially true among books that target the health and mental health care communities.[6,7]

The purpose of this book is to examine contemplative practices from a wide variety of both Eastern and Western religious and spiritual traditions and to examine their commonalities and unique approaches to improved well-being, health, healing, wholeness, and stress management. Chapters are written by experts in their fields, most of whom are affiliated with the Spirituality and Health Institute at Santa Clara University in Santa Clara, California. Each chapter will discuss the state-of-the-art science, practice, and general applications of contemplative practices in the professional workplace, educational settings, pastoral care, and medical, psychological, or other health care environments. This book hopes to be inclusive in coverage of contemplative practices, and integrate science and practice in a balanced manner and from a variety of Eastern and Western sources.

This book will discuss several different contemplative approaches to stress management and achieving well-being. Some chapters highlight approaches from Western traditions while others highlight contemplative approaches from Eastern traditions. Others are integrative of both Western and Eastern traditions. Some are more closely connected to religious traditions and practices while others are not. Several chapters will highlight application to business and health care as well.

Oman (Chapter 2) has pointed out that four similar functions are performed in diverse ways by elements within many of the contemplative systems discussed in this book. Most approaches involve setting aside time for practices that reshape and train attention; most also include elements for centering oneself throughout the day, cultivating personal character strengths, and drawing inspiration and guidance from spiritual exemplars. Oman suggests using the phrase "integrated contemplative practice system" for systems of practice that encompass all four of these elements that are highlighted in this volume.

Sadly, it is impossible to include a discussion of every contemplative practice and practice system in one book. We cannot do justice to the numerous practice systems or isolated spiritual techniques that are not represented here. For example, the role of the rosary in the Roman Catholic tradition, shamanism, and the role of chanting in Hindu Bhakti traditions are just some of the many contemplative practices that are not presented here. Rather than presenting an exhaustive review of the contemplative practices among the various religious and spiritual traditions, our hope is to provide a helpful selection by leading figures in their respective fields to assist with stress management, healing, wholeness, and well-being. The contributors met for an all-day conference with university and health care community members during October 2009. This allowed all of the authors to listen to and consult with each other as well as with diverse professionals in the local San Francisco Bay Area professional community in order to hopefully create a more thoughtful, seamless, and comprehensive book project. We hope that our efforts will encourage the reader to have a better understanding and appreciation of contemplative practices in action.

REFERENCES

1. Goleman, D. (1988). *The meditative mind: The variety of meditative experience*. Los Angeles: Tarcher.

2. James, W. (1890/1923). *The principles of psychology*. New York: Henry Holt.

3. Kabat-Zinn, J. (1990). *Full catastrophe living*. New York: Delacorte Press.

4. Kabat-Zinn, J. (2003). Mindfulness-based interventions in context: Past, present, and future. *Clinical Psychology: Research and Practice, 10*, 144–156.

5. Walsh, R., & Shapiro, S. L. (2006). The meeting of meditative disciplines and Western psychology: A mutually enriching dialogue. *American Psychologist, 61*, 227–239.

6. Plante, T. G. (2008). What do the spiritual and religious traditions offer the practicing psychologist? *Pastoral Psychology, 56*, 429–444.

7. Plante, T. G. (2009). *Spiritual practices in psychotherapy: Thirteen tools for enhancing psychological health*. Washington, DC: American Psychological Association.

8. Walsh, R. (1999). *Essential spirituality: The seven central practices*. New York: Wiley.

9. Borman, J. E., Gifford, A. L., Shively, M., Smith, T. L., Redwine, L., Kelly, A., et al. (2006). Effects of spiritual mantram repetition on HIV outcomes: A randomized controlled trial. *Journal of Behavioral Medicine, 29*, 359–376.

10. Brown, K. W., Ryan, R. M., & Cresswell, J. D. (2007). Mindfulness: Theoretical foundations and evidence for its salutary effects. *Psychological Inquiry, 18*, 211–237.

11. Benson, H. (1996). *Timeless healing*. New York: Scribner.

12. Wachholtz, A. B., & Pargament, K. I. (2005). Is spirituality a critical ingredient of meditation? Comparing the effects of spiritual meditation, secular meditation, and relaxation on spiritual, psychological, cardiac, and pain outcomes. *Journal of Behavioral Medicine, 28*, 369–384.

13. Wachholtz, A. B., & Pargament, K. I. (2008). Migraines and meditation: Does spirituality matter? *Journal of Behavioral Medicine, 31*, 351–366.

PART ONE

INTEGRATED CONTEMPLATIVE PRACTICE SYSTEMS

PREFACE TO PART ONE

Part One, "Integrated Contemplative Practice Systems," focuses on systems of practice from both East and West that are well defined and sufficiently limited in scope that they can be undertaken in their entirety by a single individual. First, Oman's short introductory chapter offers a conceptual analysis and overview, unique in this volume, that describes four shared elements that are present in many of these practice systems. His chapter includes a table that shows the specific names used to describe these elements in each of the additional chapters in this section, as well as the names used in chapters in Part Two ("Contemplative Traditions").

Each of the remaining four chapters in this part examines a single contemplative practice system. Attention is directed in turn at Mindfulness-Based Stress Reduction (Jazaieri and Shapiro), Passage Meditation (Flinders, Oman, Flinders, and Dreher), Centering Prayer (Ferguson), and repetition of a mantram or holy name (Bormann). Most of these practices can be undertaken within any major faith tradition, although Centering Prayer is essentially Christian. Bormann's mantram/holy name repetition practices were extracted from the Passage Meditation system by its developer, and contain only two of the four elements described by Oman. But as Bormann points out, the mantram/holy name is noteworthy for its portability, power, and universality. It highlights powerful but oft-forgotten practices that can be found within each major faith tradition, and which can complement these traditions' better-known elements.

CHAPTER 2

Similarity in Diversity? Four Shared Functions of Integrative Contemplative Practice Systems

Doug Oman

The reader of this volume, impressed by the rich descriptions of many diverse systems of spiritual practice, may start to wonder, "What are the shared themes? What patterns emerge amidst this inspiring profusion of perspectives?" In this chapter, I sketch one possible answer— one way of characterizing shared themes and functions that appear in many different systems of practice. Along the way, I propose using the term *integrated contemplative practice* to describe systems of practice that meet a certain functional threshold.

Four common elements or themes can be found, I suggest, in most of the practice systems described in the next eight chapters. These commonalities exist even though some chapters describe *comprehensive and clearly defined systems*, whereas others present *instructively selected highlights* from venerable traditions. More specifically, the next four chapters in Part One examine well-defined systems of interrelated practices that are challenging, but can be undertaken by individuals in their entirety. Three systems partly or wholly transcend individual faith traditions (e.g., Mindfulness, Passage Meditation, Mantram), whereas the fourth (Christian-derived Centering Prayer) arose within a particular faith tradition. In contrast, all four chapters in Part Two explore venerable schools (yoga, Zen) or major traditions (Judaism, Islam)[1] that constitute storehouses of wisdom accumulated over many centuries. Each of these schools or traditions, viewed in its entirety, has accumulated a richer repertoire of techniques than any one individual can fully implement.

One shared function of many spiritual practice systems was described in the 1980s by Daniel Goleman. He surveyed more than a dozen methods of meditation, both East and West, and reported that "the need for the meditator to retrain [his or her] attention . . . is the single invariant ingredient in the recipe . . . of every meditation system" (p. 107).[2] Indeed, it seems quite likely that almost all of the practices discussed in this book, when undertaken regularly over time, will affect— and may sometimes transform—how people habitually deploy their attention. But can we identify any specific and concrete forms of resemblance between traditions?

Several concrete resemblances can indeed be identified. Recently, my colleagues and I at the Spirituality and Health Institute (SHI) observed several elements in common between two paradigmatic systems of practice.[3,4] More specifically, we found four distinct functions that were each accomplished, in slightly different ways, by these two integrated contemplative practice systems: Passage Meditation (PM) (Flinders et al., this volume) and mindfulness-based stress reduction (MBSR) (Jazaieri and Shapiro, this volume).

Both PM and MBSR, we noted, require *setting aside time*—substantial time—approximately half an hour daily—for undertaking a powerful attention-training activity. For this purpose, PM and MBSR each use a form of sitting meditation. Similarly, PM and MBSR each recommend specific *mental centering/stabilizing practices* to be used throughout the day to stabilize and balance the mind in conditions of stress or boredom (PM uses mantram repetition, and MBSR uses informal mindfulness practices). These analogous elements do not perform functions that are fully identical matches—rather, to borrow a phrase from positive psychology, these analogous elements, and the precise functions they perform, may be said to share a "coherent resemblance" (p. 35).[5]

Table 2.1 shows that with few exceptions, variants of these four elements are prevalent not only in PM and MBSR, but in each set of contemplative practices covered in the next eight chapters. These four shared elements, or features, are as follows:

1. *Set-aside time*—time that is set aside regularly, usually daily, for a disciplined activity or exercise that has a comparatively

powerful effect on training attention.[2] Variants of sitting meditation are commonly used. Some systems in this book also use prescribed postures (e.g., yoga, Islam). Such attention training can support optimal performance in all spheres of life, since "attention is the first and often most effective line of defense in nearly every sphere of self-control" (p. 1172).[6] Most attention training fosters concentration, and "powerful concentration amplifies the effectiveness of any kind of activity" (p. 168).[2] The attention-training functions of meditation are supported by recent neuroimaging evidence.[7]

2. *Virtues and character strengths*—qualities of character and behavior, such as compassion, forgiveness, or fearlessness. In many systems, such qualities are to be cultivated throughout the day by making appropriate choices in thoughts, words, and actions. Typically, the recommended qualities involve subsets of six cross-culturally prevalent classes of virtues recently identified by positive psychologists—wisdom, courage, humanity, justice, temperance, and transcendence.[5]

3. *Practices for centering/stabilizing that are usable throughout the day*— such as during occasions of stress, anxiety, or unstructured time. Examples include returning the mind to the breath (MBSR), or returning the mind to repeating a mantram or holy name.[8,9] Here, the contemporary word "center" (small *c*) is used to designate recovery of a sense of inner strength and balance. (This contrasts with the term "Centering Prayer," which designates a specific system of Christian-derived practices,[10] described elsewhere in this volume by Ferguson.)

4. *Spiritual models*—attending to individuals whose behavior reflects desired spiritual qualities—provide a unique resource for spiritual growth. Spiritual and religious educators have long viewed spirituality as primarily "caught, not taught" (p. 149),[11] since so much of human learning is social. Spiritual and religious traditions, and many of the practice systems described in this book, transmit words of revered or instructive spiritual models, such as Jesus, the Buddha, Muhammad, or various sages and saints.[12] Attending to spiritual models' words and actions can motivate sustained practice, and guide or inspire implementation of other spiritual practices (e.g., #1–#3).

Table 2.1. Presence and Naming of Features by Contemplative Practice Type

Practice System	1 Set-Aside (/Dedicated) Attention Training	2 Virtuous/Mindful Attitudes	3 Centering Practice Usable Throughout Day	4 Spiritual Models/Exemplars[a]
Integrated Contemplative Practice Systems (Part One)				
Mindfulness (/Vipassana)[b]	Sitting meditation (on breath)	Mindfulness attitudes	Informal practices	Poetry
Passage Meditation[b]	Sitting meditation (on a passage)	Put others first; + additional	Mantram repetition	Passages; reading
Centering Prayer	Sitting meditation (with sacred word)	Implicit;[c] silence, solitude, service	Prayers: active; welcoming	Implicit[c]
Mantram[d]		Focus; slow	Mantram repetition	
Contemplative Traditions (Part Two)				
Judaism	Sabbath;[e] prayer; meditation	Implicit;[c] peace, calm, equanimity	Repeat verse (liturgy/scripture)	Implicit;[c] teachers/Rebbes[f]
Islam	Five daily prayers	Many (justice, gentleness, etc.)	Dhikr (remembrance); supplication	The Prophet/aḥādīth

| Yoga | Asanas +meditation | Yamas (truth, nonviolence, etc.) | | Lineage of teacher |
| Zen | Sitting meditation (Zazen) | Brahma Viharas (compassion, etc.) | Mindfulness; letting go | Teaching stories; teacher |

Others Combinations or Systems—Yours, Your Client's, or Your Student's

1. _____
2. _____
3. _____

Note: For a fuller explanation of each practice system, see corresponding chapter in this volume; lists of practices contained in each cell may be incomplete.

[a] The final column describes learning from traditional or prominent models, but most systems also encourage spiritual fellowship to foster learning from positive models in the local community.

[b] Mindfulness and Passage Meditation are the two paradigms used to develop the four categories.

[c] "Implicit" practice categories are typically enacted when an individual engages in traditional observance, especially communal worship. For example, Jewish and Christian services in synagogues and churches often include scripture readings about virtuous conduct and spiritual models such as Moses or Jesus.

[d] Mantram/holy name repetition as presented by Bormann lacks the full set of four elements that comprise an integral contemplative practice system, but it is extracted from such a system (Passage Meditation).

[e] The Sabbath cycle is weekly (not daily).

[f] See Silberman[25] on Rebbes as spiritual models.

Figure 2.1 shows how these four elements of practice can work together in concert to foster spiritual growth and related outcomes. In every system, these elements are intended for integration into one's daily and weekly routines of life,[13] through which they may gradually transform "character, conduct and consciousness" (p. 37).[14] As tools for retraining attention, they reinforce each other. They address multiple needs and opportunities that arise in the ordinary rhythms and textures of daily living. Like a well-designed course of instruction or a healthy physical exercise routine, they provide for periods of heightened intensity and immersion (#1, set-aside time), application of skills in diverse contexts (#2 character strengths and #3 centering/stabilizing), and overall guidance and inspiration (#4 spiritual models).

The model in Figure 2.1 suggests that these four elements function synergistically, by reinforcing each other. Like the nutritional contributions of complementary food groups,[15] these four types of practice together may generate greater benefits than obtainable separately from individual practices. Of course, the model in Figure 2.1 is far from complete in representing *all* of the psychological and spiritual processes that operate in real time. Other factors include an

Figure 2.1.   Elements Function Dynamically in Concert.

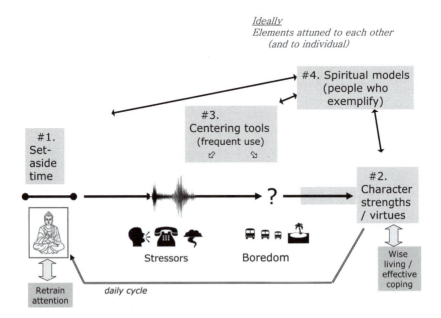

individual's need for a valid and coherent worldview,[16] and the influence of spiritual fellowship.[11,17] For this reason, forms of "spiritual
shopping" (p. 126)[18] that are blind, that incoherently mix and match
incompatible elements from discordant practice traditions, will rarely
be optimal. Spiritual benefits, one might hypothesize, are maximized
when the elements interface and cohere harmoniously with each other,
like pieces of a well-constructed musical instrument, or threads in a
well-crafted tapestry. *How* to best evaluate the coherence of a set of practices is, of course, a perennially controversial and important issue—
and one that cannot be resolved here.

Practical applications flow from recognizing the synergistic interre-
lation of elements in these four categories. For example, an individual
could use the four categories as a checklist to review the complete-
ness of his or her own practice, from the standpoint of the model in
Figure 2.1. More broadly, the four elements might function as a
checklist for a psychotherapist to help a client in reviewing his or her
practice, or for an educator to lead students in reviewing or augmenting their own practices. To distinguish it from something less
complete, my SHI colleagues and I propose that a system of practices
that encompasses elements from all four categories should be desig-
nated an *integral contemplative practice system*.

In the practice systems examined in this book, centering activities (#3)
are perhaps most commonly missing, or underemphasized in real-world
implementations. A useful resource to redress this neglect is offered by
Bormann's chapter (this volume). She highlights mantram/holy name
repetition, a cross-culturally common practice that produces centering.
When sought, variations of mantram repetition can be found in many
faith traditions and practice systems, including several described in this
volume.

For individuals who are interested or engaged in some form of spiritual practice—about 80 percent of U.S. adults, according to a recent
national survey (p. 79)[19]—the following questions may prove practically
beneficial:

1. Do I currently draw spiritual support, strength, and reinforcement
   through engaging in practices in each of the four categories listed
   earlier? That is, do I enjoy the spiritual support of an *integral
   contemplative practice*?

2. If not, can I expand my practice in ways that are personally
   appropriate and consistent with my tradition and beliefs?

3. How can I extend my practice in a way that is most harmonious and complementary to my existing practices?

Such questions may also be relevant to the growing roster of for-profit and nonprofit organizations seeking to systematically integrate spirituality into the workplace[20,21] (see also Delbecq, this volume, whose executive seminars have addressed all four elements).

Even beyond its relevance to spiritual practice, of course, many benefits can flow from identifying commonalities across faith traditions. Recognizing similarities may facilitate intercultural understanding, foster improved communication between human service professionals and diverse clients, and contribute to better education and health care. This chapter has described similarities in daily spiritual practices. Similarities also exist at other levels, ranging from the institutional[22] to the philosophical.[23] Comparatively few earlier writers, such as Walsh[24] and Easwaran,[14] have examined similarities in practices. Yet daily practice is at the core of applying spirituality to address real-world problems. Our analyses suggest that diverse faith traditions have recommended similarly integrated systems of contemplative practice. I encourage readers to consider how these four categories may apply to their own practices, and that of their clients, students, fellow congregants, and organizations, as well as to the practice systems described in the next eight chapters in this book.

REFERENCES

1. Hamdan (this volume) describes practices from Islamic Sunni tradition; also within Islam is Shia tradition, as well as Islam's mystical side, Sufism, a phenomenon "so broad [and with] appearance so protean that nobody can venture to describe it fully" (p. 3), according to Schimmel, A. (1975). *Mystical dimensions of Islam*. Chapel Hill: University of North Carolina Press.

2. Goleman, D. (1988). *The meditative mind: The varieties of meditative experience*. New York: Tarcher.

3. Oman, D., Shapiro, S. L., Thoresen, C. E., Plante, T. G., & Flinders, T. (2008). Meditation lowers stress and supports forgiveness among college students: A randomized controlled trial. *Journal of American College Health*, *56*, 569–578.

4. Oman, D., Shapiro, S. L., Thoresen, C. E., Flinders, T., Driskill, J. D., & Plante, T. G. (2007). Learning from spiritual models and meditation: A randomized evaluation of a college course. *Pastoral Psychology*, *55*, 473–493.

5. Peterson, C., & Seligman, M. E. P. (2004). *Character strengths and virtues: A handbook and classification*. Washington, DC, and New York: American Psychological Association and Oxford University Press. "To say that particular virtues . . . converge . . . is not to argue that all their features line up perfectly, but rather that they have a coherent resemblance to one another, sharing more features than not" (p. 35).

6. Baumeister, R. F., & Exline, J. J. (1999). Virtue, personality, and social relations: Self-control as the moral muscle. *Journal of Personality, 67*, 1165–1194.

7. Lutz, A., Slagter, H. A., Rawlings, N. B., Francis, A. D., Greischar, L. L., & Davidson, R. J. (2009). Mental training enhances attentional stability: Neural and behavioral evidence. *Journal of Neuroscience, 29*, 13418–13427.

8. Oman, D., & Driskill, J. D. (2003). Holy name repetition as a spiritual exercise and therapeutic technique. *Journal of Psychology and Christianity, 22*, 5–19.

9. Baesler, E. J. (2001). The prayer of the holy name in Eastern and Western spiritual traditions: A theoretical, cross-cultural, and intercultural prayer dialogue. *Journal of Ecumenical Studies, 38*, 196–216.

10. The term "Centering Prayer" was adopted in the 1970s by three Trappist monks to describe a system of practices they had codified; and one of its earliest published uses was in Pennington, M. B. (1980). *Centering prayer*. Garden City, NY: Doubleday.

11. Oman, D., & Thoresen, C. E. (2003). Spiritual modeling: A key to spiritual and religious growth? *International Journal for the Psychology of Religion, 13*, 149–165.

12. Oman, D., & Thoresen, C. E. (2007). How does one learn to be spiritual? The neglected role of spiritual modeling in health. In T. G. Plante & C. E. Thoresen (Eds.), *Spirit, science and health: How the spiritual mind fuels physical wellness* (pp. 39–54). Westport, CT: Praeger.

13. Fiese, B. H., Tomcho, T. J., Douglas, M., Josephs, K., Poltrock, S., & Baker, T. (2002). A review of 50 years of research on naturally occurring family routines and rituals: Cause for celebration? *Journal of Family Psychology, 16*, 381–390.

14. Easwaran, E. (1978/2008). *Passage meditation: Bringing the deep wisdom of the heart into daily life*. Tomales, CA: Nilgiri Press (full text: http://www.easwaran.org).

15. Robertson, L., Flinders, C., & Ruppenthal, B. (1986). *The new laurel's kitchen: A handbook for vegetarian cookery & nutrition*. Berkeley, CA: Ten Speed Press.

16. Antonovsky, A. (1987). *Unraveling the mystery of health: How people manage stress and stay well*. San Francisco: Jossey-Bass.

17. Oman, D., Thoresen, C. E., Park, C. L., Shaver, P. R., Hood, R. W., & Plante, T. G. (2009). How does one become spiritual? The Spiritual Modeling Inventory of Life Environments (SMILE). *Mental Health, Religion & Culture, 12*, 427–456.

18. Wuthnow, R. (2005). *America and the challenges of religious diversity*. Princeton, NJ: Princeton University Press.

19. Gallup, G., & Lindsay, D. M. (1999). *Surveying the religious landscape: Trends in U.S. beliefs*. Harrisburg, PA: Morehouse.

20. Giacalone, R. A., & Jurkiewicz, C. L. (2003). *Handbook of workplace spirituality and organizational performance*. Armonk, NY: M.E. Sharpe.

21. Duerr, M. (2004). The contemplative organization. *Journal of Organizational Change Management, 17*, 43–61.

22. Smart, N. (1996). *Dimensions of the sacred: An anatomy of the world's beliefs*. Berkeley: University of California Press.

23. Smith, H. (1976/1992). *Forgotten truth: The common vision of the world's religions*. San Francisco: HarperSanFrancisco.

24. Walsh, R. N. (1999). *Essential spirituality: The 7 central practices to awaken heart and mind*. New York: Wiley.

25. Silberman, I. (2003). Spiritual role modeling: The teaching of meaning systems. *International Journal for the Psychology of Religion, 13*, 175–195.

CHAPTER 3

Managing Stress Mindfully

Hooria Jazaieri and Shauna L. Shapiro

Mindfulness, a translation of the traditional Eastern words including *smrti* (Sanskrit), *sati* (Pali), and *dranpa* (Tibetan), is associated in contemporary Western psychology as the awareness one achieves through intentionally attending in an accepting and discerning way to one's current moment-to-moment experience.[1,2] Mindfulness involves an intimate knowing of what is arising as it is arising, without trying to change or control it. Thus, the process of mindfulness involves changing one's relationship to experience as opposed to changing experience itself.

Any activity can be an opportunity to practice mindfulness—walking, washing dishes, eating, conversing—anything, as long as you are bringing full attention to the present. Essentially, life itself becomes the practice as every moment is a new opportunity to train your attention, thus creating the ability to respond to stress instead of habitually reacting. Mindfulness is a natural human capacity, *and* it can be cultivated through formal practice.

Often we are told that being mindful takes too much time or effort, or at times, seems counterproductive to our culture of doing. Mindfulness does in fact require us to stop in a sense—this may feel awkward, uncomfortable, or unproductive at first. However, when practicing mindfulness, the goal is not to get anywhere or do anything. It is not about being or feeling a certain way. It is about trusting that you are already where you need to be, and you already are the way you need to be. Mindfulness requires the element of letting go and allowing things to unfold in their own natural way:

> [It is] an invitation to cease clinging to anything—whether it be an idea, a thing, an event, a particular time, or view, or desire. It is a conscious decision to release with full acceptance into the stream of present moments as they are unfolding. To let go means to give up coercing, resisting, or struggling, in exchange for something more powerful and wholesome which comes out of allowing things to be as they are without getting caught up in your attraction to or rejection of them, in the intrinsic stickiness of wanting, of liking and disliking. It's akin to letting your palm open to unhand something you have been holding on to.[3]

Although the notion of mindfulness is often associated with the rich, 2,600-year-old tradition of Buddhism, it is currently being applied as a universal technique that transcends its religious and cultural roots. With this recontextualization of mindfulness comes different aims; among them the contemporarily relevant aim of managing stress through easing suffering and improving health and well-being. In this chapter, we will briefly describe the historical and religious context from which mindfulness arose, describe the dimensions of the practice and how someone may begin some of the basic exercises, briefly review the empirical literature supporting mindfulness as a treatment intervention, discuss preexisting applications of this practice, and present ideas for new research directions. Our hope is to introduce practices and resources to help manage stress, as well as a radically different way of seeing and being in the world that naturally gives rise to greater states of happiness and ease.

CONTEXT

Although most often associated with Buddhism, mindfulness can be found in various forms in virtually all religions and spiritual practices.[4] Methods to enable individuals to focus their attention have been around for centuries, and while the approaches are different, the intention behind them is similar—to alter people's lives.[5] According to Buddhist psychology, suffering comes from our wanting things to be different from what they really are, whether that is wishing for another job, for more money, for a different appearance, or even to be happier. Neuroscientist Daniel Siegel[5] suggests that stress and suffering occur when the mind grasps onto what "should be" and creates this tension between what really is. Though we are presenting mindfulness meditation here as a means of stress management, it is important to note that in Buddhism, the intention of mindfulness training is not for "stress management" but to achieve complete liberation from suffering and compassion for all beings.[6]

However as mindfulness has gone "mainstream"—a recent Google search of the term returned 2,630,000 results—the aims and understandings have been recontextualized to fit a modern Western culture. The clinical application of mindfulness meditation (also referred to as "insight meditation" or "Vipassana") in Western psychology can largely be attributed to Jon Kabat-Zinn and colleagues at the University of Massachusetts's mindfulness-based stress reduction (MBSR)[7] program. Though MBSR was originally developed to help manage chronic pain, it is currently practiced worldwide and is used with a variety of populations ranging from grade school students to those with psychopathology. The skills one acquires through MBSR have been shown to reduce anxiety and depression symptoms[8] as well as increase positive emotional states.[9] MBSR truly is "compatible with diverse cultural and religious backgrounds."[10] Regardless of its religious and cultural origins, mindfulness-based interventions have been introduced by researchers and clinicians as an empirically supported treatment (or component of) program.

Our lives are full of chronic and acute stressors—some are predictable while others catch us off guard. Some are real while others are imagined. Mindfulness mediation is thought to affect the stress response in four stages—first, by freeing the senses from anything that is occupying them. Second, with practice, it provides the participant with tools to observe patterns of reacting or responding. Third, with even more practice, conditioned and habitual ways of reacting and responding gradually weaken. Finally, mindfulness meditation affects the stress response by allowing one to have a more effective and "wiser" response to any experience that emerges.[11]

DIMENSIONS OF THE PRACTICE

Some claim that in order to gain success in any field, one must practice the specific task for 10,000 hours.[12] We are not suggesting that you attempt to practice mindfulness meditation for 10,000 hours, through electroencephalogram studies of experienced (10,000–50,000 hours) and novice meditators have shown that meditation provides both short- and long-term benefits to health and well-being.[13] Therefore, we are simply suggesting that you practice, in whichever way happens to be *your* way.

If at first you can manage only five minutes a day, or even one minute, that is fine—there is no right way of practicing. Simply stopping and remembering to shift your attention, even momentarily, from your usual state of *doing* and into a state of *being* is enough (and even more imperative to practice when feeling stressed). This comes from one's ability to experience with a sense of curiosity and kindness instead of with judgment or preference. It requires an enormous amount of patience and practice because it is a completely different experience from what we are used to—"if you happen to stumble upon somebody who is meditating, you know instantly that you have come into the orbit of something unusual and remarkable."[14]

THE SITTING PRACTICE

Sitting meditation is one of the most frequently practiced approaches to formally exercising mindfulness. There are several sitting practices you may choose to experiment with. We will discuss three of the most common, observing the breath, body scan, and Hatha yoga.

Observing the Breath

Observing one's breathing is considered to be one of the simplest and most effective ways to begin practicing mindfulness. Observing the breath is simply that—paying attention to the inhalation and exhalation of air without changing what is currently going on. The breath is really the foundation to a mindfulness practice because with any of the exercises, one begins by focusing all of the attention on the breath. You can begin the practice of observing the breath by sitting in a comfortable, upright fashion, closing your eyes, and simply breathing naturally—making no effort to control or change the breath, just focusing all of the attention on the breath. Observing the rhythm, the length of each in-breath and each out-breath, the temperature, how the body moves—the nostrils, shoulders, chest, rib cage, and belly. Continuing to observe all of the qualities of the breath, without elaborating on its implications or creating any need for action. Practice for two to three minutes to begin with and then try extending it for longer periods of time. Some find it helpful to set an intention before beginning this sitting exercise by silently speaking something that resonates for them in the moment. "May I be nonjudgmental," or "May I be gentle with myself" are examples of such intentions.

Throughout the practice, attention will inevitably wander off the breath to thoughts, memories, fantasies, and feelings that arise. Simply notice them and let them go, gently bringing the attention back to the breath. Observe judgmental thoughts (e.g., "there are so many better things that I could be doing with my time instead of this") in a nonjudgmental manner. Steadily repeat the process of directing your attention back to your breath each time you notice your mind is wandering—this may happen dozens of times in the span of minutes. Continue to practice using your breath as an anchor, as your breath is always there and you may come back to it at anytime, whether you are feeling anxiety, stress, or even in moments of delight. Your breath is always there to help you cope with the next moment, stressful or otherwise.

Body Scan

Another form of sitting practice is the body scan where you progressively move your attention throughout the body, feeling each region. You can begin the practice by first comfortably lying down on your back with your legs extended, your arms by your sides with your palms facing up, and gently closing your eyes. If you choose, you may begin by setting an intention for this practice, speaking silently something that resonates for you in this moment; for example, "May I accept my body," or "May I cultivate greater patience." Begin by focusing your attention on the breath and observe nonjudgmentally as it moves in and out of your body.

Once you are in touch with the breath, you may start by bringing attention to the toes of the left foot, slowly moving up the foot and the leg. Upon reaching the pelvis, do the same with the toes of the right foot, gradually moving up the body to the torso, lower back, abdomen, upper back, chest, and shoulders. Upon reaching the shoulders, slowly and systematically go to the fingers of the left hand, moving up the arm and returning back to the shoulders and then repeating on the fingers of the right hand. Upon reaching the shoulders again, move to the clavicle, the neck, throat, and continuing to the face, bringing attention to the lips, nose, eyes, and ears. Conclude the body scan by moving to the back of the head and to the top of the head. Attempt to keep focus on each part of the body for at least one minute and really pay close attention to the sensations in that particular area. After moving through the regions of your body, return to the breath and focus attention to whatever arises.

Hatha Yoga

Though there are many ways of practicing being in your body, Hatha yoga is a method whereby participants incorporate gentle yoga stretches and postures that are designed to enhance mindful awareness of bodily sensations and to balance and strengthen the musculoskeletal system. Each pose and each exercise is done deliberately with the intention of paying attention to the moment-to-moment sensations that arise while keeping awareness fixated on the breath. Yoga is practiced in the same spirit and attitude that is applied to the other meditation practices, including gentleness, curiosity, nonattachment, beginner's mind, patience, nonjudging, nonstriving, and acceptance. While a by-product of mindful yoga is that it may help you become stronger, more flexible, and improve balance, it also helps with relaxing yourself and reducing stress.

For your yoga practice you may choose to use a mat or a pad and place it on the floor. Perhaps you may choose to use a manual or DVD to guide you through this practice. It is important not to compare yourself with others if doing this in a group setting or even not to compare yourself to your past performances. Instead, be aware of what is happening to your body, in that very moment. While practicing, it is essential to bring your attention to subtle thoughts or commentary running through your mind, as these unconscious notions influence our state of being and may cause great distress. This awareness and ability to continually redirect attention back to your practice will increase your sense of self and encourage your mindful yoga exercise.

INFORMAL PRACTICES

There are numerous ways of bringing mindfulness practice into your daily life outside of the formal meditation period. Remembering to simply be *being*, rather than be *doing* is a useful mantra. Just as a violinist practices his or her violin, we too must fine-tune this new skill of mindfulness so that with time, this practice of paying attention to the present moment-to-moment experience becomes effortless.

As we mentioned previously, any activity, as long as you are awake, can be an opportunity to practice mindfulness. We can be mindful during routine activities such as taking a shower, kissing our significant other good-bye, writing an e-mail, or petting our dog. Deliberately bringing the minutia of the experience into awareness—these individual moments are what make up our lives, and too often, we are not fully awake for them: feeling the sensation of water streaming through your hair in the shower as you rinse out the shampoo; truly being in the moment as you kiss your significant other good-bye as you part ways for the day; being aware of any thoughts, feelings, or physical tensions as you type an e-mail to someone; experiencing the way your dog's hair feels between your fingers as you run your hands through her coat. As Kabat-Zinn[7] writes, it is "really doing what you're doing." Intentionally choose to live your life more fully and vividly, instead of on automatic pilot, which makes our daily routines seem exhausting and monotonous. In this section we will discuss two ways of really doing what you are already doing in everyday life more mindfully—eating and walking.

Mindful Eating

One method of practicing mindfulness in an informal fashion is through eating mindfully. First, simply observe how you eat, without changing anything about it. Do you eat with someone? Do you eat standing up or sitting down? Perhaps while doing something else? Where do you eat—on a couch, in bed, at a table, in front of the computer? How much do you eat? How long does it take you to eat? How do you feel before and after you eat? How do you determine what to eat?

Eating is an activity that plays a central role in our lives—physically, emotionally, and socially. Eating provides us the nourishment and sustenance to live, and yet we often do not pay close attention to the activity of eating, or to how we decide what we are going to eat and how much. Mindful eating involves setting an intention before you eat, becoming aware of the process of choosing what to eat, listening to your body to determine what it needs, and then eating slowly, consciously with your full attention on the moment-to-moment experience of eating.

As a mindful eating exercise, try sitting down to a meal and pausing before you begin eating. Set an intention for this meal, for example, "May this food nourish me"; "May I be present for this meal"; "May I appreciate all that was involved in providing this meal." Then, noting the food on your plate, taking it in with all of your senses—notice the color, size, shape, and aroma. Note any sensations in your body or any anticipation of eating—perhaps you feel a bit of saliva building up in your mouth. Slowly take a small bite but do not begin chewing yet—continue to pay attention to anything that comes to your mind about the taste, the temperature, the texture, and any thoughts or sensations you are experiencing. Begin to chew slowly—noticing what it feels like to chew, the movement of your jaw, any changes in the texture or flavor of the food. When your mind inevitably wanders, continue to redirect your attention back to your food. Notice the feeling of the subtle transition from chewing to swallowing. Take another bite and repeat the exercise. Maybe this meal is triggering memories for you, perhaps memories of a person, a fond vacation, or the last time you had this meal. Simply note where your attention has wandered off to and gently bring it back to where you are and what you are intentionally doing. Perhaps impatience arises; simply notice it nonjudgmentally, and continue to chew and swallow slowly and mindfully. After you finish your meal, observe how you feel immediately afterward, and an hour or two later. Notice your energy level, your mood, how your belly feels.

We are not suggesting that all of your meals are consumed in this meticulous of a manner; however, we are presenting another way of practicing mindfulness in your everyday life and a way of changing your relationship to food. As an alternative to practicing mindful eating with an entire meal, you may choose to practice with a raisin or strawberry, or even the first bite of a meal—something small where you are able to direct your attention to the practice of eating even if for just a few minutes.

Walking Meditation

Most of us spend at least some of our day walking, whether it is from the car to the store, from the office to a meeting, or from our house to the park. Typically, we are just trying to get from one point to the next without paying much attention to how we are getting there. Walking is another everyday activity where you may bring the formal practice of mindfulness into this informal realm. Walking can become meditative only when we are intentionally bringing awareness to each step we take.

We invite you when you are walking to just walk. Walk purely for the sake of walking instead of combining it with your usual habit of planning, thinking, talking, and worrying. Perhaps begin by selecting a place where you can practice walking back and forth at a leisurely rate. First, become aware of yourself and your surroundings, then begin to walk. Make an effort to be fully and completely aware of each foot as it makes contact with the earth; what part of your foot comes down first? How does weight shift in your body? How long is each stride? At what point do you pick up your other foot? It may be helpful to note what you are experiencing in each movement, whether you are "lifting," "stepping," or "placing" your foot. When you reach the end of your path, briefly pause and turn around. Do this at whatever speed feels right for you and keeps your attention focused. Thoughts or judgments may arise; acknowledge their presence and gently direct your attention back to each methodical step. You may choose to practice this for 15 or 20 minutes.

Try to bring this same spirit of awareness of your walking when you park your car and go into stores to shop or run errands, when you are walking from one building to another at work, or when taking a stroll as a way to relax and decompress after a long day. We are often rushing through all of these things to the next activity, so we fail to really experience them. Through practicing walking mindfully, you are teaching yourself to walk through life more wakefully.

CULTIVATION OF ATTITUDES

In Kabat-Zinn's book *Full Catastrophe Living: Using the Wisdom of Your Body and Mind to Face Stress, Pain and Illness*,[7] he describes seven attitudinal foundations of mindfulness: *nonjudging*, the mindfulness practice that requires us to intentionally suspend judgment and evaluation and just simply be aware of whatever arises; *patience*, whereby we allow things to unfold in their own time, as there is no reason to rush one moment to get to the next; *beginner's mind*, a willingness to see everything in life as if it were being experienced for the first time; *trust*, the quality of trusting in the knowledge that there is innate wisdom in all of us and therefore looking within ourselves for guidance rather than outside for clues on how we should be; *nonstriving*, which is being fixed on achieving nothing, having no goals, going nowhere, getting nothing, detaching oneself from any particular outcome; *acceptance*, coming to terms with reality by being receptive and open to whatever is actually here in the present moment, regardless of whether we agree or approve of it; and finally, *letting go*, which was described at the beginning of the chapter as a way of just letting things be and accepting them for what they are, holding onto nothing. All seven of these attitudes are interconnected; practicing one almost always inevitably leads to practicing another.

In addition, Shapiro and Schwartz[15,16] have included the qualities of *nonattachment*, letting go of grasping or clinging to a particular outcome and allowing things to unfold; *curiosity*, a genuine interest in one's experience, being willing to explore and investigate; *gentleness*, a tender quality that is soft though not to be confused with undisciplined or passive; *nonreactivity*, the ability to respond where we come from a place of clarity and consciousness instead of automatically reacting in a conditioned or habitual way; and finally, *loving kindness*, demonstrating love, benevolence, and friendliness.

These attitudes can be thought of as the manner in which we go about our mindfulness practice. It is with these attitudes that we approach observing the breath, the body scan, Hatha yoga, eating, walking, or whatever activity we choose to be mindful while doing. Keeping these interrelated attitudes at the forefront of the practice allows us to create a space where empathy and compassion for ourselves and others may be cultivated.

Spiritual Models

Many people tend to seek and want to feel connected to something greater than themselves, without necessarily being tied to a formal religion. Since "most human behavior is learned observationally through modeling,"[17] it seems logical that we look to spiritual models. Due to the context where mindfulness arose, the Buddha is a common example of a spiritual model who exemplified seeking a clam or meditative state.

Spiritual modeling has been defined as the act of learning spiritually relevant behaviors or skills through observing other people—spirituality is "caught, not taught."[18] Through observational spiritual learning, four processes are used: attention, retention, reproduction in behavior, and motivation.[19] MBSR supports all four spiritual modeling processes and allows us to link spiritual beliefs to practices.[20] Oman and Beddoe[21] examined MBSR and suggested that it offers support for spiritual modeling in several ways. The group format through which MBSR is taught facilitates collaboration between fellow participants and allows them to draw upon each other as models. Furthermore, text from "spiritually oriented poets such as Jalaluddin Rumi, Walt Whitman, or others, are commonly used in MBSR session to illustrated and support meditative states of mind."[20]

Whether everyday models, such as a mother, a close friend, or colleague, or revered models, such as the Buddha, Jesus, Mother Teresa, His Holiness the Dalai Lama, Mahatma Gandhi, Martin Luther King, or Nelson Mandela, spiritual modeling is all around us if we pay attention. For many, these spiritual models motivate us through our daily lives or our practices as we seek meditative or calm states of mind.

OTHER CONSIDERATIONS

It is important to note that although you may be practicing mindfulness in a formal setting, you are encouraged to also bring mindfulness to seemingly ordinary activities like walking, eating, or standing. It is useful to apply these same general principles outside of the formal meditation practice as much as possible, keeping you grounded in the here and now instead of focusing on ongoing streams of thoughts that are often confused with reality, worries that tend to only increase your stress levels, or rumination that drains us of energy that can be better used elsewhere.

You may find that different practices fit you better than others; that is fine. It is important to find *your* way of practicing by experimenting— varying the length of time, the location, the time of day which you practice, the quality of your attention, and seeing how it effects your practice. For most of us, the practice of mindfulness is quite challenging and requires practice, discipline, and intentional effort. It is important to remember to set aside time for yourself to practice formal meditation, whether it is 20 or 40 minutes, once or twice a day, whatever you find to be most effective at alleviating your stress.

REVIEW OF THE THEORETICAL AND EMPIRICAL LITERATURE

Although researchers have attempted to empirically examine mindfulness through some of the constructs associated with it including the cultivation of compassion, awareness, insight, wisdom, and empathy, this rigorous investigation of mindfulness is in many ways antithetical to the rich tradition from which it stems. Nevertheless, numerous scientific research studies have examined the beneficial effects (both psychological and physiological) of mindfulness in clinical and nonclinical samples ranging from chronic-pain patients, individuals with Axis I disorders (e.g., binge eating disorder, panic, generalized anxiety, depression), Axis II disorders (e.g., borderline personality disorder), mixed clinical populations (Axis I and Axis II disorders combined), other medical disorders (e.g., cancer, fibromyalgia, psoriasis, cardiovascular disease, hypertension, HIV/AIDS), and nonclinical populations (e.g., elementary, undergraduate, graduate, and medical students; community volunteers; experienced mediators). Research has shown that mindfulness meditation promotes cognitive change, self-management, relaxation, and acceptance in participants.[22,23]

Physiologically, mindfulness mediation has shown to exhibit significant impacts on the autonomic nervous system by slowing heart rate (Cuthbert et al., as cited by Kristeller[11]) and decreasing blood pressure (Benson, as cited by Kristeller[11]). More recently, brain-imaging technology such as electroencephalogram studies have shown the positive effects of which even short mindfulness meditation-training programs are capable, such as changing the brain and immune functioning of the participant.[24] If stress decreases one's immune functioning, and mindfulness has been shown to increase one's immune functioning, then it is only natural to suggest that it is even more imperative that we practice mindfulness when we are experiencing moments of stress, acute or otherwise.

Several studies have found an increase in spirituality due to participation in MBSR. Carson, Carson, Gil, and Baucom[25] found that couples who participated in mindfulness-based relationship enhancement experienced statistically significant increases in spirituality as compared to those who did not received the treatment. When examining undergraduates who received MBSR, Astin[26] also found increase in spiritual experiences. Carmody, Reed, Merriam, and Kristeller[27] recently found that participation in MBSR intervention significantly increased spirituality, which was associated with medical and psychological improvements.

APPLICATIONS/INTERVENTIONS

There are several empirically validated interventions that are based on mindfulness and also include mindfulness as a component of the treatment program. The most well known is MBSR,[7] which is typically designed as an eight-week course with groups of up to 35 participants who meet on a weekly basis for two and a half to three hours and a six-hour weekend retreat after the sixth class. Participants are taught both formal and informal mindfulness techniques, ranging from sitting mediation, walking mediation, body scan, yoga, and informal daily practices. In addition to class, participants practice for at least 45 minutes a day, six days per week from home and are given audiotapes to assist with their practice.

MBSR has been offered to undergraduate and graduate students alike at both public and private universities. At Santa Clara University, a graduate course in the counseling psychology program entitled "Stress and Stress Management" provides training in mindfulness meditation (through an eight-week MBSR course). Likewise, in Montana State University's counseling psychology program a course called "Mind/ Body Medicine and the Art of Self-Care" provides students with stress management training through MBSR.[28] Recently, MBSR has been applied in the professional workplace, as an increasing number of companies offer the course to employees because they recognize that stress poses negative consequences on an employee's professional effectiveness in addition to his or her personal well-being. Davidson et al.[24] examined the effects of MBSR on employees at a biotechnology company compared to a wait-list group and found that antibody production measured four months after the MBSR program was significantly higher in the treatment group.

In addition, there are other therapies that draw largely on Kabat-Zinn's MBSR program with specific populations in mind, such as mindfulness-based cognitive therapy,[8] a manualized eight-week group approach to the treatment of depression. Recently, we have seen numerous other therapies emerging in the mindfulness-based field: mindfulness-based eating awareness training,[29] designed for individuals with binge eating disorder and most recently, obesity; mindfulness-based art therapy,[30] which was developed for use in medical populations and also has been applied to women with breast cancer: mindfulness-based relapse prevention,[31,32] which has been applied to alcohol and drug abuse as well used as a treatment for smoking cessation; and MBRE[25] (mentioned earlier), designed to enhance the relationships of couples.

There are also cognitive-behavioral interventions that use mindfulness as a *component* of the treatment program. Dialectical behavior therapy[33,34] is a manualized, multifaceted group and individual therapeutic approach originally developed for the treatment of borderline personality disorder and is now currently being used with a variety of clinical and nonclinical populations. One of the modules in DBT is mindfulness, where patients are instructed on how to pay attention to the present moment in a nonjudgmental manner. Acceptance and commitment therapy[35] is a treatment whose core principles include acceptance and being in contact with the present moment while also taking into consideration one's goals and values. It is typically delivered in an individual format but can also be delivered in a group format. Acceptance and commitment therapy has been shown to be successful when applied to individuals with a broad range of psychological problems.

NEW RESEARCH DIRECTIONS

Many have attempted to define the term mindfulness for the purposes of Western psychology. Brown and Ryan[9] define mindfulness as "the presence or absence of attention to and awareness of what is occurring in the present" (p. 824). Wallace and Bodhi have stated that mindfulness is simply "bare attention" (as cited by Shapiro and Carlson).[23] Bishop and colleagues,[36] presented mindfulness as having two components, the first involving the ability to self-regulate attention and maintain focus on present experience, and the second, the adaptation of an open, curious, and accepting orientation to one's present-moment experiences. Shapiro and colleagues[2,23] have proposed that mindfulness is both an outcome (mindful awareness) and a process (mindful practice) that involves three key elements: intention (e.g., why you are practicing), attention (e.g., observing moment-to-moment experiences both internal and external), and attitude (e.g., how you attend—the qualities that are brought)—collectively referred to as IAA (Intention, Attention, Attitude).

Current research, as demonstrated previously, suggests that mindfulness practice is an effective means of reducing stress and enhancing well-being across a wide range of populations. Future research, however, is needed to determine the mechanisms of action for how mindfulness works. In addition, examining how to best teach mindfulness to diverse populations is crucial, and determining any adverse effects of mindfulness on certain clinical and nonclinical populations would be beneficial to the field.

Another area for future research is to expand the measures used to assess the effects of mindfulness intervention. The majority of the outcome measures in mindfulness studies have been self-report, while some have expanded research to more objectively observable and quantifiable measures such as electroencephalogram, functional magnetic resonance imaging, and cortisol levels—leading the research in mindfulness to strive toward more objective outcome measures. Though the neuroscientific study of mindfulness meditation has shown exciting preliminary results, it is still in its infancy. Current findings must be supplemented with longitudinal randomized clinical trials to examine the long-term effects mindfulness has on the participant.

CONCLUSION

Four decades of empirical research suggest that mindfulness practice has numerous positive effects such as enhancing physical health, increasing spiritual and psychological well-being, and lowering stress. The intention of this chapter was to introduce mindfulness both as a way of being and as a practice to help with the management of stress. Through the cultivation of mindfulness, we are better able to effectively respond with greater awareness instead of automatically reacting to stress. As our mindfulness builds and becomes more integrated into our moment-to-moment experience, we have greater degrees of free-dom of how we choose to respond, how we choose to live and be in the world. Building a new relationship with our experiences is necessary to finding peace, as Germer[37] illustrates:

> While striving may allow us to acquire physical comforts, living in the present enables us to live more fully. Everyone feels stress to one degree or another. The conditions of our lives never seem quite right, because our inner experience of them is unsatisfactory. We find ourselves either running headlong toward the future for relief or dwelling in the past, or both. A changed relationship to our experience is needed to find lasting peace. (p. 114)

We believe mindfulness offers one avenue to cultivate this "changed relationship to experience"—and that through this, we will be better able to manage stress and ultimately lead more joyful and fulfilling lives.

REFERENCES

1. Kabat-Zinn, J. (2003). Mindfulness-based interventions in context: Past, present, and future. *Clinical Psychology: Science and Practice*, *10*(2), 144–156.

2. Shapiro, S. L., Carlson, L. E., Astin, J. A., & Freedman, B. (2006). Mechanisms of mindfulness. *Journal of Clinical Psychology, 62*, 373–386.

3. Kabat-Zinn, J. (1994). *Wherever you go there you are*. New York: Hyperion.

4. Walsh, A. B., & Shapiro, S. L. (2006). The meeting of meditative disciplines and Western psychology. *American Psychologist, 61*(3), 1–13.

5. Siegel, D. J. (2007). *The mindful brain: Reflection and attunement in the cultivation of well-being*. New York: Norton.

6. Begley, S. (2007). *Train your mind change your brain: How a new science reveals our extraordinary potential to transform ourselves*. New York: Ballantine Books.

7. Kabat-Zinn, J. (1990). *Full catastrophe living: Using the wisdom of your body and mind to face stress, pain and illness*. New York: Delacorte.

8. Segal, Z. V., Williams, J. M. G., & Teasdale, J. D. (2002). *Mindfulness-based cognitive therapy for depression: A new approach for preventing relapse*. New York: Guilford Press.

9. Brown, K. W., & Ryan, R. M. (2003). The benefits of being present: Mindfulness and its role in psychological well-being. *Journal of Personality and Social Psychology, 84*, 822–848.

10. Oman, D., Shapiro, S. L., Thoresen, C. E., Plante, T. G., & Flinders, T. (2008). Meditation lowers stress and supports forgiveness among college students: A randomized controlled trial. *Journal of American College Health, 56*, 569–578.

11. Kristeller, J. (2007). Mindfulness meditation. In P. Lehrer, W. Sime, & R. Woolfolk (Eds.), *Principles and practice of stress management* (3rd ed., pp. 393–427). New York: Guilford Press.

12. Gladwell, M. (2008). *Outliers*. New York: Little, Brown.

13. Lutz, A., Greischar, L. L., Rawlings, N. B., Ricard, M., & Davidson, R. J. (2004). Long-term meditators self-induce high-amplitude gamma synchrony during mental practice. *Proceedings of the National Academy of Sciences, 101*, 16369–16373.

14. Kabat-Zinn, J. (2005). *Coming to our senses: Healing ourselves and the world through mindfulness*. New York: Piatkus.

15. Shapiro, S. L., & Schwartz, G. E. (2000a). Intentional systemic mindfulness: An integrative model for self-regulation and health. *Advances in Mind-Body Medicine, 16*, 128–134.

16. Shapiro, S. L., & Schwartz, G. E. (2000b). The role of intention in self-regulation: Toward intentional systemic mindfulness. In M. Boekaerts, P. R. Pintrich, & M. Zeidner (Eds.), *Handbook of self-regulation* (pp. 253–273). New York: Academic Press.

17. Bandura, A. (1986). *Social foundations of thought and action: A social cognitive theory*. Englewood Cliffs, NJ: Prentice-Hall.

18. Oman, D., & Thoresen, C. E. (2003). Spiritual modeling: A key to spiritual and religious growth? *International Journal for the Psychology of Religion, 13*(3), 149–165.

19. Bandura, A. (2003). On the psychosocial impact and mechanisms of spiritual modeling. *International Journal for the Psychology of Religion, 13*(3), 167–173.

20. Oman, D., Shapiro, S. L., Thoresen, C. E., Flinders, T., Driskill, J., & Plante, T. G. (2007). Learning from spiritual models and meditation: A randomized evaluation of a college course. *Pastoral Psychology, 55*(4), 473–493.

21. Oman, D., & Beddoe, A. E. (2005). Health interventions combining meditation with learning from spiritual exemplars: Conceptualization and review. *Annals of Behavioral Medicine, 29*, S126.

22. Baer, R. A. (2003). Mindfulness training as a clinical intervention: A conceptual and empirical review. *Clinical Psychology: Science & Practice, 10*, 125–143.

23. Shapiro, S. L., Carlson, L. E., Astin, J. A., & Freedman, B. (2006). Mechanisms of mindfulness. *Journal of Clinical Psychology, 62*, 373–386.

24. Davidson, R. J., Kabat-Zinn, J., Schumacher, J., Rosenkranz, M., Muller, D., Santorelli, S. F., Urbanowski, F., Harrington, A., Bonus, K., & Sheridan, J. F. (2003). Alterations in brain and immune function produced by mindfulness meditation. *Psychosomatic Medicine, 65*, 564–570.

25. Carson, J. W., Carson, K. M., Gil, K. M., & Baucom, D. H. (2006). Mindfulness-based relationship enhancement in couples. In R. A. Baer (Ed.), *Mindfulness-based treatment approaches: Clinician's guide to evidence base and applications* (pp. 309–331). London: Academic Press.

26. Astin, J. A. (1997). Stress reduction through mindfulness meditation. *Psychotherapy and Psychosomatics, 66*, 97–106.

27. Carmody, J., Reed, G., Merriam, P., & Kristeller, J. (2008). Mindfulness, spirituality and health-related symptoms, *Journal of Psychosomatic Research, 64*(4), 393–403.

28. Christopher, J. C., Christopher, S. E., Dunnagan, T., & Schure, M. (2006). Teaching self-care through mindfulness practices: The application of yoga, mediation, and quigong to counselor training. *Journal of Humanistic Psychology, 46*, 494–509.

29. Kristeller, J. L., Baer, R. A., & Quillian-Wolever, R. (2006). Mindfulness-based approaches to eating disorders. In R. A. Baer (Ed.), *Mindfulness-based treatment approaches: Clinician's guide to evidence base and applications* (pp. 75–91). London: Academic Press.

30. Monti, D. A., Peterson, C., Kunkel, E. J., Hauck, W. W., Pequignot, E., Rhodes, L., et al. (2005). A randomized, controlled trial of mindfulness-based art therapy (MBAT) for women with cancer. *Psycho-Oncology, 15*, 363–373.

31. Marlatt, G. A., & Gordon, J. R. (Eds.). (1985). *Relapse prevention: Maintenance strategies in the treatment of addictive behaviors*. New York: Guilford Press.

32. Marlatt, G. A., & Witkiewitz, K. (2005). Relapse prevention for alcohol and drug problems. In G. A. Marlatt & D. M. Donovan (Eds.), *Relapse prevention* (pp. 1–44). New York: Guilford Press.

33. Linehan, M. M. (1993a). *Cognitive-behavioral treatment of borderline personality disorder*. New York: Guilford Press.

34. Linehan, M. M. (1993b). *Skills training manual for treating borderline personality disorder*. New York: Guilford Press.

35. Hayes, S. C., Strosahl, K., & Wilson, K. G. (1999). *Acceptance and commitment therapy*. New York: Guilford Press.

36. Bishop, S. R., Lau, M., Shapiro, S., Carlson, L. E., Anderson, N., Carmody, J., Segal, Z., Abbey S., Speca, M., Velting, D., & Devins, G. (2004). Mindfulness: A proposed operational definition. *Clinical Psychology: Science and Practice, 11,* 230–241.

37. Germer, C. K. (2005). Teaching mindfulness in therapy. In C. K. Germer, R. D. Siegel, & P. R. Fulton (Eds.), *Mindfulness and psychotherapy* (pp. 113–129). New York: Guilford Press.

CHAPTER 4

Translating Spiritual Ideals into Daily Life: The Eight-Point Program of Passage Meditation

Tim Flinders, Doug Oman, Carol Flinders, and Diane Dreher

An inspirational passage turns our thoughts to what is permanent, to those things that put a final end to insecurity. In meditation, the inspirational passage becomes imprinted on our consciousness. As we drive it deeper and deeper, the words come to life within us, transforming all our thoughts, feelings, words, and deeds. (p. 48)[1]

Passage Meditation (PM) is an eight-point contemplative program whose foundational meditation practice is designed to help practitioners deepen their spirituality and manage the pressures of contemporary life by drawing directly upon the words and wisdom of the world's spiritual traditions. A growing number of adherents across all the major faith traditions use the PM program, as do many seekers who characterize themselves as "spiritual but not religious." Together, the program's eight tools constitute what Oman (this volume) calls a "fully integrated contemplative practice."

In this chapter we will describe the historical development of PM, also known as the Eight-Point Program, outline its special features, and then describe the basic instructions for the practice of each of its eight points. The chapter will emphasize two particular strengths of PM. The first is PM's appeal to seekers who draw inspiration from the saints and sages of their own religious traditions as well as perhaps

Table 4.1.   Distinctive Features of the Eight-Point Program

Feature	Explanation
Universal	PM can be used by members of any religious faith, or by those who identify as "spiritual, but not religious."
Comprehensive	PM provides a comprehensive program for spiritual living, offering a classical meditative practice with supporting tools for practitioners with families and careers.
Wisdom Based	PM offers direct daily contact with the world's wisdom traditions.

from other traditions. Preliminary evidence suggests that PM fosters learning from spiritual wisdom figures such as the Psalmist, St. Francis, and the Buddha. We outline the psychological theory of *spiritual modeling*,[2] which identifies ways that PM may support assimilating attitudes and wisdom embedded in the words of these revered figures.

The second strength we will emphasize is PM's potential usefulness to educators, physicians, psychologists, caregivers, and other human service professionals who are increasingly called upon to respond to the diverse spiritual needs of their clientele. We will suggest that PM provides significant added value to psychological or educational interventions, especially when set alongside more familiar professional resources such as mindfulness methods. In this way, PM may expand the ability of health and human service professionals to address more effectively the spiritual needs of diverse clientele. This added value is in part due to several of PM's distinctive features highlighted in Table 4.1.

We then describe several controlled empirical studies of PM that suggest a wide range of benefits, including enhanced professional work skills, increases in empathy, forgiveness, and mindfulness, improved mental health, and substantial reductions in stress (see fuller reviews elsewhere).[3,4] Finally, we describe several recent applications of the program among two highly stressed populations, workplace professionals and college students.

HISTORY AND CONTEXT

PM was first systematized and taught at the University of California–Berkeley, during the 1960s by Fulbright scholar Eknath Easwaran (1910–99), to support students entering professional life. Since that

Table 4.2.   Eight-Point Program of Passage Meditation (PM) and Contemporary Challenges

PM Point	Modern Challenges It Addresses
1. Passage Meditation	Distraction, spiritual alienation
2. Mantram Repetition	Negative thinking, chronic, obtrusive thoughts
3. Slowing Down	Chronic hurry/"Hurry Sickness"[a]
4. One-Pointed Attention	Compulsive multitasking/"Polyphasic thinking"[a]
5. Training the Senses	Sensory overload, overconsumption
6. Putting Others First	Self-absorption, egocentricity
7. Spiritual Association	Social and spiritual isolation
8. Inspirational Reading	Disillusion, pessimism
Total PM program	Chronic stress, lack of meaning, lack of spiritual growth

[a]Quotation marks show how this challenge was characterized in research on Type A Behavior Pattern.

time, thousands of practitioners of all religious faiths, as well as nonreligious seekers, have used PM throughout the United States and elsewhere to help them deepen their spirituality and manage the stresses of contemporary life with greater clarity and calm.[5] The PM program has been used in college and seminary education,[6] substance abuse recovery,[7] and psychotherapy.[8] Translations of PM instructional materials by independent publishers appear in more than 20 languages in two dozen countries in North and South America, Europe, and Asia.[9] But possibly because the appeal of PM cuts across and transcends the most common categories of religious and sectarian identity, it has only intermittently appeared on lists of popular meditation practices such as Transcendental Meditation, Vipassana, and Zen. Table 4.2 summarizes the eight points and places them alongside some major modern lifestyle challenges that each addresses.

PASSAGE MEDITATION PROGRAM

POINT 1—MEDITATION ON AN INSPIRATIONAL PASSAGE

Among contemporary forms of concentrative meditation, Passage Meditation may be unique in focusing attention on the words of inspirational passages, rather than on the breath (Vipassana), sounds (Transcendental Meditation), or brief spiritual phrases (Centering

Prayer). This feature of the program may help explain why PM has been used by members of all the major religious faiths traditions, including various branches of Protestant Christianity, Judaism, Roman and Eastern Catholicism, Buddhism, Islam, and Hinduism.[5] As such, the practice might be characterized as "multisectarian" in that many observant religious practitioners readily embed PM fully within their religious practice without conflict. Figure 4.1 presents sample passages from the world's major religious traditions.

Since practitioners of PM may select their meditation passages from theistic or nontheistic sources (or both), many nonreligious seekers

Figure 4.1. Theistic Inspirational Passages.

Source	Passage	Tradition
Psalm 23	*The Lord is my shepherd, I shall not want.* *He makes me lie down in green pastures,* *He leads me beside quiet waters,* *He restores my soul...*	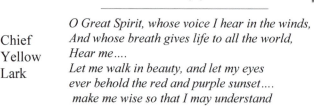
Prayer of St. Francis of Assisi	*Lord, make me an instrument of thy peace,* *Where there is hatred, let me sow love;* *Where there is injury, pardon,* *Where there is doubt, faith,* *Where there is darkness, light,* *Where there is sadness, joy ...*	
Chief Yellow Lark	*O Great Spirit, whose voice I hear in the winds,* *And whose breath gives life to all the world,* *Hear me....* *Let me walk in beauty, and let my eyes* *ever behold the red and purple sunset....* *make me wise so that I may understand* *the things you have taught my people.*	
Bhagavad Gita	*The Lord dwells in the hearts of all creatures,* *And he whirls them round on the wheel of time.* *Run to him for refuge with all your strength,* *And peace profound will be yours,* *through his grace.*	

Note. Passages are drawn from Easwaran's (2008) *Timeless Wisdom: Passages for meditation from the world's saints and sages* or from his (2003) *God Makes the Rivers to Flow* (Tomales, CA: Nilgiri), sourcebooks containing passages drawn from the major wisdom traditions.

find PM especially appealing. Recent surveys show that as many as one-third of Americans place themselves in the category of "spiritual, but not religious," rejecting traditional organized religion as the sole means of furthering their spiritual growth.[10] While they profess belief in a spiritual reality, many prefer nontheistic representations. Figure 4.2 shows examples of inspirational passages from nontheistic traditions that have been used in PM.

Figure 4.2. Nontheistic Inspirational Passages.

Source	Passage	Tradition
Discourse on Good Will	*May all beings be filled with joy and peace.* *May all beings everywhere, the strong* *and the weak, the great and the small,* *May all beings everywhere . . .* *May all be filled with lasting joy*	
Tao Te Ching	*Break into the peace within,* *Hold attention in stillness,* *And in the world outside.* *You will ably master the 10,000 things.* *All things rise and flourish.* *Then go back to their roots.* *Seeing this return brings true rest...*	
Rumi	*Everything you see has its roots.* *In the unseen world.* *The forms may change,* *Yet the essence remains the same.* *Every wondrous sight will vanish,* *Every sweet word will fade.* *But do not be disheartened,* *The source they come from is eternal.*	
Upanishads	*The all-knowing Self was never born,* *Nor will it die. Beyond cause and effect,* *This Self is eternal and immutable.* *When the body dies, the Self does not die...* *When the wise realize the Self...* *They go beyond all sorrow*	

Note. From Easwaran's recommended passage sourcebooks (see Fig. 4.1 note)

While these brief instructions below are sufficient to begin the practice of PM, those interested in a more detailed presentation should look at Easwaran's *Passage Meditation: Bringing the Deep Wisdom of the Heart into Daily Life*, the definitive description of PM.[1]

1. Memorize an inspirational passage from a scripture or major spiritual figure that is positive, practical, inspiring, and universal.

2. Choose a time for meditation when you can sit for half an hour in uninterrupted quiet. (It is not recommended to meditate for more than 30 minutes without personal guidance from an experienced teacher.) Sit with your back and head erect, on the floor or in a straight-backed chair.

3. Close your eyes and go through the words of an inspirational passage *in your mind* as slowly as you can and with as much concentration as possible. For instance, the first line from Rumi's "A Garden Beyond Paradise" would be repeated like this: "*Everything . . . you . . . see . . . has its . . . roots . . . in . . . the . . . unseen . . . world . . .*" Concentrate on each word, without following any association of ideas or allowing your mind to reflect on the meaning of the words. When distractions come, do not resist them, but give more attention to the words of the passage.

4. If your mind strays from the passage entirely, bring it back gently to the beginning of the verse and start again.

5. In time, develop a repertoire of inspirational passages to keep them from becoming automatic or stale. They may be selected from within a single religious tradition, or from several traditions.

Two Dimensions of Meditating on an Inspirational Passage

Meditating on an inspirational passage has two dimensions, according to its developer: training attention and the absorption of spiritual content (pp. 12–13).[1] When fused these dimensions make the practice transformational. Training attention is achieved by the discipline of returning the mind back to the words of the passage each time it becomes distracted. Over time, this develops a capacity for sustained concentration that can be used outside of meditation, to remain focused during interruptions, in times of emotional stress, and in making wise lifestyle choices.

The second dimension, content absorption, focuses on values-laden, inspirational passages. Popular practices like Vipassana or Transcendental Meditation have a concentrative dimension, but PM more systematically couples the power of focused attention to the spiritual content of wisdom-based inspirational passages. This does not occur by thinking about or reflection on the words of the passage, which, in PM, would constitute a distraction. Rather, as concentration on the words deepens, the values embedded within these passages from the world's great sages, mystics, and seers become absorbed so that their values and qualities may become accessible in the lives of practitioners.

POINT 2—HOLY NAME (MANTRAM) REPETITION

To help practitioners refocus themselves during the day, repetition of a mantram is highly recommended. A mantram is a hallowed word or phrase that is silently repeated or chanted aloud; versions of this practice appear in all major spiritual traditions, both East and West.[1,11] In PM, mantram repetition acts as a bridge for integrating the calm and clarity gained from sitting meditation into the remainder of the day. Unlike the sitting practice, the mantram can be invoked almost anywhere, any time, at home or in the workplace, to help maintain clarity and wisdom. Such a portable practice is a core component of what Oman (this volume) calls an integral contemplative practice system, and is a key coping resource for those living in a fast-paced, highly competitive society. The following are instructions for using the mantram:

1. Choose a mantram that appeals to you (see Figure 4.3), from a traditional source that has been widely used over time (for a fuller discussion of mantram instructions, see Bormann, this volume.)
2. Repeat your mantram silently in the mind ("*Rama, Rama, Rama*" … "*Jesus, Jesus, Jesus*") as opportunities arise: while walking, waiting in line, stopped at a traffic light, while falling asleep, etc.
3. Remember to repeat your mantram in times of stress, to calm the mind when pressured by time urgency, or to interrupt negative thinking when angry or afraid.

Note that in PM, the mantram is *not* used during sitting meditation. Consequently, PM's use of mantram repetition should be contrasted with other recent popularizations of mantram repetition, such as in

Figure 4.3. Selected Mantrams.

Tradition	Mantram	Meaning
Buddhist	*Om mani padme hum*	"The jewel in the lotus of the heart"
Christian	*Jesus* *My God and my all*	(St. Francis of Assisi is reported to have used this.)
Hindu	*Rama* *Om Bhavani*	"Joy" (Gandhi's mantram) A mantram in honor of the Divine Mother
Jewish	*Barukh attah Adonai* *Ribono shel olam*	"Blessed are you, O Lord" "Lord of the universe"
Muslim	*Allah* *Bismillah ir-Rahman ir-Rahim*	"In the name of Allah, the merciful, the compassionate"

Herbert Benson's *Relaxation Response*, and in Transcendental Meditation. Contrary to PM, these methods use mantrams as the focus of sitting meditation practice. In PM, the mantram is used as a *bridging tool* between meditation on an inspirational passage (typically done in the early morning), and the remainder of the day.

Studies suggest that the use of a mantram at free times throughout the day is effective in decreasing stress, anger and anxiety (see Bormann, this volume).

POINT 3—SLOWING DOWN

In PM, Slowing Down denotes the practice of moving with care and deliberation through the day to minimize the stress caused by hurry and time pressures. It does not necessarily mean going slowly, but rather setting priorities and limiting activities so as not to live with the constant time urgency of contemporary life. Excessive time urgency not only undermines quality of life, but has been linked to coronary illness. For example, a recent 15-year longitudinal study of young adults ($n = 3,142$) found that the "time/urgency and impatience syndrome" was a "strong predictor" of developing hypertension. Another recent study ($n = 340$) found that a heightened sense of the time/urgency and impatience syndrome was associated with a dose-response increase in the risk of nonfatal myocardial infarction.[12]

The practice of Slowing Down includes looking at and adjusting daily patterns and habits that may contribute to increased time urgency, such as driving patterns, eating habits, responses to workplace pressures, and technology use. Recommendations for altering these patterns to a healthier lifestyle include setting a more relaxed pace by getting to work earlier, setting limits, and avoiding over scheduling. As such, Slowing Down may represent a buffer against the pressures of the time/urgency and impatience syndrome.

POINT 4—ONE-POINTED ATTENTION

In PM, the practice of One-Pointed Attention involves trying to do only one thing at a time, and giving it full attention. Suggestions for practicing One-Pointed Attention include not listening to the radio while driving or studying, and not checking e-mail while talking to someone on the phone. While this practice may appear counterintuitive in a multitasking, workplace culture, it offers a way to remain centered amid the continuous assault of interruptions that characterize contemporary life.

Multitasking has become a commonplace phenomenon of contemporary life, especially in the modern workplace. Yet serious questions are increasingly being raised about its actual benefits (e.g., Gallagher, 2009).[13] Recent research suggests, for example, that trying to do more than one thing at a time may, in fact, have adverse consequences on learning and efficiency. Using functional magnetic resonance imaging to examine brain activity, researchers in one recent study found that while multitasking participants' learning was less flexible and less easily retrieved.[14] Another study reported that "heavy media multitaskers" who attend simultaneously to two or more media (e.g., phone, e-mail, print, etc.) performed "*worse* on a test of task-switching ability" and are "more susceptible to interference from irrelevant environmental stimuli and irrelevant . . . memory" (emphasis added; p. 15583).[15]

Traditional Indian yoga stresses one-pointed concentration (*ekagratha*) as do certain forms of Buddhist meditation. One-Pointed Attention and Slowing Down can be understood as the two primary dimensions of mindfulness, which work together to assist PM practitioners in staying focused and calm while managing competing demands and interruptions. Indeed, PM appears at least as effective for increasing mindfulness as Mindfulness-Based Stress Reduction (MBSR), according to evidence described later.[16] Furthermore, a recent randomized, controlled study of American veterans ($n = 29$) with symptoms of posttraumatic stress disorder (PTSD) combined PM mantram repetition, Slowing Down, and One-Pointed Attention in a five-week intervention and found significant reductions in PTSD symptom severity, psychological distress, and increasing quality of life.[17]

POINT 5—TRAINING THE SENSES

Training the Senses directs practitioners to discriminate in lifestyle choices. It is not presented as a moral injunction, but as a corrective to compulsive behaviors like smoking, excessive drinking, and overeating, which are strongly implicated by research in chronic conditions such as cancer and coronary illness.

The goal of Training the Senses is to develop a balanced lifestyle, in which we make wise and healthy choices in the foods we eat and the exercise we get, while avoiding unhealthy habits like smoking and overeating. Training the Senses also includes being discriminating in our entertainment choices. Some form of sense discrimination can be found in all major religious and contemplative systems, both East and West, and is referred to as the "Middle Path" in the Buddhist tradition. Such moderation can help support a contemplative practice, even as it promotes better health.

POINT 6—PUTTING OTHERS FIRST

Putting Others First encourages practitioners to move their concern and attention to the needs of others—family, colleagues, community, world—and away from serving only private self-interest. Putting Others First recasts into a contemporary formulation the early Christian concept of *agape*, universal love, as well as Buddhist *metta*, compassion.

Several decades of research have demonstrated the therapeutic value of helping others, showing positive relations between volunteerism and health, including increased longevity. A recent review suggested that the benefits of volunteering may be greatest when it is complemented by other practices, such as PM, that offer resources for coping with important life tasks.[18]

POINT 7—SPIRITUAL ASSOCIATION

Like Christian fellowship or the Buddhist *Sangha*, Spiritual Association emphasizes the importance of coming together on a regular basis with other PM practitioners to offer and receive support. Social support has long been recognized as a factor in both physical and psychological health, and is associated with longevity.[19]

POINT 8—INSPIRATIONAL READING

Daily spiritual reading from the world's wisdom traditions is recommended as a source of inspiration and motivation for PM practitioners. *Lectio divina*, for instance, is an ancient Christian devotional practice centered on reading and reflecting on scripture.

AN INTEGRATIVE PROGRAM

Each of the eight points has analogues in other traditional contemplative systems as well as among contemporary practices (see Table 4.3). However, the PM points are not isolated protocols, independent of each other. Rather, as codified and used in PM, they are structurally integrative. They jointly reinforce each other in a web of supportive strategies that draw on the calm and clarity of meditation to help practitioners deepen their wisdom, and more effectively face the challenges of daily life. For example, in meditation, practitioners are instructed to repeat the words of the inspirational passage as slowly as they can, and with as much concentration as possible. Slowing Down and One-Pointed Attention replicate these interior practices during the day, supporting efforts in meditation to slow down and focus attention. The repetition of the mantram at moments of stress helps the mind refocus and regain some of the calm and clarity of meditation.

Some of the processes by which PM points complement each other are suggested by Oman's (this volume) concept of four synergistic elements that together comprise an integrated contemplative practice system.[20] However, the developer of the PM program has described a wide range of additional processes by which PM points appear to complement each other.[21] Some PM points are flexible tools for self-regulation and problem-focused coping;[22] others help participants

Table 4.3. Elements of Easwaran's PM and Similar Practices in Traditional Religion and Health Interventions

Element of PM	Similar Practices in Religious Traditions	Similar Existing Health Interventions
1. Meditation	Raja Yoga, Kavvanah, Prayer of the Heart, higher *Lectio Divina*	Benson's Meditation, Transcendental Meditation
2. Mantram	Jesus Prayer; Dhikr, Japa Yoga	Affirmations
3. Slowing Down	Right Mindfulness	Treating Type A (alleviate sense of time urgency); Mindfulness—informal practices
4. One-Pointed Attention	Right Mindfulness	Treating Type A (avoid polyphasic thinking), Mindfulness—informal practices
5. Training the Senses	Pervasive (e.g., Middle Way in Buddhism; Temperance in Christianity)	Pervasive (e.g., 12-Step programs)
6. Putting Others First	Pervasive (e.g., "Love Thy Neighbor"; humility)	Treating Type A (be compassionate)
7. Spiritual Association	Pervasive (e.g., faith communities; scriptural study groups; Sangha)	Social support, 12-Step programs
8. Inspirational Reading	Pervasive (e.g., scriptural study; preparatory *Lectio Divina*)	Reading sacred writings in counseling

draw on spiritual wisdom traditions to cultivate adaptive goals.[23] Users sometimes state that PM helps them frame almost any situation as an opportunity for growth—for example, one reported that PM "can take any experience and work with it.... it no longer has a static presence—it's clay in your hands to shape into something more."[24] Participants in one research study described 15 distinct ways that PM points worked together to promote work effectiveness.[25]

INTERPRETATION: LEARNING FROM SPIRITUAL MODELS

One of PM's distinctive features, noted earlier, is its systematic support for assimilation of key elements of spiritual wisdom traditions.

Most distinctively, meditating on a passage supports assimilating the attitudes and perspectives of revered spiritual wisdom figures such as the Buddha, Jesus, and others. Inspirational Reading (Point 8) also supports learning from such spiritual models. An intuitive appreciation of these features may account for some of PM's appeal across cultures and faith traditions. A recent review reported that among meditation-based health interventions, PM offered the highest level of support for learning from exemplars from spiritual wisdom traditions.[26]

Scientifically, the process of learning from exemplars is known as spiritual modeling, an extension of Albert Bandura's social cognitive theory (SCT), the most highly cited and widely applied theory in contemporary psychology. Bandura's SCT helps illuminate from a scientific perspective how PM may foster spiritual growth through spiritual modeling. Spiritual and religious traditions have long recognized that "spirituality is caught, not taught." But decades of SCT-guided research have extensively documented four major psychological processes that underlie all types of learning from human models of behavior: *attention* to the model, *retention* of information about the model's behavior and attitudes, *reproduction* of what is learned in behavior, and *motivation* to persist. By extension, Bandura and other psychologists have theorized that these same four processes underlie the effective transmission of spiritual behaviors and attitudes. Not surprisingly, therefore, evidence suggests that religious traditions have sought to foster these four processes throughout history (e.g., fostering *retention* through frequent repetition at worship services of key verses from scripture).[2,10,27]

These four modeling processes are also clearly evident in PM, which appears to foster them systematically. For example, memorizing and meditating on an inspirational passage gives focused *attention* to the modeling information contained in the passage. Repeatedly meditating on the words builds *retention*. This, in turn, enhances the *reproduction* of the ideals in the passages during the day. Many passages also recount positive experiences that come to those who persist in spiritual practice, thereby supporting *motivation* to practice ("It is in giving that we receive"). Anecdotal evidence shows that meditation passages are sometimes recalled later in the day, in the midst of daily stressors, when they can facilitate improved coping and self-control.[28]

Passage Meditation's support for spiritual modeling is corroborated by controlled empirical research in college populations. A recent study reported that practicing PM enhances the influence and number of revered spiritual models, as well as one's self-efficacy for learning from spiritual models.[6] Self-efficacy is a technical term for a person's self-confidence for carrying out tasks in a particular skill domain, and is a central construct in Bandura's SCT. Self-efficacy is typically among the strongest predictors of objective performance for any type of activity, and is increasingly used to evaluate programs for education, training, and behavioral modification.[22] These documented gains in self-efficacy represent a pioneering application of Bandura's theory to spirituality, and support PM's theorized capacity to foster learning from spiritual models.

For this reason, we have argued that PM holds interest not merely as a health intervention,[10] but as a model of a more general educational approach. That is, PM demonstrates a nonsectarian approach, feasible in appropriate settings in a pluralistic society, for reintegrating spiritual modeling into education and other human service professions. In what follows, we describe three applications of PM to educational settings—one for the continuing education of health professionals, and two for college undergraduates. We also describe research that documents beneficial impacts for stress reduction and gains in professional skills, forgiveness, mindfulness, and spirituality, and other outcomes. Fuller reviews of research on PM are available elsewhere.[3,4]

PM APPLICATION #1: WORKPLACE PROFESSIONALS

Health care workers, like many modern professional groups, often experience chronically high stress levels. Unfortunately, sustained stress experiences are a risk factor for accelerated rates of biological aging,[29] as well as major chronic health conditions such as hypertension and coronary heart disease. Among health care professionals, stress has also been directly linked to problems ranging from depression, decreased job satisfaction, and disrupted personal relationships, to reduced concentration, impaired decision making, and poorer relationships with patients.[30]

Could training in Passage Meditation help hospital-based professional caregivers to better manage the formidable stresses and challenges of their workplace? To study this question, an eight-week, 16-hour course was taught to health professionals in a large midwestern urban hospital. Study participants included nurses, physicians, chaplains, and other health care professionals who were randomly assigned to a treatment group receiving PM classes (*n* = 27), or to a wait-list control group (*n* = 31).

Treatment group participants met together weekly in one large group. Part of each week's activities took place in facilitated subgroups of six to eight persons. The classes emphasized using all eight points of PM to manage the challenges common to health care professionals with patient contact. Each weekly meeting lasted two hours, and included time for presentation, discussion, a break, and a group meditation.

Several outcomes of interest were measured using validated self-report questionnaires. All participants completed questionnaires on four occasions: prior to the beginning of the course, immediately after it concluded, 8 weeks later, and again 19 weeks after the course ended.

FINDINGS

The study found large and statistically significant reductions in stress which remained significant nearly five months after the course ended (see Figure 4.4a). Stress reductions were actually slightly larger eight weeks after the course ended than they were at postintervention, despite the lack of social support from the weekly classes. And at the 19-week follow-up assessment, nearly five months after classes ended, PM group reductions in perceived stress relative to the control group remained statistically significant. These stress reductions are quite large when compared with the effects seen in most intervention studies, and the effects on stress were mediated (explained) by adherence to PM practices.[30]

The PM group also showed statistically significant benefits on several other outcome measures, in comparison with the control group. Mental health, assessed with a widely used scale, showed significant improvement, although changes were less dramatic than for stress.[30] Smaller benefits, not statistically significant, were observed for burnout. But larger and statistically significant benefits for PM group participants were found for compassion[31] (Figure 4.4b), empathy, forgiveness, and confidence in their professional caregiving skills (technically called relational caregiving self-efficacy) (Figure 4.4c).[32,25] All of these benefits were nearly fully retained at the final 19-week follow-up assessment.

These quantitative results were corroborated by semistructured interviews with 24 of the participants (5 physicians, 12 nurses, and 7 others),

Figure 4.4.   Effect of Passage Meditation Practice by Health Professionals on (a) Stress, (b) Compassion, (c) Caregiving Self-Efficacy, and by College Students on (d) Forgiveness, in Comparison with Controls: Group Means Over Time.

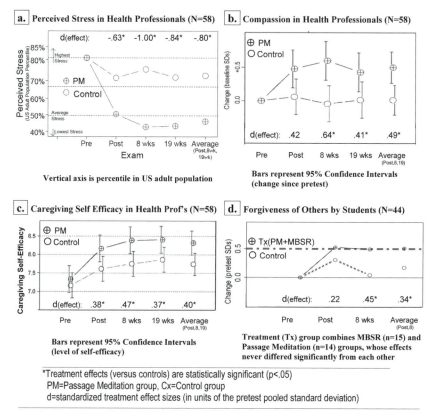

an average of three months after the intervention. The interviews revealed that most participants could recount specific ways in which program points had helped them to be more effective in their work. For example, one caregiver reported:

> I'll tell you a couple of things that have happened to me recently from the [PM] Program. I'm more focused and I also feel like I'm making a conscious effort to look in people's eyes so that I feel like they are hearing me and I'm hearing them. Recently someone said to me that my eyes show my compassion. So that

made it very real to me that I am coming across, that I do care. (p. 1129)[25]

Another said this about the mantram:

The mantram calms me down, slows me down and I feel that I can deal with whatever the situation is that got me upset. (p. 1129)[25]

PM APPLICATION #2: AN EIGHT-WEEK "STAND-ALONE" COLLEGE COURSE

Today's college students cope with a variety of academic, social, and personal challenges that leave many of them feeling overwhelmed.[16] Recently, undergraduates at a private university in California were taught PM in an eight-week course in which PM was taught along with spiritual modeling theory. Participants ($n = 44$) were randomly assigned to one of three groups: one group received PM training, a second group received training in MBSR, and a third control group was wait-listed. PM and MBSR groups were conducted concurrently, and each met over eight weeks for 90 minutes each week. Questionnaire self-report measures were administered to all study participants immediately before and after the intervention, and eight weeks following its completion. Each week in the PM group, students were taught to use one or more of PM's points, were familiarized with a prominent spiritual model, and participated in a 10- to 30-minute session of meditating on a passage. A detailed description of the PM course pedagogy has been published elsewhere.[33]

FINDINGS

For several outcomes, changes in PM and MBSR groups did not significantly differ from each other, suggesting very similar effects, and were pooled together in analyses of how they differed from controls. Compared to controls, the intervention groups showed significant reductions in stress and significant increases in the ability to forgive others (Figure 4.4d).[16]

PM and MBSR *differences* were also noted with regard to spiritual modeling. Compared to controls, PM participants showed significant increases in self-efficacy for learning from famous/traditional spiritual models, the availability of pre-1900 spiritual models, and the influence of famous/traditional spiritual models (these findings were mentioned earlier). Furthermore, the PM group gained significantly more than the MBSR group on these measures, and the MBSR group did not gain more than the controls. These findings were expected because of the higher support offered by PM for learning from spiritual models, especially traditional models.[6]

Interestingly, on a measure of *mindfulness*, the PM group showed slightly larger gains than the MBSR group, which itself gained substantially in comparison to controls (Figure 4.5). According to the researchers, findings suggest that "mindfulness . . . can be trained through a variety of different practices that differ in . . . level of explicit emphasis on mindfulness" (p. 858).[34] These findings hold important implications, since mindfulness methods have recently inspired a variety of effective psychological interventions. Apparently benefits associated with mindfulness need not be obtained only from Buddhist-derived mindfulness practices; these findings suggest that such benefits might equally be derivable from methods, such as PM, that draw spiritual content from other sources, including Western faith traditions.

Figure 4.5.   Changes in Mindfulness Over Time for College Students Trained in Passage Meditation (PM), in Mindfulness-Based Stress Reduction (MBSR), and for Controls (Cx).

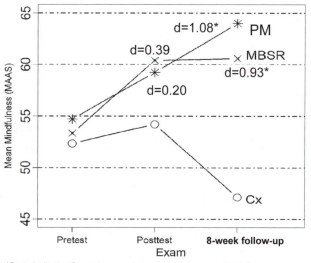

*Statistically significant changes since pretest vs controls (p<.05).
d's are changes since pretest in PM-Cx or in MBSR-Cx, in pooled pretest SDs.
Adapted from Shapiro et al. (2008) (#34 in references)

PM APPLICATION #3: PM EMBEDDED WITHIN A 10-WEEK TRADITIONAL ACADEMIC COURSE

Along with experiencing enhanced stress, U.S. college students have become increasingly anxious, depressed, and uncertain about what to do with their lives.[35] In response, a private California university in 2006 developed a 10-week academic course, English 189: Vocation. Offering ongoing support from PM along with role models from Renaissance lives and guest speakers,[6] the course fulfills both English major and core religious studies requirements, attracting a wide range of students annually. This successful course demonstrates how PM can make a valuable contribution at the heart of liberal arts education.

Easwaran's *Passage Meditation* is used as the primary course text, along with Dreher's *Your Personal Renaissance*, which presents a process for vocational discernment blending passage meditation with research from Renaissance biography and positive psychology. Several other historical and literary texts are also used.[1,36]

On the first day of class, after introductions and a short lecture, students begin their meditative practice, as described in Chapter 1 of *Passage Meditation*. They spend 10 minutes silently meditating on the first four lines of the Prayer of St. Francis, followed by time for questions and comments. They are then assigned to read the first chapter of *Passage Meditation* and memorize the St. Francis prayer or another passage from their own spiritual tradition. For the rest of the quarter, they practice daily passage meditation, starting with 10 minutes and working up to 30 minutes a day, recording their experience in paragraph assignments.

In the second class, students practice PM, discuss their practice and readings on vocation, and select one Renaissance biography for their research paper and oral report from a list that includes St. Teresa of Avila, Leonardo da Vinci, John Milton, and Sor Juana Inés de la Cruz. The paper is due at the end of the term, along with a personal vocation narrative.

Each class begins with 10 minutes of passage meditation. Classes include regular check-ins with a professor who follows PM, offering personal insights and time for students' questions.[37] Throughout the course, students learn and practice each of the eight points, discuss them in class, and write about their experience. They read chapters in *Your Personal Renaissance* about discovering their gifts, detaching from distractions, discerning their values, and charting their direction, while learning about how Renaissance role models, such as John Donne, St. Teresa of Avila, and St. Ignatius Loyola, used meditation to discern their vocations.

During the second week, students read about vocation, learn about how Giotto, Cimabue, and Botticelli discovered their gifts, look for parallels in their own lives, and take a survey to discover their gifts.[38] In the third week, students review Chapter 1 of *Passage Meditation*, and consult the description of PM at www.Easwaran.org, another supportive guide for their practice. They read about da Vinci and other Renaissance artists, and learn about a guest speaker's spiritual journey.

During the fourth week students read Chapter 2 of *Passage Meditation*, learn about using the mantram to relieve stress (see Bormann, this volume), then select and begin using their own mantram. They also learn about detachment, reading meditations by Traherne and Marvell. In the fifth week, students take a midterm on course readings and concepts. Then they focus on Chapter 3 of *Passage Meditation*, "slowing down," along with reading on discernment and the life of St. Ignatius Loyola. The sixth week focuses on Chapter 4 in *Passage Meditation*, "one-pointed attention," the search for direction, John Donne's struggle, and the spiritual journey of another guest speaker. The seventh week focuses on Chapters 5 and 6 in *Passage Meditation*, "training the senses," and "putting others first," and the life and sonnets of Michelangelo.

During weeks eight and nine, students read Chapters 7 and 8 in *Passage Meditation*, focusing on "spiritual association" and "inspirational reading," learn about the lives of George and Magdalen Herbert, and give their oral reports. In the tenth week, they meet individually with their professor for conferences on course papers. Course portfolios (research paper, personal vocation narrative, and final paragraphs) are due at the end of the week.

The final grade is based on the midterm, paragraphs, oral report, class participation, research paper, and personal vocation narrative. The daily paragraphs (written for each class period) provide a convenient means to assess student progress in their PM practice. For the personal vocation narrative, a grading rubric with key concepts and expectations helps students relate course lessons to their own lives.

OUTCOMES

Numerical evaluations for English 189 are high, averaging 4.7 on a 5-point scale. Student comments in paragraphs and narrative evaluations reveal their appreciation for PM, which provides valuable tools for dealing with stress as well as a common culture and vocabulary to support students' quest for vocation.

Although initially some students found it difficult to meditate, after a few weeks most looked forward to their daily meditation, finding peace and comfort in their practice. They appreciated the 10-minute meditation before each class, even requesting it the day of the midterm. Some students sought further meditation opportunities, joining a student-faculty Wednesday evening meditation group. Students repeatedly referred to "hurry sickness," realizing when they needed to slow down, and reported that the mantram helped them deal with exam stress and to get to sleep at night. Many also found spiritual models in the course through PM, the guest speakers, and Renaissance lives.

CONCLUSIONS

We have suggested that PM's use of inspirational passages from the world's wisdom traditions gives it a distinctive appeal to many religious and nonreligious spiritual seekers. PM appears unique among nonsectarian contemplative practices in its systematic support for learning from spiritual models, especially revered saints, sages, and founders. The inspired deeds and words (Figures 4.1 and 4.2) of such revered spiritual models represent a global legacy that many modern seekers continue to find relevant. The PM program's support for learning from such models provides potentially important "added value" not only to individual seekers, but also to health and human service professionals who are increasingly called upon to respond to the diverse spiritual needs of their clientele.

We have described several applications of the PM program, including two educational courses for college undergraduates, as well as a continuing education course for health professionals. We outlined empirical research findings that confirmed that these PM-based courses helped participants to draw upon their spiritual resources to manage the challenges of the workplace and of college life with more clarity, resolve, and compassion. Benefits were promising and sometimes dramatic. Stress reductions could plausibly translate into better physical health and longer life.[29] Yet much remains to be discovered about how the PM program may be applied in other educational, health, and human service settings. Can PM support diabetics and other chronic-disease victims in adhering to lifesaving health behaviors, despite the stresses and distractions of modern life? Can PM assist business executives to recover a spiritually grounded sense of purpose in the midst of challenging and stressful careers (see Delbecq, this volume)? Do PM-based courses offered through colleges or other organizations foster increased cross-cultural and interfaith understanding?

Because of its nonsectarian character, its comprehensive set of tools, its support for direct engagement with spiritual wisdom traditions, and its appeal to diverse populations, PM warrants careful consideration from all human service professionals, including caregivers, campus health services, and educators.

REFERENCES

1. Easwaran, E. (2008). *Passage meditation: Bringing the deep wisdom of the heart into daily life* (3rd ed.). Tomales, CA: Nilgiri Press. Full text also online at http://www.easwaran.org.

2. Bandura, A. (2003). On the psychosocial impact and mechanisms of spiritual modeling. *International Journal for the Psychology of Religion, 13,* 167–174.

3. Flinders, T., Oman, D., & Flinders, C. L. (2007). The eight-point program of passage meditation: Health effects of a comprehensive program. In T. G. Plante & C. E. Thoresen (Eds.), *Spirit, science and health: How the spiritual mind fuels physical wellness* (pp. 72–93). Westport, CT: Praeger.

4. Flinders, T., Oman, D., & Flinders, C. L. (2009). Meditation as empowerment for healing. In J. H. Ellens (Ed.), *The healing power of spirituality* (Vol. 1, pp. 213–240). Santa Barbara, CA: Praeger.

5. Two of the authors (Tim Flinders and Carol Flinders) have presented PM workshops over several decades to thousands of individuals observant in every religious tradition. The website www.easwaran.org lists over 100 current PM fellowship groups around the world.

6. Oman, D., Shapiro, S. L., Thoresen, C. E., Flinders, T., Driskill, J. D., & Plante, T. G. (2007). Learning from spiritual models and meditation: A randomized evaluation of a college course. *Pastoral Psychology, 55,* 473–493.

7. AA Meditators (n.d.). *Passage meditation & the eleventh step: The method of meditation developed by Eknath Easwaran* [booklet, 24 pages]. http://www.meditationandrecovery.org (accessed December 13, 2009).

8. Plante, T. G. (2009). *Spiritual practices in psychotherapy: Thirteen tools for enhancing psychological health*. Washington, DC: American Psychological Association.

9. Dutch, English, French, German, Greek, Hungarian, Italian, Lithuanian, Portuguese, Russian, Slovenian, Spanish. Asian languages: Bahasa Indonesian,

Chinese (PRC), Chinese (Taiwan), Hebrew, Japanese, Korean, Malayalam (India), Marathi (India), Telugu (India).

10. Oman, D., & Thoresen, C. E. (2007). How does one learn to be spiritual? The neglected role of spiritual modeling in health. In T. G. Plante & C. E. Thoresen (Eds.), *Spirit, science and health: How the spiritual mind fuels physical wellness* (pp. 39–54). Westport, CT: Praeger.

11. For holy name repetition through the day in Christianity, see Oman, D., & Driskill, J. D. (2003). Holy name repetition as a spiritual exercise and therapeutic technique. *Journal of Psychology and Christianity*, *22*, 5–19.

12. Cole, S. R., Kawachi, I., Liu, S., Gaziano, J. M., Manson, J. E., Buring, J. E., & Hennekens, C. H. (2001). Time urgency and risk of non-fatal myocardial infarction. *International Journal of Epidemiology*, *30*(2), 363–369.

13. Gallagher, W. (2009). *Rapt: Attention and the focused life*. New York: Penguin Press.

14. Foerde, K., Knowlton, B. J., Poldrack, R. A., & Smith, E. E. (2006). Modulation of competing memory systems by distraction. *PNAS Proceedings of the National Academy of Sciences of the United States of America*, *103*, 11778–11783.

15. Ophir, E., Nass, C., & Wagner, A. D. (2009). Cognitive control in media multitaskers. *Proceedings of the National Academy of Sciences of the United States of America*, *106*, 15583–15587.

16. Oman, D., Shapiro, S. L., Thoresen, C. E., Plante, T. G., & Flinders, T. (2008). Meditation lowers stress and supports forgiveness among college students: A randomized controlled trial. *Journal of American College Health*, *56*, 569–578.

17. Bormann, J. E., Thorp, S., Wetherell, J. L., & Golshan, S. (2008). Spiritually based group intervention for combat veterans with posttraumatic stress disorder: Feasibility study. *Journal of Holistic Nursing*, *26*, 109–116.

18. Oman, D. (2007). Does volunteering foster physical health and longevity? In S. G. Post (Ed.), *Altruism and health: Perspectives from empirical research* (pp. 15–32). New York: Oxford University Press.

19. Taylor, S. E. (2007). Social support. In H. S. Friedman & R. C. Silver (Eds.), *Foundations of health psychology* (pp. 145–171). New York: Oxford University Press.

20. Oman (this volume) defines an "integrative contemplative practice system" as including (1) set-aside time for attention training practice (e.g., sitting meditation), (2) cultivation of character strengths or virtues (e.g., Putting Others First), (3) centering practices for use throughout the day (e.g., the mantram), and (4) learning from spiritual models.

21. Easwaran published an extensive set of practical commentaries on Western and Eastern spiritual figures and scriptures. Many describe ways that PM points are complementary tools for coping with challenges of daily living and spiritual growth. His most comprehensive discussion is the *Bhagavad Gita for Daily Living* (1977–1984, 3 vols., Tomales, CA: Nilgiri Press).

22. Bandura, A. (1997). *Self-efficacy: The exercise of control.* New York: Freeman.

23. Sheldon, K. M., Ryan, R. M., Deci, E. L., & Kasser, T. (2004). The independent effects of goal contents and motives on well-being: It's both what you pursue and why you pursue it. *Personality & Social Psychology Bulletin, 30,* 475–486.

24. Anonymous (2008). Life persists. *Blue Mountain, 19(4),* 7. (This journal, at http://www.nilgiri.org/page/140, regularly publishes anecdotal accounts of PM coping and results.)

25. Oman, D., Richards, T. A., Hedberg, J., & Thoresen, C. E. (2008). Passage meditation improves caregiving self-efficacy among health professionals: A randomized trial and qualitative assessment. *Journal of Health Psychology, 13,* 1119–1135.

26. Oman, D., & Beddoe, A. E. (2005). Health interventions combining meditation with learning from spiritual exemplars: Conceptualization and review. *Annals of Behavioral Medicine, 29,* S126.

27. Oman, D., & Thoresen, C. E. (2003). Spiritual modeling: A key to spiritual and religious growth? *International Journal for the Psychology of Religion, 13,* 149–165.

28. For example, see an account of improved automobile driving after remembering a passage: Anonymous. (2008). "Finding peace on the road." *Blue Mountain, 19(1),* 12.

29. Epel, E., Daubenmier, J., Moskowitz, J. T., Folkman, S., & Blackburn, E. (2009). Can meditation slow rate of cellular aging? Cognitive stress, mindfulness, and telomeres. *Annals of the New York Academy of Sciences, 1172,* 34–53.

30. Oman, D., Hedberg, J., & Thoresen, C. E. (2006). Passage meditation reduces perceived stress in health professionals: A randomized, controlled trial. *Journal of Consulting and Clinical Psychology, 74,* 714–719.

31. Changes were observed in a measure of "compassionate love," a form of "other-focused" love or concern that is the subject of an emerging scientific research field—see Fehr, B. A., Sprecher, S., & Underwood, L. G. (2008). *The science of compassionate love: Theory, research, and applications.* Malden, MA: Blackwell.

32. Oman, D., Thoresen, C. E., & Hedberg, J. (2010). Does passage meditation foster compassionate love among health professionals? A randomized trial. *Mental Health, Religion & Culture, 13,* 129–154. DOI: 10.1080/13674670903261954.

33. Oman, D., Flinders, T., & Thoresen, C. E. (2008). Integrating spiritual modeling into education: A college course for stress management and spiritual growth. *International Journal for the Psychology of Religion, 18,* 79–107.

34. Shapiro, S. L., Oman, D., Thoresen, C. E., Plante, T. G., & Flinders, T. (2008). Cultivating mindfulness: Effects on well-being. *Journal of Clinical Psychology, 64,* 840–862.

35. Twenge, J. M. (2000). The age of anxiety? Birth cohort change in anxiety and neuroticism, 1952–1993. *Journal of Personality and Social Psychology, 79,* 1007–1021.

36. Additional course texts include Dreher, D. E. (2008). *Your personal renaissance: 12 steps to finding your life's true calling.* New York: Da Capo; Vasari, G. (1998). *The lives of the artists.* J. C. Bondanella & P. Bondanella (Trans.). New York: Oxford University Press (originally published 1550); Perkins, W. (1970). *A treatise of the vocations or callings of men.* In I. Breward (Ed.), *The work of William Perkins* (pp. 441–476). Abington, Berkshire, England: Sutton Courtenay Press (originally published 1603); Hardy, L. (1990). *The fabric of this world.* Grand Rapids, MI: Eerdmans.

37. As Kabat-Zinn explains, the support of an experienced meditator is vital when learning a new contemplative practice: Kabat-Zinn, J. (2003). Mindfulness-based interventions in context: Past, present, and future. *Clinical Psychology: Science & Practice, 10,* 144–156.

38. The VIA-IS survey, based on Peterson, C., & Seligman, M. E. P. (2004). *Character strengths and virtues: A handbook and classification.* New York: Oxford University Press, is available online at http://www.authentichappiness .org, and also in Seligman, M. E. P. (2002). *Authentic happiness.* New York: Free Press.

CHAPTER 5

Centering Prayer: A Method of Christian Meditation for Our Time

Jane K. Ferguson

Thousands of people from a variety of backgrounds and ethnicities are gradually becoming aware of the Christian tradition of contemplative prayer as a quieting practice in a fast-paced world. Having been exposed in the 1960s and 1970s to the value of meditation from Eastern religious practices, a steadily growing number of Christians are often surprised to learn that a meditation practice exists in their own faith tradition, based on the classical mystical theology of the church.[1]

This chapter focuses on a contemporary form of contemplative prayer known as Centering Prayer, which is based on the ancient Christian tradition of resting in God. The chapter explores the religious context in which Centering Prayer arose, its historical roots in early Christianity, the method of the prayer, and its distinctive qualities and accompanying practices. Emerging empirical research about the spiritual and health effects of Centering Prayer is highlighted, including a study in progress on Centering Prayer's effects on the brain's neural networks and a published account of the prayer's impact on stress. Everyday applications of Centering Prayer are reviewed within a variety of settings, from churches to prisons, hospitals to

Sections of Chapter 5 are reprinted with kind permission from Springer Science+Business Media: *Pastoral Psychology*, "Centering Prayer as a Healing Response to Everyday Stress: A Psychological and Spiritual Process," June 9, 2009, Jane K. Ferguson, Eleanor W. Willemsen, and MayLynn V. Castaneto. Copyright (c) Springer Science+Business Media, LLC 2009.

psychotherapy sessions, and 12-step recovery workshops to college classrooms. Cross-cultural considerations of the practice in different settings also are touched upon.

Of course Centering Prayer is not the only form of Christian meditation. Modern teachers and authors who have helped advance understanding of a practical method to access the Christian mystical path are Benedictine monks and priests John Main and Laurence Freeman of the World Community for Christian Meditation, as well as Episcopal priest Tilden Edwards and psychiatrist and spiritual director Gerald May of the Shalem Institute. The contemplative practice of the Jesus Prayer that grew out of Eastern Christianity in the early sixth century endures today. This chapter focuses on Centering Prayer because of my own familiarity with it as a trained presenter and my personal daily prayer practice the past nine years. I helped establish two Centering Prayer groups in my professional ministry at St. Mary Parish in Los Gatos, California, and conducted a doctoral study on the prayer's spiritual and health effects in the lives of parishioners, discussed below.

RELIGIOUS CONTEXT

Centering Prayer's emphasis on a personal relationship with God distinguishes it from some Eastern approaches to meditation that seek still-mind or observation of the present moment. While acknowledging this distinction, the terms contemplative prayer and meditation are used interchangeably in this chapter to recognize their similarity as a quieting practice.

Importantly, the Centering Prayer movement encourages dialogue with the contemplative dimension of other religions and sacred traditions. In this climate, Centering Prayer developed in the mid-1970s when Fr. Thomas Keating, then abbot of St. Joseph's Abbey in Spencer, Massachusetts, became engaged in interreligious dialogue with Buddhist and Hindu teachers and their students. What impressed Keating during these dialogues was a psycho-spiritual wisdom presented in Buddhist meditative disciplines that was not as readily available in the Christian contemplative framework in the same detailed and practical way.[2] Keating believed that he and his fellow Trappist monks, Basil Pennington and William Menninger, might be able to distill the essence of the Christian contemplative tradition into an accessible method, too, based on the Egyptian Desert experience that was the basis of St. Benedict's Rule. They were responding to Pope Paul VI's request of monastics to share the contemplative life with the laity to encourage the spirit of church renewal promoted by Vatican II.

The method became known as Centering Prayer to reflect the classical contemplative experience of interior silence described in the sixteenth century by St. John of the Cross: "We are attracted to God as to our center, like a stone toward the center of the earth."[3] When through ongoing surrender to God we reach the very core of our being, there remains one more center that is deeper and greater than us, Keating adds. "This center is the Trinity, Father, Son, and Holy Spirit, who dwells at the inmost center of our being. It is out of that Presence that our whole being emerges at every moment."[4]

An estimated 150,000 people are now practicing Centering Prayer individually and in hundreds of small prayer groups throughout the United States and in 39 countries in Latin America, Africa, the Asia Pacific, Europe, and the Middle East. Keating's books have been translated from English into French, Korean, Spanish, Croatian, Czech, and Polish. The Centering Prayer movement has grown largely through the grassroots efforts of laity and religious who are affiliated with Contemplative Outreach, the nonprofit organization Keating founded in 1984 to support the growing ecumenical base of practitioners from mainstream denominations, principally Roman Catholic, Episcopalian, Methodist, and Presbyterian. Centering Prayer introductory workshops are being offered on the Internet internationally, and Fr. Keating can be found on YouTube teaching the method of Centering Prayer.

While interest and practice of Centering Prayer is steadily growing, it generally is perceived as a peripheral practice within mainstream Christianity today, even though contemplative prayer was commonly practiced by devout lay men and women, as well as clergy, during the first 16 centuries of the church. Today's ordained clergy and their congregants generally have not been introduced to the Christian contemplative prayer tradition in seminaries and churches, and so it is not well understood. Some fundamentalist sectors remain to be convinced that Centering Prayer is authentically Christian, viewing it as a New Age knock-off of Eastern meditation practices. Yet it is a rich and living vein of the Christian experience. The *Catechism of the Catholic Church*, for example, likens contemplative prayer to entering into the Eucharistic liturgy to abide in the dwelling place of the Lord: "We let our masks fall and turn our hearts back to the Lord who loves us, so as to hand ourselves over to him as an offering to be purified and transformed. . . . Contemplative prayer is silence, or 'silent love.' "[5] Rev. Cynthia Bourgeault, PhD, an Episcopal priest, author, and teacher of contemplative prayer, sees theological congruence between Centering Prayer and the biblical concept of *kenosis* (Greek for "to let go" or "to empty oneself"), which describes the very nature of Christ, who emptied himself to become human, and again in the Garden of Gethsemane turned his will over to God. This is the gesture of Centering Prayer: "It's a surrender method, pure and simple, a practice based entirely on the prompt letting go of thoughts as they arise. I often think of it as *kenosis* in meditation form, a way of patterning into our being that continuously repeated gesture of, 'let go,' 'let go,' 'let go,' at the core of the path that Jesus himself walked."[6]

HISTORICAL ROOTS OF CENTERING PRAYER

The biblical basis of Centering Prayer is Jesus's intimate experience of God as *Abba* (Mark 14:36), his teaching of the prayer in secret (Matthew 6:6), and the final discourse of the Gospel of John describing the divine indwelling (John 17:21–23a). Centering Prayer also is rooted in the spirituality expressed in the third and fourth centuries by the Desert Fathers and Mothers in Egypt, Palestine, and Syria who informed mainstream Christianity. The essence of desert spirituality is expressed by the term *hesychia*, the Greek word for rest as well as stillness or silence in prayer. This rest, however, has little to do with the absence of conflict or pain. It is a rest in God in the midst of intense daily struggle. Desert spirituality as an effective response to the tensions of daily existence came not through escape but from cultivating an interior "peace of the heart"[7] during one's trials. This spirituality is particularly fitting for contemporary Christians who seek respite from daily turmoil because "the real desert lies within the heart."[8] Here, one learns from the Desert Mother Syncletica of Egypt (380 to ca. 460) that "it is possible to be solitary in one's mind while living in a crowd, and it is possible for one who is a solitary to live in a crowd of personal thoughts."[9]

This awareness that one's thinking has a profound effect on the body, mind, and soul is characteristic of the desert spirituality that was exported to Western Christendom by the desert monk John Cassian in the fifth century when he moved from Egypt to France and founded two monasteries near Marseilles. Cassian's instructions on silent prayer, drawn from his interviews of other desert monks and chronicled in his influential *Conferences*, focus on the prayer in secret that informs the method of Centering Prayer:

> We need to be especially careful to follow the gospel precept which instructs us to go into our room and to shut the door so that we may pray to our Father. And this is how we can do it.
>
> We pray in our room whenever we withdraw our hearts completely from the tumult and the noise of our thoughts and our worries and when secretly and intimately we offer our prayers to the Lord.
>
> We pray with the door shut when without opening our mouths and in perfect silence we offer our petitions to the One who pays no attention to words but who looks hard at our hearts. Hence, we must pray in utter silence.[10]

Contemplative spirituality became the norm for the devout Christian and for clergy. This slowly began to change over the centuries with a continuing shift in emphasis from the experiential to the intellectual in spirituality beginning with the rise of Scholasticism in Western Europe in the thirteenth century. With the suppression of monasteries in many European countries during the Reformation, and the Inquisition's prosecution of individuals who practiced certain forms of quiet prayer that were deemed suspect by the church, contemplative prayer faded into a rarefied practice appropriate for cloistered monks well advanced on the spiritual journey but not for laity.

THE METHOD OF CENTERING PRAYER

To revive the Christian contemplative tradition within the wider church, Keating and his fellow monks developed an accessible method for modern-day seekers. The method of Centering Prayer is recommended for 20 minutes, two times a day to deepen one's intimacy with God and to manifest the prayer's healing effects in one's life. These are the four guidelines:

1. Choose a sacred word as the symbol of your intention to consent to the presence and action of God within.
2. Sitting comfortably and with eyes closed, settle briefly and silently introduce the sacred word as the symbol of your consent to God's presence and action within.

3. When engaged with your thoughts, return ever so gently to the sacred word.

4. At the end of the prayer period, remain in silence with eyes closed for a couple of minutes.

Guideline 1. The sacred word is a one- or –two-syllable word selected beforehand. It may be a word of scripture, like "Jesus," "Peace," "*Abba*," "Mary," "Shalom," or some other word that is meaningful but does not stimulate thought—for example, "let go," "calm," or "be." The sacred word is "sacred" not because of its meaning but because it symbolizes one's intention to consent to God's presence and action within.[11] Generally, one does not change the sacred word after it has been chosen because with use over time it becomes infused in the depths of one's being, leading one to enter more willingly into contemplative prayer.

Guideline 2. The posture is relaxed yet aware. One sits upright. The eyes are closed to reduce external stimulation. The basic disposition is receptive and diffuse. One silently introduces the sacred word, without using the lips or vocal cords. "The sacred word comes from the heart and reverberates in the imagination only momentarily."[12] The method of Centering Prayer is not a technique that can be used to automatically produce either a relaxation response or a mystical experience. Instead, it is both a method and a form of prayer in itself to help dispose the practitioner to receive the divine *gift* of contemplation by quieting the mind through the use of a sacred word.

Guideline 3. Thoughts refer to any perception. This might be a feeling, sensation, emotion, image, memory, reflection, concept, commentary, or even spiritual experience. When one becomes aware of "engaging," that is to say, becoming overly interested in, any kind of thought other than the original intention to consent to God, one renews the intention by returning to the sacred word *ever so gently*. The loving attitude toward oneself in this prayer is based on advice given to spiritual seekers 400 years ago by St. Francis de Sales: "Act with great patience and gentleness toward ourselves. . . . We must not be annoyed by distractions or our failures but start over without further ado."[13]

Guideline 4. The additional two minutes serve as a bridge to ease back into ordinary awareness and sustain the effects of silence into the day.[14]

For those interested in exploring the method more deeply, read Keating's *Open Mind, Open Heart* and Bourgeault's *Centering Prayer and Inner Awakening* (referenced).

THREE DISTINGUISHING FEATURES

1. Centering Prayer is often called a prayer of intention rather than attention, making it a receptive as opposed to a concentrative form of meditation. The only "action" on the part of the practitioner is to consent to one's intention to open to God by returning to the sacred word as necessary. The sacred word does not function as a mantra in that it is not constantly repeated or used to focus one's attention. Instead, it is introduced only on those occasions when one is "engaged" in thoughts. Otherwise, one simply lets the thoughts drift by as one continues to rest in God.

2. Centering Prayer is an *apophatic* (Greek for negative), as opposed to *cataphatic* (positive) form of prayer within the two classic streams of Christian theology. Cataphatic prayer is positive because it is everything that can be said or imagined of God, typical of the prayers recited in church. Apophatic prayer, by contrast, is a prayer of "no-thinking," that is, without images or ideas of any kind, asserting the ultimate incomprehensibility of God, the mystery of mysteries whom we meet in a cloud of unknowing like Moses did on Mount Sinai. Though distinct, cataphatic and apophatic forms of prayer are profoundly complementary. Centering Prayer, for example, can enhance one's experience of spoken prayer and overall faith commitment.

3. Keating has developed a conceptual framework of Centering Prayer called the divine therapy to offer an understanding of the classical spiritual path of purification that is accessible to today's laity. He uses the jargon of popular psychology to unpack the spiritual insights of Thomas Aquinas, Teresa of Avila, and St. John of the Cross in light of the modern theory of the unconscious and developmental psychology. This has helped many people incorporate the Christian spiritual tradition more easily into their twenty-first-century lives.

Thus, while Centering Prayer may promote deep relaxation as a side effect it does not stop there: the deep rest one experiences in the prayer encourages the healing of an individual's emotional wounds of a lifetime through the purification of the unconscious. This process of purification is itself prayer, "not a preparation for the (divine) relationship but the relationship itself,"[15] leading to one's true self in

God, as St. Paul describes, "It is no longer I who live but it is Christ who lives in me" (Galatians 2:20).

Those interested in a more extensive presentation of the divine therapy may reference Keating's *Intimacy with God* as well as a lecture he delivered at Harvard Divinity School on *The Human Condition: Contemplation and Transformation*.[16] As an individual progresses in a regular practice of Centering Prayer, both psychotherapy and spiritual direction may be supportive adjuncts in helping to integrate this transformational process. While Centering Prayer does not appeal to everyone because of its radically receptive method it is available to all who are attracted to it.

ACCOMPANYING PRACTICES

The positive effects of Centering Prayer are to be found not so much in the actual prayer period but rather in the transformation of one's attitudes and behaviors in daily life. Friends and co-workers often notice these changes before the practitioner does, for example, greater peacefulness, patience, kindness, wisdom, compassion, and a desire to serve others. To help extend the effects of the prayer into daily life, several other spiritual practices have been elaborated by Contemplative Outreach to accompany a Centering Prayer practice.

1. Cultivation of Silence, Solitude, and Service

These traditional values of Christian monks are translated in practical ways for lay people who live and work in the world. Silence means avoiding making a lot of noise when one is walking, sitting, or working, and refraining from unnecessary chatter or gossip in order to be tranquil and open to God's presence. Solitude is not a withdrawal from ordinary life but taking moments apart like Jesus did when he withdrew from crowds to be with God, for it is in solitude that God renews one. Contemplative service is prayer in action. It is comprised of forming an intention to be open to God's will as the "why" of one's activity at a business meeting, for example, teaching a class, or reaching out to the homeless; and paying attention to "how" one is doing the activity through listening and presence, which allows one's relationship with God to be developed at the contemplative level even as one is actively engaged.[17]

2. *Lectio Divina*

One of the classical sources of Centering Prayer is the monastic practice of *lectio divina*, Latin for "sacred reading," characterized by four interwoven moments: *lectio* (reading), *meditatio* (reflecting), *oratio* (praying), *contemplatio* (resting). The process involves a deep listening from one's heart to the word of God in scripture, leading to moments of simply resting in God, beyond words and thoughts.

Practitioners of Centering Prayer often use *lectio divina* as a way to end a prayer period. The quiet time spent in Centering Prayer prepares one to savor scripture, or even a poem, more deeply, either individually or in small groups. At the small prayer group at my parish, for example, we practice *lectio divina* for a half hour after a 20-minute Centering Prayer period. The scriptural passage is selected from the lectionary for the upcoming Sunday Gospel, linking the prayer practice to participants' overall worship life.[18]

3. Welcoming Prayer

The Welcoming Prayer is a nonsitting practice known as "consent on the go." It describes a way to surrender to God in the present moment during the activity of daily life, inspired by the eighteenth-century spiritual classic, *Abandonment to Divine Providence*, by Jean-Pierre de Caussade. The method of the Welcoming Prayer includes noticing the feelings, emotions, thoughts, and sensations in one's body, welcoming them, and then letting them go. Practicing the Welcoming Prayer helps a person respond instead of react to the present moment. I have found it to be useful in transforming inner turmoil to greater peace and acceptance when I am emotionally upset. Here is the method:

- Focus, feel, and sink into the feelings, emotions, thoughts, sensations, and commentaries in your body.
- Welcome the divine indwelling in the feelings, emotions, thoughts, commentaries or sensations in your body by saying, "Welcome, welcome, welcome."
- Let go by repeating the following sentences:
  "I let go of my desire for security, approval, and control."
  "I let go of my desire to change this situation or person."
- Repeat the prayer as often as you need it.

4. Active Prayer Sentence

The active prayer is also a nonsitting practice involving a phrase or short sentence drawn from scripture and comprised of five to nine syllables, which one says aloud or silently in harmony with one's heartbeat. Examples include, "O Lord, come to my assistance"; "Abide in my love"; "Jesus, my light and my love." The advantage of repeating the active prayer phrase frequently during the day is that, "it eventually becomes a 'tape' similar to the 'tapes' that accompany one's upsetting emotions. When this occurs, the aspiration has the remarkable effect of erasing the old tapes, thus providing a neutral zone in which common sense or the Spirit of God can suggest what should be done."[19]

EXPERIMENTAL STUDIES

While extensive research exists on the health benefits of Eastern religious practices, only a small number of experimental studies have explored the bio-psycho-social correlates of Judeo-Christian practices. Empirical research is beginning to emerge on the promising impact of Centering Prayer, exemplified in three instances:

1. The subtle but distinguishing feature of intention in Centering Prayer is being studied by Michael Spezio, a social neuroscientist at Scripps College and the California Institute of Technology. Spezio, who is also an ordained Presbyterian minister, is investigating the effects of Centering Prayer on the brain's neural networks, using magnetic resonance imaging and other methods to discover how the brain contributes to such complex activities as returning to one's intention to be with the divine in Centering Prayer and how this compares to an attentive practice. Spezio's hypothesis is that the brain activation in Centering Prayer is statistically different than an attentive practice. Experimental research is in progress.

2. A study funded by the Templeton Foundation and the Fetzer Institute is investigating how involvement in spiritual practices such as Centering Prayer—and the lay communities that support them—influence people's health, life, and well-being over a one-year period. The study, called the "Spiritual Engagement Project," is directed by psychologists John Astin and Cassandra Vieten of the Mind-Body Medicine Research Group at California Pacific Medical Center in San Francisco. It involves 50 practitioners of

Centering Prayer, as well as 100 practitioners from two other groups, Religious Science/Science of Mind, and Contemplative Non-Dual Inquiry.

3. A published study based on a doctoral dissertation by this author, in collaboration with Eleanor Willemsen, PhD, professor of psychology and advanced statistics at Santa Clara University, and May Lynn Castañeto, a PhD candidate in psychology at Pacific Graduate School of Psychology, reports the impact on Catholic parishioners ($n = 15$) of a three-month program focused on Centering Prayer.[20] The study explores the connection between health, stress, and the unconscious using Keating's paradigm of the purification of the unconscious and psychologist Richard Lazarus's theory of stress. It hypothesizes that a regular practice of resting in the arms of a loving God may inspire an unburdening of emotional wounds from the past, which in turn may lower a person's susceptibility to stress.

To test this hypothesis, participants received guidance in twice-daily Centering Prayer. The project used quantitative and qualitative measures to assess the prayer's effects. The quantitative measures included Kenneth Pargament's Relationship-With-God Coping Styles (Collaborative, Self-Directing, Deferring). Qualitative measures involved open-ended questionnaires and observation of participants by the author and an interdisciplinary team. A comparison group of other parishioners ($n = 15$) filled out pre- and postmeasures but did not have a Centering Prayer experience.

The study concludes that participants in the first three months of their introduction to a twice-daily Centering Prayer practice experienced:

(a) Change in their style of relationship to the divine as measured by an increased Collaborative Style. The Collaborative Style is based on an interactive relationship with God that is consistent with Centering Prayer's theological grounding where those praying establish an increasingly intimate relationship with God. It is associated with reduced stress and the greatest overall sense of well-being among the three styles.

(b) Healing of stress through the effects of this relationship, corroborated by qualitative results indicating signs of purification of the unconscious and positive coping behavior. For example, unexpected tears emerged "all of a sudden" for one participant—"I just needed to let go and let it flow." Several

participants said thoughts "came up, and were let go," of child-
hood flashbacks and of people and events that they had not
entertained in years.

Participants relayed that their detachment from thoughts during the
prayer period also became a habit in daily life as they disengaged from
reactive patterns of behavior with their children, co-workers, and
spouses. This resulted in less conflict and greater intimacy in their
interactions with others, which indicates an overall reduction in stress
since interpersonal relationships are a prime source of source.[21]
For example, one participant reported the experience of a double
awareness of her outward behavior on the one hand, and her inward,
observing self, on the other: "I'm not as 'engaged' in my children's
dramas like I used to be. I can step back more, and if I do start arguing
unproductively with my kids, I can catch myself sooner, and stop."

Many of the participants found that in letting go of their expectations
for stress relief or other goals, they were better able to relax by surrendering to God, which brought them rewards beyond their expectations.
This included a desire for a relationship with God in and of itself.

APPLICATIONS

It is primarily laity who practice the prayer and have found ways to
share it in a variety of settings as church members and as psychotherapists; volunteers in prisons and 12-step recovery workshops; health
professionals in hospitals and educators in high schools, universities,
and seminaries. Here are some examples:

TEACHING MODEL IN A UNIVERSITY CLASSROOM

Vincent Pizzuto, PhD, professor of theology and religious studies at
the Jesuit University of San Francisco, teaches Centering Prayer in his
semester-long course, "Mystery of God." The course involves thirteen
three-and-a-half-hour sessions that revolve around the theology of
Keating with references to his inspiration from the scriptural and traditional roots of Christian mysticism. Each class opens with a 10-minute
Centering Prayer group practice. This is followed by lecture and dialogue on required readings that include Keating's books and texts by
other authors such as Martin Laird's *Into the Silent Land* and selections
from Harvey Eagan's *Anthology of Christian Mysticism*. A series of

20-minute DVDs featuring interviews with Thomas Keating sets the weekly class themes of Centering Prayer, the human condition, the pursuit of happiness, sin, suffering, redemption, Trinitarian love, divine indwelling, and divine transformation. The course also invites students to attend a day-long field trip in nearby Marin County to hike in meditative silence on nature trails leading to a mountaintop. The point of the trip is to get students away from cell phones and text messaging in order to experience nature as a sacred place to encounter the divine.

Grading is based on class participation (40%), written critical reflections on all of the readings (50%), and a final exam (10%) in which students are observed practicing Centering Prayer for 15 minutes in order to demonstrate their "skill set" of being able to quiet the body, mind, and emotions—to "be" instead of "do." Students especially appreciated integrating Centering Prayer meditation into the classroom experience because it helped them experience the theological concepts and ideas that they were studying, and appropriate the course material on a deeper level contributing to their own personal development and learning.

Centering Prayer Support Groups

There are Centering Prayer groups worldwide to support individuals in the daily practice of the prayer. Most of them meet in churches, generally for an hour a week, but Centering Prayer groups also gather in prisons, hospitals, and other locations. Typically, groups range from 6 to 12 participants, with chairs arranged in a circle in a quiet place. Formats include a 20-minute period of Centering Prayer followed by either *lectio divina* (described above) or a walking meditation in which participants walk slowly and mindfully before returning to a second Centering Prayer period.

In a Prison

Prison outreach has been integral to the Centering Prayer movement for decades, currently involving 187 volunteers who teach contemplative prayer to inmates in 69 state, county, and federal prisons across the United States. Reduced recidivism and a lessening of violent behavior among inmates who practice Centering Prayer has been observed by prison staff, but firm statistics have not been compiled to corroborate this.

Savario Mungo began volunteering in prisons after his retirement as a college professor. He now leads a Centering Prayer group attended by 180 inmates of different ethnicities and religious backgrounds who gather each week and sit together in silence in the gym at the McConnell Prison Unit in Beeville, Texas: "It's amazing how they respond to silence because it gets them away from the chaos. This is a private prayer they can do on their own." Prisoners themselves have written about the inner freedom and healing they have found through a Centering Prayer practice.

IN A HOSPITAL

At Santa Fe's Christus Saint Vincent Regional Medical Center, hospital chaplain Susan Rush leads a weekly Centering Prayer group on Wednesday evenings for patients, their caregivers, hospital staff, and the wider community. Participants have found the practice to be restorative on all levels in a hectic medical setting. The chaplain also teachers the prayer to her hospice patients: "In Centering Prayer, we consent to God's presence and action within. In dying, it is the same consent, the very same surrender. We do the prayer in life, we become the prayer in death." At the final stages of death, Rush does not teach Centering Prayer to patients, but through her own practice of the prayer she is able to extend to the dying her own compassionate and contemplative presence.

AS AN ADJUNCT IN PSYCHOTHERAPY

Len Sperry, clinical professor of psychiatry and behavioral medicine at Florida Atlantic University, used Centering Prayer and other spiritual interventions in his treatment of a 45-year-old Roman Catholic woman with chronic depression and an eating disorder.[22] The focus of the therapy was reducing the stressors related to the patient's symptoms. Several spiritual disciplines were employed during the three-year psychotherapeutic treatment process, including Centering Prayer, a focusing body awareness practice, journaling, and participation in a faith community. Sperry attributes the spiritual practices to the quieting effect that helped derail his patient's ruminative, internal mental chatter. At the beginning of therapy, the woman indicated that her image of God was, "judge and taskmaster . . . emotionally withholding, unsupportive, and critical."[23] By the end of therapy this image gradually changed to that of a "smiling, caring grandmother."[24] Her depression and eating disorder lessened considerably and she stopped taking antidepressants.

12-STEP RECOVERY

Contemplative Outreach offers Centering Prayer workshops for people in 12-Step Recovery groups. The 11th Step seeks "through prayer and meditation to increase our conscious contact with God." Workshop presenters are people in recovery themselves, and their vocabulary is tailored to the culture of Alcoholics Anonymous, for example, surrendering to God as a Higher Power. The purpose is to integrate the 12 Steps with the Christian contemplative tradition of Centering Prayer in order to elaborate a journey of healing. Recommended further reading is Keating's *Divine Therapy and Addiction: Centering Prayer and the Twelve Steps*.

CROSS-CULTURAL CONSIDERATIONS

While the method of Centering Prayer itself remains the same across cultures, it sometimes is contextualized differently depending on the country or denomination. For example, a Pentecostal pastor found that his congregation did not like the term Centering Prayer and so he renamed it "Abiding Prayer," which they embraced. In France Centering Prayer is called *Prier dans le Secret* (Prayer in Secret).

The choice of language in conveying the theology of the prayer can be crucial in making it "tasty" enough to try, observes Hee-Soon Kwon, professor of pastoral care and counseling at the Methodist Theological University in Seoul, Korea, where Kwon has offered Centering Prayer to seminary students and the wider community. Kwon considered the first Korean translation of *Open Mind, Open Heart* to be abrasive to some South Korean Protestants because of its Catholic terminology. So she translated a second version with a Protestant sensibility. For example in South Korea, the Catholic name for God is "God in Heaven" (Ha*nu*nim), while the Protestant name is "Only One God" (Ha*na*nim).

At a workshop in the Philippines, Fr. Carl Arico, cofounder of Contemplative Outreach, remembers needing to use the affective practice of *lectio divina* first in order to engage participants in Centering Prayer; whereas in Great Britain, his audience preferred a more intellectual theological discussion of the prayer's value before they warmed up to the prayer.

One has to be open-minded in teaching the prayer in order to meet people where they are, concludes Isabel Castellanos of Extensión Contemplativa Internacional, the Spanish-speaking arm of

Contemplative Outreach. Latin America has a strong charismatic movement and sometimes people come to the Centering Prayer workshops looking for experiences when they begin the prayer: " 'I see these clouds and angels,' they say. 'Well if you see clouds and angels, you let them go and return to the sacred word,' " Isabel responds. " 'What?!' " participants incredulously ask. "Yes," Isabel replies, ever so gently.

CONCLUSION

Centering Prayer is a form of Christian meditation that provides a practical way to rest in God in a hectic world and offers a psycho-spiritual healing paradigm that has been embraced by thousands of individuals from a variety of backgrounds, ethnicities, denominations, and countries. Centering Prayer's ancient biblical and theological sources prove it to be an integral Christian practice that is easily accessible using four guidelines, with recommended accompanying daily practices. Promising empirical research into the prayer's beneficial bio-psycho-spiritual effects include its healing impact on stress. The relevance of Centering Prayer to today's world is shown in examples of its applications inside the church setting and outside in a university classroom, psychotherapeutic treatment plan, prison, hospital, and 12-Step recovery workshop.

The cross-cultural aspects of this prayer, while lightly touched upon in this chapter, open a vista to research that remains to be done in this area, for example, looking at the importance of cultural context in the appeal of beginning and sustaining a contemplative prayer practice. Another promising area is exploration of the similarities of the theologies that undergird the meditation practices of different mystical traditions, for example the emptying practices in Buddhist *Śūnyatā*, Jewish *Ayin*, and Christian *Kenosis*.[25] What implications does a shared experience of silence through different meditation methods have in healing a world broken by wars and theologies?

REFERENCES

1. For a scholarly treatment of the ancient origins of Christian mysticism, see McGinn, B. (2007). *The foundations of Christian mysticism: Vol. 1. The presence of God: A history of Western Christian mysticism*. New York: Crossroad. For a pastoral treatment of the subject, see Arico, C. (1999). *A taste of silence: A guide to the fundamentals of centering prayer*. New York: Continuum.

2. Miles-Yepez, N. (Ed.) (2005). *The common heart: An experience of interreligious dialogue* (p. 41). New York: Lantern Books.

3. Kavanaugh, K., & Rodriguez, O. (Trans.) (1991). *The collected works of St. John of the Cross* (p. 645). Washington, DC: Institute of Carmelite Studies.

4. Keating, T. (1981). *The heart of the world: An introduction to contemplative Christianity* (p. 233). New York: Crossroad.

5. *Catechism of the Catholic Church*. (1997). 2nd ed. (pp. 651–652). United States Catholic Conference. Washington, DC: Libreria Editrice Vaticana.

6. Bourgeault, C. (2008). *The wisdom Jesus: Transforming heart and mind— a new perspective on Christ and His Message* (p. 142). Boston: Shambhala.

7. Wong, J. (2005). The Jesus Prayer and inner stillness. *Religion East and West, 5,* 86.

8. Ibid., 88.

9. Swan, L. (2001). *The forgotten desert mothers: Sayings, lives, and stories of early Christian women* (p. 58). New York: Paulist Press.

10. Cassian, J. (1985). *Conferences* (pp. 123–124). C. Luibheid, Trans. New York: Paulist Press.

11. Keating, T. (1986). *Open mind, open heart: The contemplative dimension of the Gospel* (p. 43). New York: Continuum.

12. Keating, T. (1994). *Intimacy with God* (p. 68). New York: Crossroad.

13. Keating, T. (2008). A traditional blend. In *Spirituality, contemplation, & transformation: Writings on centering prayer* (p. 5). New York: Lantern Books.

14. Keating, T. (n.d.). The method of centering prayer: The prayer of consent. [Brochure]. Butler, NJ: Contemplative Outreach. Available online at http://www.contemplativeoutreach.org/site/PageServer?pagename =about_practices_centering.

15. Bourgeault, C. (2004). *Centering prayer and inner awakening* (p. 94). Cambridge: Cowley.

16. Keating, T. (1999). *The human condition: Contemplation and transformation*. The Harold M. Wit Lectures, Harvard University Divinity School. New York: Paulist Press.

17. Frenette, D. (Speaker). (n.d.). Contemplative service: Intention/ attention. In *The practices that bring the fruits of centering prayer into daily life* (CD recording available at http://www.contemplativeoutreach.org/site/ PageServer?pagename=store). Butler, NJ: Contemplative Outreach.

18. A brochure published by Contemplative Outreach outlining a format for both individual and group practice of *lectio divina* may be found online at http://www.contemplativeoutreach.org/site/PageServer?pagename =about_practices_lectio.

19. Keating, *Open mind, open heart* (pp. 133–134).

20. Ferguson, J., Willemsen, E., & Castañeto, May Lynn V. (2009). Centering prayer as a healing response to everyday stress: A psychological and spiritual process. *Pastoral Psychology*, DOI: 10.1007/s11089-009-0225-7. See also J. K. Ferguson. (2006). *Centering prayer as a healing response to everyday*

stress at a Roman Catholic parish in Silicon Valley. Unpublished doctoral dissertation, Pacific School of Religion, Graduate Theological Union, Berkeley.

21. Kabat-Zinn, J. (1990). *Full catastrophic living: Using the wisdom of your body and mind to face stress, pain, and illness* (p. 368). New York: Dell.

22. Sperry, L. (2004). Integrative spiritually oriented psychotherapy: A case study of spiritual and psychosocial transformation. In P. Scott Richards (Ed.), *Casebook for a spiritual strategy in counseling and psychotherapy* (pp. 141–152). Washington, DC: American Psychological Association.

23. Ibid., 144.

24. Ibid., 146.

25. Cynthia Bourgeault is exploring the similarities of contemplative prayer practices from different world religions in her work at Spiritual Paths Institute in Santa Barbara, California, http://www.spiritualpaths.net/.

CHAPTER 6

Mantram Repetition: A "Portable Contemplative Practice" for Modern Times

Jill E. Bormann

Living in today's world with a steady stream of interruptions from wireless cell phones, iPods, and hand-held organizers, the notion of contemplation seems nearly impossible. Yet, the ancient practice of silently repeating powerful, sacred words throughout the day to slow down and center oneself is truly a modern-day *stress buster*. This chapter will describe mantram repetition as a portable contemplative practice. Recommendations for choosing and using a mantram will be described. Research supporting application of mantram repetition for managing stress in a variety of groups will also be presented. Family caregivers, women in labor, health care providers, adults living with HIV, and combat veterans coping with posttraumatic stress disorder (PTSD) will describe their experiences of using this simple tool that deepens spiritual and psychological well-being.

Living in societies that value speed, productivity, and multitasking, leave very little room for thoughtful contemplation or reflection. What was once unavoidable "pause time," such as waiting an hour to bake potatoes, is now a five-minute "zap" in the microwave. If we want or need to pause, we must plan for it. We feel stressed from the pressure of deadlines or the pace we believe is expected. With computers and

Sections of Chapter 6 are reprinted from Bormann, Jill, "Frequent, Silent Mantram Repetition: A Jacuzzi for the Mind," *Advanced Emergency Nursing Journal*, Volume 27, Issue 2 (Wolters Kluwer Health, 2005). Reprinted with permission from Wolters Kluwer Health.

the Internet, there is a never-ending stream of perceived demands that all seem urgent. Nevertheless, throughout history, people have managed to survive the ever-changing challenges in their lives and have discovered ways to find inner peace. To do this today requires some innovative strategies. One of these strategies is *Mantram Repetition*.

WHAT IS MANTRAM REPETITION?

In this chapter, the guidelines and language of mantram repetition is taken from Eknath Easwaran, a spiritual teacher from India who came to the United States in 1959 and created the Eight-Point Program—a set of guidelines for living a spiritual life[1] (see the chapter "Finding Balance in a Hurried World: The Eight-Point Program of Passage Meditation" by Flinders et al.). The word "mantram" originates from the Sanskrit words "manas" (mind) and "trai" (to set free or protect from). Thus, one traditional definition of the word is "to set free from the mind" (p. 39),[2] and another is "the thought that liberates and protects" (p. 2).[3]

The word "mantram" does not differ in meaning from the word "mantra," which is more familiar to Westerners. Easwaran's preference for mantram is simply a reflection of the Sanskrit he studied as a boy, but the slight difference in spelling is helpful insofar as it underscores his understanding of the power of the mantram and the remarkable range of circumstances in which he suggests it be repeated.

In Easwaran's Eight-Point Program of Passage Meditation, the mantram is one of eight points that are taught and practiced together as a comprehensive and integrated program for spiritual seekers. Even so, repetition of a mantram or sacred word is a practice that goes back thousands of years in virtually all faiths—it has a life of its own. While not all of us are willing or able to commit to a daily meditation practice, repetition of a mantram may be the ideal portable contemplative practice for modern times.

Easwaran defined the mantram as a "short, powerful spiritual formula, for the highest power we can conceive of—whether we call it God, or the ultimate reality, or the Self within. Whatever name we use, with the mantram we are calling up what is best and deepest in ourselves" (p. 8).[4] In Western culture, the word "mantra" is commonly used to mean *any* thought or phrase that is repeated ("I want to be a millionaire"). So another advantage of using Easwaran's preferred term "mantram" is that it preserves the traditional meaning: a *sacred* or *holy* word or phrase chosen to be the object of one's mental focus with the goal of connecting to inner positive resources that help in managing stress.

Mantram repetition is virtually available at any and every moment. Unlike a meditation practice such as bringing attention to one's breath throughout the day, focusing on a mantram—a sacred name or exalted word—provides a more concrete, mental tool, which brings pause to the mind. The mantram can be described as a form of "divine communication" that opens us to the sacred Spirit within. Some call this Spirit their Higher Power, God, Mother Nature, Universal Consciousness, Heavenly Father, and so on. Mantram repetition has been described as a direct call to stillness. Regardless of the language used, the mantram repetition program is based on the assumption that human beings possess a mind, body and spirit. Attributes of the spirit include characteristics of goodness, compassion, well-being, peacefulness, and kindness. Unfortunately, most do not tap into these inner characteristics due to racing thoughts, unending interruptions, and a focus on past memories or future worries.

As a contemplative practice, mantram repetition is completely portable, invisible, inexpensive, readily available, nontoxic, and nonpharmacological. It can be repeated anywhere, anytime, and in any position with eyes open or closed. It can be repeated throughout the day to serve as a rapid focusing tool for the mind or even at night to help deal with insomnia or nightmares. For stress management, it is used to redirect attention away from intrusive, negative thoughts and allow observation and reflection. Thus, it provides "pause time" to reevaluate one's behavior, habits, and addictions. It fosters equanimity, being able to stand in the middle of a situation and observe.

AUTHOR'S EXPERIENCE WITH MANTRAM REPETITION

Personally, this author has been repeating a mantram as part of the Eight-Point Program since 1988, when first introduced to the Blue Mountain Center of Meditation in Tomales, California. A greater sense of well-being and quality of life are benefits attributed to practicing the entire Eight-Point Program. However, some specific experiences related just to the mantram are noteworthy and may be helpful to readers.

Initially, it took some time to thoughtfully choose a mantram. A word or phrase related to my prior beliefs and religious upbringing was preferred, but not a word associated with any negative personal memories. I chose a less familiar, non-English word with a neutral, soothing sound and rhythm meaning "Lord of the Heart" or "Come, Lord."

Then, I had some resistance to repeating the mantram, as it seemed too simplistic and mechanical. Over time and with persistence, however, I felt a growing sense of inner security and distinct feelings of safety when repeating it. Until then, I had little awareness of the chronic fear and anxiety I experienced daily. Over time, mantram repetition began to generate an increased awareness of emotional detachment and stability. An ability to watch the mind, to recognize automatic behaviors of reactivity versus intentional, thoughtful action was cultivated. The mantram gradually became familiar, like an old friend. Amusingly, it became a game to see how long I could repeat the mantram without drifting away to other thoughts. I enhanced my ability to concentrate on tasks at hand and dismiss unwanted distractions.

After several years of consistent mantram practice, I experienced some mantram dreams. Such dreams are described as protecting people from nightmares,[4] and they illustrate the depth at which the practice can impact a person. These nightmares consisted of being chased either by a large grizzly bear or by angry men with dangerous knives. In each dream, at the point of being overcome by enemies and unable to escape, I surrendered by repeating the mantram as sincerely and focused as possible. This freed me from feeling threatened and terrorized. Immediately, in the dream, I felt peacefulness. I was not harmed in the dream and upon waking, I felt relieved and secure.

DIMENSIONS OF THE PRACTICE

How to Choose a Mantram

There are specific guidelines for choosing and using a mantram that are highlighted here, but for more comprehensive instructions, see *The Mantram Handbook*[4] by Easwaran. Choosing a mantram is not to be taken lightly. It is wise to take extra time and choose one that offers strength and support. Avoid words or phrases that evoke negative associations or bad memories. Do not make up your own. Mantrams are distinctive and time honored. They have been handed down from generation to generation and repeated by millions over time. Their power is not so much related to their concrete meaning, as it is to the resulting effects they have on individuals through repetition. Some people choose a mantram because of the person who used it. Those who are inspired by Mahatma Gandhi, for example, may choose his mantram, which was "Rama" meaning "to rejoice." A small list of recommended mantrams is shown in Table 6.1.

It is not necessary to be affiliated with a religion or have religious/spiritual beliefs in order to benefit from mantram repetition. However, those with strong religious and/or spiritual beliefs often choose a mantram that complements their beliefs. Others are surprised to find that a mantram from a different spiritual tradition may be more beneficial than one from their own tradition.

Some people have no difficulty choosing a mantram. A word or phrase jumps out at them immediately. Others have to *try it on* and practice repeating it silently for a few days, weeks, or months to see how it sounds and feels. From a psycho-spiritual perspective, the choice of a mantram is extremely important because "we are shaped by what gains our attention and occupies our thoughts."[5]

Once chosen, keep the same mantram, despite any temptation to choose another. Unlike some traditions where a different mantram is recommended for different situations, in this practice *one mantram fits all* situations. One advantage of having only one mantram is its rapid accessibility when needed immediately. It becomes an automatic *speed*

Table 6.1.   List of Common Mantrams from Traditional Sources

Sample Mantrams	Common Meanings
Jesus, Jesus, or Lord Jesus Christ	Savior or Son of God
Hail Mary or Ave Maria	Mother of Jesus or Divine Mother
My God and my All	Used by St. Francis of Assisi in his prayers
Om mani padmé hum	The jewel in the lotus of the heart
Namu Amidabutsu	An invocation of the Buddha of Infinite Light
Rama Rama	To rejoice or joy within
So Hum or So Ham	I am That
Ribono shel olam	Lord of the universe
Barukh attah Adonai	Blessed art thou, O Lord
Bismillāh ir-rahmān ir-rahīm	In the name of God, the merciful, the compassionate
Allah	One true God

Note: See other instructional resources at http://www.easwaran.org.

bump that slows reaction time in stressful moments. It is a doorway to equanimity.

How to Use a Mantram

The mantram is to be repeated with sincerity, concentration, and intention as often as possible. "As with anything else in life, the more effort and concentration you give, the greater and more dramatic the results may be" (p. 58).[2] For example, if the mind were analogous to a muscle that you wanted to strengthen, then repetition is the key. Just as an athlete lifts weights repetitively to build that muscle, we strengthen our ability to concentrate by repeating a mantram— returning our attention to it over and over. Moreover, the good news is that we can practice the mantram anytime, anywhere, without a gym, a trainer, a weight or a medicine ball, etc. It is important to repeat the mantram silently at every possible opportunity throughout the day, during routine activities such as washing dishes or when walking to the car, and even during the night, particularly just before sleep. Even though the mantram can be chanted, spoken, sung out loud, whispered, hummed, or written, repeating it silently is highly recommended. Then it can be used rapidly when needed and when others are present.

It is also helpful to repeat a mantram in times of distress or emotional upheaval such as anger, fear, panic, and/or grief. The mantram can be repeated intensely while walking briskly to transform unwanted emotions into positive energy. This is called a *mantram walk*. In addition to eliciting the relaxation response, the mantram serves as an immediate connection to one's higher Power, or inner, higher Self. It is a shortcut to awareness of the present moment and one's inner resources. Thus, it becomes a convenient form of contemplation.

The mantram can also be written, over and over, to capture one's entire attention. Writing the mantram is particularly helpful when the mind is very scattered, when emotions are out of control, or when struggling with an addiction. Mantram writing in these situations serves as a *pause button* to allow space between thought and action.

Repeating a mantram involves two additional points of Easwaran's program: skills of intentionally slowing down one's thinking and engaging in one-pointedness or focused concentration. These three skills work together synergistically to create a quiet, contemplative state of mind.

Using a Mantram to Slow Down Thinking and Set Priorities

Our culture values speed and multitasking. Instant results are expected with the technology of computers, e-mail, cell phones, and fax machines. Although we benefit from these so called time-savers, they also create an enormous demand on our attention and energy. People groan that there are not enough hours in the day to accomplish all they want. Stress is felt when we perceive there is not enough time. Such thinking promotes a sense of urgency and the need to hurry through life.

Given our culture, it may seem ridiculous to even consider slowing down. After all, everyone and everything around us appears to be accelerating at high speed. It seems as if we must hurry to survive. After awhile, most of us are not even aware we are hurrying. We become automatic robots with no time to reflect, to observe or examine our lives, and no time for contemplation.

One result of going faster and faster is that we become insensitive to others' needs. Furthermore, speed fosters physical ailments that can be linked to stress and hurry. Easwaran claims, "If we want freedom of action, good relations with others, health and vitality, calmness of mind, and the ability to grow, we have to learn to slow down" (p. 102).[1] This is an enormous task when everything around us is speeding up and making demands on us to do the same.

Slowing down involves discrimination. Discrimination means setting priorities and learning to let go of the nonessentials. Yes, there are many things to attend to—daily maintenance of household and career, caring for relationships with family and friends, etc. Discrimination is needed to determine what is most important, and then to do those things at a moderate pace to avoid mistakes and error. Contrary to what most people believe, slowing down means greater efficiency! There are fewer mistakes, fewer accidents, and more creativity.

Repeating a mantram can actually help a person go slower and allows time for discrimination. Initially, it may feel threatening to evaluate one's speed and realize the need to change and slow down. Nevertheless, slowing down has the reward of making a conscious effort to choose wisely each day in all aspects of life. The end result is living more fully, consciously, and intentionally.

USING A MANTRAM TO DEVELOP ONE-POINTED ATTENTION OR MINDFULNESS

Mantram repetition requires the mind to inherently become one-pointed with focused attention. Mantram repetition raises our awareness of the thinking process and how poor decisions and bad habits are fostered. The mantram is a very concrete, practical tool where you know when you *are* repeating it, and you know when you are *not*. Each time the mind wanders and you bring it back to focus and repeat the mantram, you have controlled your attention *internally*. Each time you pay attention to what you are doing, you control your attention *externally*. Attention is a valuable resource that often goes wasted. Just as sunlight can be focused through a magnifying glass to create a laser-sharp point capable of burning a leaf, attention that is focused on completing one task at a time creates efficiency and carefulness.

To summarize, all three skills are needed to be successful—mantram repetition, slowing down, and one-pointed attention. Repetition of each, especially mantram, is the key. Over time, repetition of the mantram increases in its power and effectiveness. "One drop of water can accomplish very little, but hundreds of millions of drops can cut through rock or, indeed, change the face of the earth" (p. 4).[3] Finally, the best way to evaluate the effectiveness of mantram practice, is to observe one's reactivity to the usual, stressful things and to evaluate the time it takes to recover from such stressors. Usually, the speed of reactivity is reduced and recovery time diminishes.

HISTORICAL PERSPECTIVES

Some form of word repetition has been discovered in nearly every culture and spiritual tradition throughout history. It has been documented as early as the seventh or eighth century BCE in the Upanishads and from the fourth or fifth century BCE in Judaism. In Christianity, mantram repetition is a form of holy name repetition used for healing and devotional purposes.[6]

The practice may not necessarily be central to the religious institutions in which it is found. Catholics use the rosary but that is only one small part of the faith tradition. Many times, in contrast, lay persons have reported that they discovered, on their own, the benefit of repeating a soothing word or phrase in times of distress. The practice appears to be universal, despite the many variations that can range from community vocal chanting or singing as a form of worship to quiet individual mental repetitions that some might call prayer.

REVIEW OF THEORETICAL AND EMPIRICAL LITERATURE

Theoretically, there are several explanations of how mantram repetition works to enhance health and well-being. These explanations are usually described using physical, mental/cognitive, psychological/emotional, and religious/spiritual mechanisms. Some of these mechanisms are briefly summarized below. More research is needed, however, to support these theories and address the impact of mantram repetition as a unique, portable practice.

PHYSICAL MECHANISMS

One of the earliest explanations for the health benefits of repeating a word, phrase, or sound is derived from research on the "relaxation response," a term coined by cardiologist Dr. Herbert Benson and defined as the opposite of the stress response.[7] The relaxation response is initiated by repeating a word, sound, prayer, phrase, or muscular activity and passively disregarding any intruding thoughts that come to mind. Ample research has been conducted on the effects of the relaxation response on anxiety, stress, cardiovascular, and neuroendocrine function.[7]

Benson recommends sitting with eyes closed repeating a chosen word or phrase for 20 minutes daily. This practice resembles Transcendental Meditation (TM), a form of sitting mantra meditation, which has also been studied in relation to health outcomes.[8] TM, however, should not be confused with mantram repetition. It differs in that the TM mantra is assigned by a paid TM practitioner rather than personally chosen. TM is a sitting meditation with eyes closed rather than a portable practice. Its goal to "transcend" beyond conscious thought in contrast to training attention and remaining conscious.

But Benson also spoke of "mini's" or brief moments throughout the day of repeating the word, sound or phrase and releasing tension while taking a deep breath. He suggested initiating the relaxation response as often as possible throughout the day and even while exercising.[7] This use most resembles mantram repetition.

Other mechanisms of mantram repetition are linked to the neural pathways in the brain. Such theories are based on preliminary data found using functional magnetic resonance imaging scans. With repetition, one is theoretically using the same neural networks over and over. This is believed to cause structural changes in the brain, particularly the structures involved with attention and control. Researchers have found that the cortical thickness in the brain is also thickened with long-term meditation practice.[9]

MENTAL/COGNITIVE

From a mental/cognitive perspective, mantram repetition works by interrupting negative, anxious, or irrational thoughts. For example, one way to restructure maladaptive thinking is by using the mnemonic acronym of the three C's: "Catch it, Check it, Change it." The mantram provides a tool or mechanism to "catch it" (meaning, recognize the unwanted thought). Then one can "check it" (assess if it is an irrational thought). This may be referred to as meta-cognitive awareness. Only when the thought is recognized can one "change it" (or replace it with a more realistic thought). Thus, mantram repetition may be a useful aid in teaching cognitive-behavioral skills.

This process has been explored in a study of positive reappraisal coping as it relates to anger in a sample of HIV+ persons. Using mixed model statistics, results suggested that the mechanism for reducing anger in the mantram group was increasing positive reappraisal coping. Those who used their mantrams were better able to pause and reappraise the situation, which in turn, led to less anger over time.[10]

PSYCHOLOGICAL/EMOTIONAL MECHANISMS

A psychological explanation for mantram repetition is called the "associative network" theory of memory and emotions.[6] Certain words generate either positive or negative feelings. Through associations, the mantram fosters what is called a "spreading activation," making related memories and emotions more mentally available. So when a mantram is paired with feelings of calm and peacefulness as in nonstressful times, such as before sleeping, it becomes associated with positive mental and physical memories. These positive feelings are then more easily accessed when the mantram is repeated during stressful, annoying moments.

RELIGIOUS/SPIRITUAL MECHANISMS

Another mechanism explaining how mantram repetition works is related to spirituality. Existential spiritual well-being is defined as having meaning and purpose in life. Because the mantram helps us connect to our inner spiritual resources, it fosters a sense of well-being. In several mantram studies that measured spiritual well-being, the mantram groups improved significantly more than controls, supporting the notion that mantram repetition enhances spiritual well-being.

In the HIV study, there were 71 participants who gave saliva samples for a secondary analysis to look at relationships between faith/assurance and the stress hormone of salivary cortisol. The mantram group participants had significant improvements in faith/assurance from pre- to postmantram treatment. Faith/assurance, in turn, was found to be inversely associated with a lagged reduction in average salivary cortisol levels over time compared to the control group.[11]

MANTRAM REPETITION PROGRAM OF RESEARCH

A program of research, conducted by this author and colleagues, has been exploring the health benefits of a mantram-based group intervention since 2001. The program is now established as an eight-week (90 minutes per week) group course called "Mantram Repetition for Relaxation." It has been adapted for a variety of audiences and consists of teaching mantram repetition, slowing down, and one-pointed attention. The textbook used is *Strength in the Storm*,[12] along with a course manual that has recommended readings and exercises.

The following section describes a series of research studies that highlight the health benefits reported by various groups practicing mantram repetition. The groups include veterans with chronic illness and combat veterans coping with PTSD, health care providers, family caregivers of veterans with dementia, women in labor, and adults living with HIV disease. For an overview of these and other studies, see Table 6.2.

Table 6.2. Published Research Studies on Mantram Repetition

Reference	Studies	Findings
13	62 veterans in mantram group assessed at pre- and posttreatment (without comparison group)	Significant improvements were found in stress, anxiety, anger, spiritual well-being, quality of life, and PTSD. Mantram practice fully mediated changes in anxiety and spiritual well-being, and partially mediated improvements in all other outcomes.
16	29 combat veterans randomized to mantram ($n = 14$) and wait-list control ($n = 15$)	Mantram group (compared to controls) decreased PTSD symptom severity, psychological distress, and improved quality of life and spiritual well-being.
17	136 combat veterans with PTSD randomized to usual care with mantram group ($n = 66$) or usual care only ($n = 70$).	Mantram group had significant improvements in self-reported PTSD, spiritual well-being, quality of life, and mental health function compared to controls. 32% of veterans in mantram group were no longer classified by clinicians as having PTSD diagnosis at posttreatment compared to 15% of veterans in control group.
Health Care Provider and Veteran Qualitative Study		
15	30 veterans and 36 health care employees were interviewed about mantram use at follow-up	Most participants (83%) reported situations where the mantram was useful for managing stress, other negative emotions, sleep/insomnia, and unwanted thoughts.
Health Care Provider Studies		
14	42 health care employees assessed at pre- and posttreatment (without comparison group)	Significant improvements in stress, anxiety, anger, spiritual well-being, and quality of life. Mantram practice mediated favorable changes in anxiety and spiritual well-being.

Table 6.2. (continued)

Reference	Studies	Findings
21	13 health care providers completed the entire Eight-Point Program and were interviewed on the impact of the program and its specific points, including mantram repetition.	7 of 13 (54%) providers reported that use of mantram helped them slow down and focus attention on the tasks at hand.
	Family Caregiver Study	
18	16 family caregivers of Veterans with dementia completed a mantram program with added cognitive-behavioral skills and were assessed at pre-, post-, and 8 weeks posttreatment with phone interviews at 36-week follow-up (without comparison group).	Caregivers reported significant improvements in caregiver burden, perceived stress, rumination, depression, and quality of life.
		94% of caregivers reported still using mantram at 36 weeks posttreatment and 100% reported that mantram repetition was helpful.
	First-time Mothers During Labor	
19	9 first-time mothers were randomized to childbirth classes plus mantram ($n = 5$) or childbirth class only controls ($n = 4$) and were telephone interviewed at 6 months postdelivery.	All 5 mothers in mantram group reported using mantram to manage pain and moments of uncertainty during complicated labors. One used mantram during delivery. All 5 reported still using mantram at 6 months postdelivery.
	HIV Studies	
20	93 HIV-infected adults randomized to mantram ($n = 46$) and educational controls ($n = 47$). Both groups had similar levels of attention and were followed for 22 weeks.	Mantram group (compared to controls) had favorable changes in anger, faith/assurance, and spiritual connectedness.
		Mantram practice was associated with increased quality of life, faith/assurance, spiritual meaning/peace, and decreased non-HIV intrusive thoughts.

10	93 HIV-infected adults randomized to mantram (n = 46) and educational controls (n = 47) for a secondary analysis that examined positive reappraisal and distance coping as mediators of anger reduction.	Mantram group reported a 25% increase in positive reappraisal and 15% reduction in anger from baseline. Positive reappraisal appeared to mediate the effect of mantram on decreased anger at 22-week follow-up. Controls reported decreased positive reappraisal coping. Distance coping was not related to anger reduction.
11	71 HIV adults randomized to mantram (n = 36) and educational controls (n = 35) for a secondary analysis of relationships among faith/assurance and daily average salivary cortisol levels over time.	Faith/assurance increased among mantram group but not controls. There was a lagged relationship between faith/assurance and average daily cortisol levels, which may have been enhanced by mantram use.
	Community-Dwelling Adults	
22	61 healthy community volunteers were randomized to mantram group (n = 23), placebo mantram group (n = 19), and no-treatment controls (n = 19).	Maha mantra repetition was associated with significantly less stress and depression compared to active controls or no-treatment controls at posttreatment and even after 4-week follow-up.

Note: PTSD = posttraumatic stress disorder.

APPLICATIONS/INTERVENTIONS

Early research on the benefits of frequent, silent mantram repetition has shown improvements in lowering perceived stress, anxiety, and anger while increasing quality of life and spiritual well-being in veterans with chronic illnesses[13] and in health care providers.[14] In these first two pilot studies, participants who received the mantram program were self-selected (not randomly assigned) and were not compared to a control group. Therefore, these positive outcomes may have been related to the therapeutic effects of group social support. These studies did provide, however, initial support needed to conduct larger, randomized controlled trials and qualitative research yet to be described.

Another group of veterans and health care providers ($N = 66$) were interviewed approximately two months after completing the mantram course. They were asked about the kinds of situations in which they used mantram repetition and found it helpful. Fifty-five (83%) reported a total of 139 helpful incidents including (a) managing emotions (54% of incidents) such as impatience, anger, frustration, feeling upset, disgruntled, or out of control; (b) managing stress (25% of incidents); (c) managing sleep/insomnia (14% of incidents); and managing unwanted thoughts (7% of incidents).[15] Some examples are provided below:

To manage grief:

I recently lost my father to cancer and I have found it [mantram repetition] very helpful in coping with his death.

—health care employee

To focus attention:

The mantram helps me slow down, helps me think and reason because it allows me to focus. And without that focus, I might be thinking three to four things at the same time.

—veteran with chronic illness

To find perspective:

The mind always blows things out of proportion and so my reciting the mantram, it seems to settle everything down and keep it in perspective, because again, reality is never as bad as what you imagine it to be.

—veteran with chronic illness

MANTRAM FOR COMBAT VETERANS WITH PTSD

While there have been numerous studies of pharmacological and cognitive-behavioral interventions for treating PTSD, little attention has been given to spiritually based approaches for managing symptoms of PTSD. Spirituality may be important to the treatment of PTSD because of research indicating that combat trauma may challenge veterans' religious faith and beliefs about life's meaning and purpose.

Because earlier research in veterans showed promising results, a feasibility study in a small sample of combat veterans was conducted. Thirty-three veterans with PTSD were recruited and 29 completed the study. They were randomly assigned to the mantram group ($n = 14$) or a wait-list control group ($n = 15$). Results demonstrated that mantram repetition was acceptable in this population and that the mantram group improved significantly more than controls in a number of psychological measures including a clinician assessment of having a PTSD diagnosis.[16]

These results supported a larger randomized trial testing the effects of the mantram program compared to usual care. A cohort of 136 outpatient veterans with PTSD were assigned to either the mantram program ($n = 66$) or the delayed-treatment control ($n = 70$). There were significant reductions in self-reported PTSD symptom severity in the mantram group compared to controls. Clinician assessment of PTSD diagnosis in the mantram group was reduced in 32 percent of the veterans compared to 15 percent in the control group. Mental health function and quality of life also improved in the mantram group. Spiritual well-being increased in the mantram group compared to a decrease in controls.[17]

Some examples of how veterans with PTSD used mantram are as follows:

To think clearly and rationally:

If I find myself getting into a bad mood or depressed . . . how can I say it . . . when I have no patience with myself and I find myself going back and beat myself up over issues or whatever, I have to . . . I do my mantram at that point in time. . . . I get more relaxed where I can start thinking other thoughts.

—veteran with PTSD

To manage anger:

I'm glad I learned the mantram. I don't stay mad. I'm not angry. I'm not all stressed out. So I try and use the mantram the best

I can to relieve the pressure, you know, 'cause we're like ...
steam, you know, once you turn the fire up ... you got to get rid
of it, you know, and the mantram really works well.

—veteran with PTSD

To manage various PTSD symptoms:

[I use mantram] any time I get agitated ... any time I have any
PTSD triggers ... driving ... situations in relationships ... anywhere I feel uncomfortable. Those types of things ... in crowds
when I am not comfortable in crowds ... If I wake up in the night
from a dream or nightmare ... I wake up in sweat ... I say my
mantram and relax.

—veteran with PTSD

Mantram for Family Caregivers of Veterans

Family caregivers are another group who are in danger of poor
health due to the stress of care giving. Caregivers frequently have total
responsibility for their loved ones and are often unable to obtain
support services because of their reluctance to leave care recipients
alone. Therefore, a family caregiver support program was created
using the structure of the mantram course and adding some cognitive
behavioral skills. The program was delivered using teleconference
calls in order to reach more caregivers, especially those from a
distance.[18]

The caregiver study resulted in significant reductions in caregiver
burden, depression, perceived stress, and rumination. There were significant improvements in quality of life satisfaction and enjoyment
over time. The teleconference delivery of the mantram program was
feasible, and improved access and participation for one caregiver
who lived 160 miles away. All caregivers reported moderate to high
satisfaction with the intervention.[18] The following quotes were taken
from telephone interviews to illustrate how mantram was used by
caregivers:

To manage impatience:

I use mantram repetition during impatient incidences when my
husband needs my attention.

—spouse as caregiver of veteran with dementia

To manage stressful situations:

Using my mantram has helped me to ward off any possible stress-ful situations, but when I do get stressed out over something, I concentrate on repeating my mantram numerous times ... then I feel relaxed.

—family caregiver of veteran with dementia

MANTRAM REPETITION FOR MOTHERS IN LABOR

Another small pilot study was conducted to assess the effects of mantram repetition on labor in first-time pregnant women.[19] Using mixed methods of quantitative and qualitative research, 9 out of 14 mothers (64%) completed the study. Five were assigned to the mantram group and four to the control group. Qualitative telephone interviews were conducted at six-month postdelivery with open-ended questions to assess mantram use.

Results of the interviews revealed that all five of the treatment group mothers had used mantram repetition during labor. They reported that mantram helped them clear their minds and not get con-sumed by experiences of pain, fear, stress, and anxiety. In return, they were able to use other measures such as deep breathing to help reduce the intensity of their physical and emotional experiences. The man-tram was also used to deal with moments of uncertainty. Mantram repetition gave them something "to do" during a time when they had no idea of what was going on. It also helped them be present to work with the doctors and the medical staff:

To manage labor:

The mantram has helped me make hard decisions ... to think clearly and rationally. [It gave me] a platform to make good deci-sions and in return, know what is truly important.

—first-time mother during labor

ADULTS LIVING WITH HIV

The last study presented here provides the most rigorous test of ben-efits. With funding from the National Center of Complementary and Alternative Medicine, a randomized controlled trial of a mantram inter-vention on health outcomes in HIV-infected adults was conducted.[20]

Ninety-three participants interested in stress management were recruited using flyers distributed in the community. They were randomly assigned to either the mantram intervention ($n = 46$) or an educational control group ($n = 47$) with equal group support. Questionnaires were administered before, during, and after the intervention and at three months follow-up. Compared to controls, the mantram group improved significantly more on anger, faith/assurance, and spiritual connectedness. Over time, both groups had significant reductions in perceived stress, anxiety, and depression.

As in earlier studies, mantram dose was measured using wrist counters and logs. More frequent mantram practice was significantly associated with reduced non-HIV intrusive thoughts, increased quality of life enjoyment and satisfaction, faith/assurance, and sense of spiritual meaning/peace. Although these relationships could not be explained by demographics, baseline spiritual well-being, involvement in a religious group, or frequency of other religious practices, mantram practice appeared to contribute to these improvements, but more research is needed. Examples of mantram practice include the following:

To help with nightmares or insomnia:

I was having trouble with nightmares . . . and those dreams were terrifying. I would wake up shaking and my hands would be clenching to my chest, stopping the blood circulation to my hands. And since I took the second week of class, the mantram started taking over and as of today, I no longer have those scary nightmares anymore.

—adult living with HIV

To manage frustration while waiting:

When I am really frustrated or in a line or something, I don't let that bother me; I just say my mantram and before you know it, I am right up at the front of the line. It has really worked for me. I liked it. I really, really liked it.

—adult living with HIV

NEW RESEARCH DIRECTIONS

With findings that mantram repetition can enhance health and well-being in many people, new directions for research would be to examine the confidence one has in using a mantram for symptom management, i.e., self-efficacy of mantram practice for various conditions. For example, there is no measure of self-efficacy for managing PTSD symptoms. Future research could assess the degree to which patients have confidence that mantram repetition can help them manage their illness.

Another area for investigation is Comparative Effectiveness Research, a description used by the Institute of Medicine for research to improve the health care system in the United States. The Institute has published a list of research topics and priorities including complementary therapies. Although the mantram program is a complementary therapy and not a stand-alone treatment, the mantram program could be compared to the Mindfulness-Based Stress Reduction program by Jon Kabat-Zinn. Although both are meditative-related practices, there may be subtle differences in health outcomes between these interventions that would be interesting to identify.

CONCLUSIONS

Because mantram repetition is simple, inexpensive, and portable, it is an ideal contemplative practice for nearly everyone. It can be used actively with a *mantram walk* or quietly before sleep. Health-related outcomes from practicing mantram are most frequently reported as inner feelings of calm or peacefulness. Evenness of mind under stress and having more patience with others has been reported by many research participants. This is the trait of equanimity sought after by contemplatives. One final tip before sharing this technique with friends, family, patients, or students: make mantram repetition a regular part of your life and test its benefits on your own.

ACKNOWLEDGMENTS

Studies cited in this chapter were conducted with support from the VA Office of Academic Affiliations; VA Office of Research and Development, Health Services Research and Development, Nursing Research Initiative (04-041-4); National Institutes of Health/National Center for Complementary and Alternative Medicine (R21AT01159); Gamma Gamma Chapter of Sigma Theta Tau International Research Award; Nurses of Veterans Affairs (NOVA) Foundation; and the San Diego State University School of Nursing's Institute of Nursing Research (#900521). The views are those of the author and do not necessarily represent the official views of the Department of Veterans Affairs, the U.S. government, or the National Center for Complementary and Alternative Medicine.

REFERENCES

1. Easwaran, E. (2008a). *Passage meditation: Bringing the deep wisdom of the heart into daily living* (3rd ed.). Tomales, CA: Nilgiri Press.

2. Ashley-Farrand, T. (1999). *Healing mantras*. New York: Ballantine.

3. Radha, S. (1996). *Mantras: Words of power* (revised ed.). Spokane, WA: Timeless Books.

4. Easwaran, E. (2008b). *The mantram handbook: A practical guide to choosing your mantram and calming your mind* (5th ed.). Tomales, CA: Nilgiri Press.

5. Easwaran, E. (2005a). *Words to live by*. Tomales, CA: Nilgiri Press.

6. Oman, D., & Driskill, J. D. (2003). Holy name repetition as a spiritual exercise and therapeutic technique. *Journal of Psychology and Christianity, 22*(1), 5–19.

7. Benson, H. (1996). *Timeless healing*. New York: Scriber.

8. Walton, K. G., Cavanaugh, K. L., & Pugh, N. D. (2005). Effect of group practice of the Transcendental Meditation program on biochemical indicators of stress in non-meditators: A prospective time series study. *Journal of Social Behavior and Personality, 17*, 339–373.

9. Lazar, S. W., Kerr, C. E., & Wasserman, R. H., et al. (2005). Meditation experience is associated with increased cortical thickness. *Neurological Report, 16*(17), 1893–1897.

10. Bormann, J. E., & Carrico, A. W. (2009). Increases in positive reappraisal coping during a group-based mantram intervention mediate sustained reductions in anger in HIV-positive persons. *International Journal of Behavioral Medicine, 16*, 74–80.

11. Bormann, J. E., Aschbacher, K., Wetherell, J. L., Roesch, S., & Redwine, L. (2009). Effects of faith/assurance on cortisol levels are enhanced by a spiritual mantram intervention in adults with HIV: A randomized trial. *Journal of Psychosomatic Research, 66*(2), 161–171

12. Easwaran, E. (2005b). *Strength in the storm: Creating calm in difficult times*. Tomales, CA: Nilgiri Press.

13. Bormann, J. E., Smith, T. L., Becker, S., Gershwin, M., Pada, L., Grudzinski, A., et al. (2005). Efficacy of frequent mantram repetition on stress, quality of life, and spiritual well-being in veterans: A pilot study. *Journal of Holistic Nursing, 23*(4), 394–413.

14. Bormann, J. E., Becker, S., Gershwin, M., Kelly, A., Pada, L., Smith, T. L., et al. (2006). Relationship of frequent mantram repetition to emotional and spiritual well-being in healthcare workers. *Journal of Continuing Education in Nursing, 37*(5), 218–224.

15. Bormann, J. E., Oman, D., Kemppainen, J. K., Becker, S., Gershwin, M., & Kelly, A. (2006). Mantram repetition for stress management in veterans and employees: A critical incident study. *Journal of Advanced Nursing, 53*(5), 502–512.

16. Bormann, J., Thorp, S., Wetherell, J. L., & Golshan, S. (2008). A spiritually based group intervention for combat veterans with posttraumatic stress disorder: Feasibility study. *Journal of Holistic Nursing, 26*(2), 109–116.

17. Bormann, J. E., Thorp, S., Wetherell, J. L., Golshan, S., Fellows, I., Lang, A., et al. (February 11–13, 2009). *Efficacy of a spiritually-based mantram intervention on quality of life in veterans with military-related PTSD.* Paper presented at the Health Services Research & Development 2009 National Meeting, Balitmore.

18. Bormann, J. E., Warren, K. A., Regalbuto, L., Glaser, D., Kelly, A., Schnack, J., et al. (in press). A spiritually-based caregiver intervention with telephone delivery for family caregivers of Veterans with dementia. *Journal of Family and Community Health, 32*(4), 345–353.

19. Hunter, L., Bormann, J., Belding, W., Sobo, E. J., Axman, L., Reseter, B. K. Hanson, S. M., & Miranda, V. (in press). Satisfaction with the use of a spiritually–based mantram intervention for childbirth-related fears in couples, *Journal of Applied Nursing Research*, online: DOI:10.1016/j.apnr.2009.06.002.

20. Bormann, J. E., Gifford, A. L., Shively, M., Smith, T. L., Redwine, L., Kelly, A., et al. (2006). Effects of spiritual mantram repetition on HIV outcomes: A randomized controlled trial. *Journal of Behavioral Medicine, 29*(4), 359–376.

21. Richards, T. A., Oman, D., Hedberg, J., Thoresen, C. E., & Bowden, J. (2006). A qualitative examination of a spiritually-based intervention and self-management in the workplace. *Nursing Science Quarterly, 19*(3), 231–239.

22. Wolf, D. B., & Abell, N. (2003). Examining the effects of meditation techniques on psychosocial functioning. *Research on Social Work Practice, 13*(1), 27–42.

PART TWO

CONTEMPLATIVE TRADITIONS

PREFACE TO PART TWO

Part Two, *Contemplative Traditions*, examines practice traditions that have been transmitted for many centuries or millennia within major faith traditions. The earlier chapter by Oman (Part One, Chapter 2) noted that four shared elements are present within many of these traditions, as well as in the integrated systems described in Part One. What distinguishes the chapters in this part is that they emphasize traditions that are too vast and deep for any one person to practice them in their entirety. For example, each tradition may contain so many variants of sitting meditation, or of formalized prayer, that an individual would almost never seek to practice them all on a regular, ongoing basis. In some cases (e.g., yoga), many practices can be easily used by people outside of the original religious tradition, and perhaps combined with adherence to a different religious tradition.

In the four chapters in this section, we are treated to key elements and highlights from the Jewish tradition (Weiss and Levy), Islam (Hamdan), the yoga school of practice that developed within Hinduism (Richards), and the Zen school within Buddhism (Tamayo-Moraga and Cohen Roshi).

CHAPTER 7

"The Eternal Is with Me, I Shall Not Fear": Jewish Contemplative Practices and Well-Being

Zari Weiss and David Levy

Over the centuries, most religious traditions have developed practices that support the cultivation of a contemplative approach to life. Judaism is no exception. Indeed, many of the practices that have traditionally been considered central to living a Jewish life have a strong contemplative orientation, and such practices can be helpful in alleviating the stress of everyday life. In the following pages, we will look at three practices in particular—prayer, meditation, and Sabbath time—that we have found valuable not only in our own practice, but also in teaching and counseling others.

The coauthors of this paper come to this exploration with distinct but overlapping backgrounds. Rabbi Zari Weiss was ordained at the Hebrew Union College-Jewish Institute of Religion in 1991, a five-year postgraduate educational institution, and has served as a rabbi in a number of capacities. Trained in the art and practice of Spiritual Direction at the Mercy Center in Burlingame, California (a Catholic-based institution), she also has worked as a spiritual director/companion with individuals and groups since 1993. She was a founding instructor, and taught for six years in a national program to train other Jews in Spiritual Direction from a Jewish perspective, and she has offered workshops and classes to rabbis and rabbinic students.

David Levy is a professor in the Information School at the University of Washington. Trained originally as a computer scientist (with a PhD from Stanford University), he too has been trained in Spiritual Direction at Mercy Center, and has practiced as a spiritual director, although to a lesser extent than Rabbi Weiss. In his academic work for the past decade, he has explored how contemplative practices and perspectives may help us to understand and alleviate the stress of information overload and the acceleration of daily life.

Both authors, then, are teachers, spiritual directors, and practicing Jews. The religious and spiritual practices we explore in this chapter are ones that that we ourselves have engaged in and experienced. Because our backgrounds and practices are not identical, we ask the reader to understand that we have adopted the first-person plural—"we"—with consideration and care. In most of the issues addressed in this chapter, it is probably less important to know which of us has the greater experience with a particular practice than that we both stand behind the assertion we are making. In certain cases, however, which will be clear below, we have found it useful to use "I" for both rhetorical and pedagogical purposes.

THE PRACTICES IN CONTEXT

It is challenging to summarize a long-standing and widespread religious tradition such as Judaism in just a few words. But it might be said that Judaism's central concern over the thousands of years of its existence has been in maintaining the sacred relationship between the Jewish people and God. Its central sacred texts, which include the Torah and the Talmud, recount the history of this relationship in its formative years and provide laws and guidance (called *mitzvot*, which we prefer to translate as "sacred obligations") intended to maintain the vibrancy and sanctity of the relationship with the Divine. One of the central mitzvot, for example, obligates Jews to "love the Eternal your God, with all your heart, with all your soul and with all your might" (Deut. 6:5). Jews are told to speak this truth at all times, when they sit in their house and when they go out on the street, when they go to sleep at night and arise in the morning. In other words, they are to love God at *all* times. Many of the other laws and customs of Judaism reinforce the importance of fulfilling this sacred obligation in all areas of life: in their interactions with others, in their care of those less fortunate, in their responsibility toward the environment and natural world.

It needs to be said, however, that not all Jews—not even all *practicing* Jews—observe all the mitzvot. Modern Judaism is divided into a number of "movements," the best known of which are Orthodox, Conservative,

Reform, and Reconstructionist Judaism. These differ in a number of ways, including the extent to which they prescribe adherence to traditional practices. The vast majority of American Jews, however, are unaffiliated: they do not belong to any movement, do not attend religious services regularly, and observe few if any Jewish holidays. Such individuals may report that they are "spiritual" rather than "religious," and to the extent that they recognize their Jewish identity, it may be more as cultural Jews (appreciating the food and the humor, for example) or in terms of a commitment to social justice, which remains a strong Jewish value.

Yet without question, Judaism's rich treasure trove of practices has been a source of comfort and solace, strength and stability for thousands of years. Its texts, rituals, and daily practices have offered many people support in stressful and uncertain circumstances. One charming anecdote illustrates this well:

> Sam happened to meet his rabbi on the street one day, and told him of all the troubles he had suffered during the past year. He wound up with: "I tell you right now, rabbi, it's enough to make a man lose his religion." "Seems to me, Sam," the rabbi told him quietly, "it's enough to make a man use his religion!"[1]

Not all people, however, know how to "use religion" in a way that offers comfort and solace, strength and stability. Particularly in our modern, assimilated world, where many have been distanced, or worse, alienated from the rich resources that are a part of Jewish tradition, these texts, rituals, and practices may seem inaccessible or foreign. As Plante and Thoresen write, "The lack of skills in using spiritual practices may be the single missing ingredient that inhibits the kind of spiritual growth that leads to better health and well-being";[2] this is as true for those in the Jewish community as it is for the broader population.

In our work as teachers and spiritual companions to others, we have had the opportunity and privilege of helping others gain access to these practices and make use of them in their own lives. In particular, it has been our growing understanding of what might be called a more contemplative approach to Jewish practice that has provided a valuable means to access the tradition in new ways. It is clear that a more contemplative approach can help bring about comfort and solace, strength and stability, and can reduce stress.

In this chapter, we will focus on three areas of Jewish practice: prayer, meditation, and Sabbath time. We could easily have chosen three other practices, or three *dozen* examples of Jewish religious and spiritual practices. The tradition is vast, and many of the customs and rituals that make up Jewish life provide opportunities for adding meaning and dimension to life.

Each of the contemplative practices we discuss has a long and diverse history. For most of Jewish history they were embedded in a complete Jewish "way of life" that was largely inseparable from the larger Jewish patterns of day-to-day living. Today, except for the most Orthodox Jews, this is no longer the case, and in today's consumerist society, many Jews are likely to choose certain practices and reject or ignore others.

Jewish prayer is a form of both verbal and nonverbal communion that can be used to praise, petition, thank, or simply communicate with God. In biblical times prayer was largely spontaneous and unscripted (the Torah records, for example, that "Isaac went out into the fields and prayed" [Gen. 24:63]). In time, these spontaneous prayers were recorded and collected, and eventually organized into a set order of specific prayers to be recited at three different times of the day. It is this form of prayer that is most familiar to Jews today. However, there are various places within the tradition where other forms of prayer are described and even encouraged. These include spontaneous prayers from the heart, recitation of a verse from the liturgy or Scripture, and personal *kavannot*, or introductory meditations. The contemplative approaches to prayer that we will discuss below are largely from this latter group.

Jewish meditation has a long, complex, and somewhat confusing history. The first problem is simply the meaning of the term meditation. An often-cited passage in the Talmud (Berachot 5:1) states that in preparation for prayer the ancient rabbis used to "incline their hearts to God" for an hour. This is now taken as evidence that some form of preparatory meditation was practiced more than 2,000 years ago. Others have suggested that the Tetragrammaton, the Divine name spelled out with the four Hebrew letters Yod Hay Vav Hay (often indicated in Roman letters as YHVH), was the sound of the breath, perhaps providing some further evidence for the existence of a form of breath meditation. Today, especially under the influence of Western Buddhist practice, a number of Jewish practitioners have rediscovered or reinvented a wide variety of forms of Jewish meditation, including meditating on a phrase or verse (mantra meditation), visual focusing on the letters of God's divine name (YHVH), and chanting. In the section on meditation below, we will highlight a few of these approaches.

Finally, probably no practice has deeper historical or spiritual roots than the observance of the Sabbath. Genesis, the first book of the Hebrew Bible, states that God created the world in six days and rested on the seventh. From this came the understanding that Jews must emulate the Divine by themselves resting every seventh day. While the nature and extent of Sabbath practice differs widely today, the basic idea of separating one day a week from the hustle and bustle—and the stress—of daily living seems well suited for today's 24/7 living.[3] In our discussion of incorporating Sabbath time into our current busy lives, we suggest several contemplative practices that are based on traditional ways of observing the Sabbath.

DIMENSIONS OF THE PRACTICES

Before looking at the specific practices, we want to suggest that their role in health, well-being, and stress-reduction can be viewed and understood from three perspectives: spiritual or theological, physical or physiological, and emotional.

SPIRITUAL/THEOLOGICAL

Any particular practice may help the practitioner put life into a broader or more spiritual perspective. Various studies have shown that gaining a broader perspective is helpful in encouraging well-being and reducing stress. In their essay on meditation, for example, Shauna L. Shapiro and Roger Walsh write: "From a growth perspective, it is essential to learn ways to free ourselves from the artificial and unnecessary limits we impose, as well as to learn to expand our world views. This liberation involves recognizing and letting go of old structures and boundaries and evolving to more complex worldviews."[4] We will see that various Jewish practices—such as meditating on a verse or line from Scripture, or observing Sabbath time—can help people experience freedom from artificial limits and expand their worldviews.

At times a broader perspective is attained in a generalized way; it may entail a specific feeling or sense of God's presence. In his article "Prayer and Health," Kevin S. Masters writes that "persons who during their prayers felt like they were experiencing an interaction with God or had feelings of increased peace were also the ones more likely to report greater levels of well-being."[5] Indeed, cultivating a sense of connection to God or God's Presence is a core component of many Jewish practices: prayer, meditation, even Sabbath time.

PHYSICAL OR PHYSIOLOGICAL

Various studies have shown that spiritual practices create physiological changes or responses in the body, which by their very nature, reduce stress. In their article "Prayer as Medicine: How Much Have We Learned?" Marek Jantos and Hosen Kiat describe "the relaxation response," one of the effects of meditation first characterized and named by Herbert Benson.[6] "Meditation," Jantos and Kiat observe, "is known to produce desirable physiological changes, such as slowed breathing, reduction in heart rate, a drop in blood pressure, peripheral warming, slower brain wave activity (marked by an increase in alpha and theta activity), and a hypometabolic state. People practicing meditation, irrespective of their religious persuasion, report feeling more spiritual and experiencing an enhanced sense of psychological and physiological wellbeing, peace and tranquility."[7] As we will see, a variety of Jewish practices, including prayer, meditation, and Sabbath time, can also create physiological changes in the body, leading to a state of wellbeing, a phenomenon that was noted by rabbis and teachers thousands of years ago.

EMOTIONAL

It is believed that religions and spiritual practices can also have a positive impact on our emotions. Jantos and Kiat write: "A third mechanism by which prayer is seen as exerting its positive impact on wellbeing is by means of the positive emotions it engenders."[7] One of the studies they cite is that of M. E. McCullough, whose research suggests that prayer improves mood and leads to a state of calm that extends to other areas of the life of the person praying.[8] They also cite the work of Candace Pert, whose book *Molecules of Emotion: The Science Behind Mind-Body Medicine* lays out some of the effects of positive emotions in the body; and they observe that "positive emotions generate physiological changes that have far-reaching consequences on our health and wellbeing. The positive emotions of peace, joy, hope, faith, trust and love, associated with prayer, can lead to physiological changes affecting a person's state of wellbeing."[9] Such emotions are fostered by a variety of Jewish practices, including prayer, meditation, and Sabbath time.

A CONTEMPLATIVE APPROACH
TO JEWISH PRACTICE

What constitutes a contemplative approach to Jewish practice? Rather than starting by referencing what has been written on this topic over the ages, we prefer to illustrate it by drawing an example from our own work as spiritual directors and teachers. It concerns the use of a verse—"The Eternal is with me, I shall not fear"—as the subject of prayer and meditation.

Often in our work as spiritual companions, our directees (i.e., clients) come to the session frazzled from the stress of the day: their bodies are tense, their hearts are racing. Sometimes they are filled with anxiety, sometimes with fear; they may be coping with illness—their own or that of a loved one; they may be anticipating a major life change, such as a loss of employment or the end of a relationship. The stress is palpable—recognizable in their shallow breathing, their tense muscles, their rigid body posture.

In our role as spiritual directors, our job is not to fix, nor even necessarily to make people feel better—though often that happens as a result of this work. Rather, it is to help people see their lives or situations from a broader, spiritual perspective.

Most people who arrive with a high level of stress, anxiety, or fear have a desire—expressed explicitly or implicitly—to reduce their level of stress and live with a greater sense of peace, calm, or equanimity. When asked directly, they may acknowledge that they wish they could feel a sense of trust—in God, in the Universe, in Something Bigger—but they also admit that they do not have any idea how to access, or cultivate, such a sense. This is the opening for which we look and listen. It is an opening no bigger than the eye of a needle: the longing of the heart (or soul) for a connection to Something Beyond the Self. From a Jewish perspective, it is the longing for a life lived in relationship with God/The Mystery/Ein Sof. (Ein Sof, one of the Hebrew names for God, literally means "That Which is Without End.") To live in this way is to live the contemplative life.

Though there are times that belief leads to experience, most often, we have seen, it is experience that leads to belief. And if experience doesn't arise on its own, it can be invited, or perhaps better, awakened.

The following example illustrates this. It is based on a session one of us conducted with a directee who had entered the office feeling very stressed.

"I wonder," I say out loud to the directee, "if there is a prayer or a phrase or some verses from a prayer that might help you feel that sense of calm or peace that you are seeking?" Many times, I haven't thought consciously about any particular prayer or verses when posing the question; it is only afterward that something comes to mind. Sometimes, the last four lines of a well-known prayer known as *Adon Olam* may come. It is a prayer that is traditionally said at the end of a service. (In some communities, it is also said at the beginning.) We don't know for certain when the prayer was written or by whom; scholars believe that it is at least 1,000 years old. It has been a part of the service since the fifteenth century. During services, it is often sung to a very upbeat or even boisterous melody (perhaps because everyone is so relieved that the service is finally over!); as a result, the beauty and power of the words' meaning is often lost. The last four verses of the prayer are quite beautiful; they suggest, almost more than any other verses from Jewish liturgy, the sense of trust that many of us long for—and the comfort that often comes with that trust.

"B'yado afkid ruchee"—"in His hand, I place my spirit." I recite the first phrase to my directee. "Of course we know that God doesn't have a hand and isn't a He—it's just a metaphor." The person usually nods. "But can you imagine, for just a moment, placing your soul in God's hand, in The Eternal's hand?" I watch as the person shuts her eyes and brings the image to mind. "It's such a beautiful image, isn't it? Now . . . can you allow yourself to rest in it?" I continue gently. I watch as the directee's breath becomes slower and her body begins to relax. "B'eyt eeshan v'ah'ee'rah—when I sleep and when I wake," I continue translating. "Imagine what you would feel like, if you started and ended each day this way, allowing yourself to rest, for just a few minutes, in God's hand." "V'im ruchee g'vee'a'tee,—and with my spirit my body too." The release of tension in her body is now visible. "Adonai lee, v'lo ee'rah—The Eternal is with me, I shall not fear." I pause, and ask: "What would it be like not to feel fear?" My directee's eyes well up with tears. "It means that no matter what happens, everything will be okay." "Okay," I repeat the word, knowing that it doesn't necessarily mean that everything will be great, or even good, but simply that, on some level, against the larger backdrop of the greater Mystery of the world and of life, everything will be all right.

"Finally," I then say, "I wonder if this is something you can return to throughout the day, when you are feeling stressed or anxious. Maybe you can recite these verses, which I'd be happy to write out for you, or perhaps you might just return to the image of resting in God's hand.

Is this something that might be helpful?" She answers yes; our time together has given her access not only to Jewish Tradition, but also to God, in a new way. It is a way that is meaningful not only in terms of her Jewish way of life, but also in terms of specific practices that may help reduce her stress and, as a result, bring about a greater sense of peace and calm.

A life lived in relationship with Something Beyond the Self: for most people caught up in our rushed, overly busy, and stress-filled culture, this is an ideal that is hard to achieve. Many people assume that to live in such a way they must seclude themselves in a monastery or convent, or disengage from their daily routines by attending an extended retreat. And while these choices certainly can be helpful for some, they are not realistic for most. There are other ways that one can cultivate a more contemplative life, even in the midst of our ordinary, everyday activities. Indeed, in our work as spiritual companions and teachers, we have found three Jewish practices that are particularly helpful in cultivating the contemplative life: prayer, meditation, and Sabbath time. We now turn to these practices.

THREE JEWISH CONTEMPLATIVE PRACTICES

PRAYER

Traditional Jewish practice specifies that one pray three times a day: morning, afternoon, and evening (these prayer services are known as *shacharit*, *minchah*, and *ma'ariv*). Today, generally only those who are at the more observant end of the spectrum fulfill this obligation; most contemporary Jews probably do not pray at all, and only a small percentage may set aside time for daily prayer.

Because people bring the real stuff of their lives to spiritual direction, and the stuff of life is, by nature, stressful, most people enter our office filled with stress. While the purpose of Spiritual Direction is not to alleviate the stress, alleviating it and living with greater calm and equanimity is often part of the person's longing or desire.

In our work as Spiritual Directors, then, we might ask in our first session if the person has any sort of a daily or regular spiritual practice. Most often, people do not. We ask if it might be reasonable to set aside some time, as little as five minutes and as much as an hour, for such a practice. Even a few minutes, particularly at the start and at the end of the day, we explain, can go far in creating a sense of greater calm or equanimity, which can be accessed throughout the day. Together with the directee we think of what might be the most realistic time of the day to build it in, given the actual circumstances of their lives (family, work, etc.).

We have found prayer to be particularly helpful in leading to feelings of calm and equanimity. As Kevin Masters writes, "The English word prayer comes from the Latin *precari* meaning to entreat or ask earnestly. Curiously, this is the same root found in the word precarious. Indeed, many pray when life seems precarious and it is during times of illness or great need that prayer is perhaps most widely acknowledged and practiced. There seems to be an almost intuitive notion among people of faith in many cultures that prayer and health are related."[5]

There are three prayers from Jewish tradition that we have found to be particularly helpful. The first prayer, part of the morning liturgy, is found in a section known as *Birchot HaShachar*, Blessings of the Dawn. Traditionally this prayer is said immediately upon awakening in the morning: "*Modeh* (*modah* for a woman) *ani lifanecha*: I am grateful before You, Sovereign that lives and endures, *she'he'chezarta bi nishmati b'chemlah*, for you have restored my soul to me in graciousness, *rabbah emunatecha*, great is your lovingkindness." Though many Jews may, in fact, have grown up saying this prayer, most are unaware of its deeper meaning. They probably have always recited it in a rote or formulaic way.

We often begin with this prayer as a starting point for building a meaningful spiritual practice. The prayer can be said in just a minute, but its effects can last throughout the day.

We invite the directee to consider why the prayer might be recited immediately upon awakening. If they don't know, we explain that upon awakening, a person realizes that she has not died during the night; on the contrary, she has been blessed with another day of life. Furthermore, we point out, the word *nishmati*, a contraction of *neshamah sheli*, my soul, is related to the word *nishimah*, breath: when we breathe in, we can become aware of our soul, the unique soul that is implanted within each one of us. As we then pause to become aware of the life-breath that flows through us, we also can become aware of the Ultimate Breath-of-Life, God/the Source, which has granted us the gift of another day. Often, as our awareness expands, the burdens which all-too-often weigh us down lighten, and our hearts somehow feel lighter, filled with gratitude instead. Gratitude is an almost guaranteed antidote to stress: when we take the time to become aware of the gift of life, of the life-breath that fills us, our breathing slows and grows deeper, our "hearts" (in reality, probably, our muscle and nerve systems) become less tight, instead opening to whatever gifts the day may bring. This awareness may result in positive emotional feelings, which in turn may have physiological effects. As the feelings help reduce stress and anxiety, they can promote a more positive outlook, which in turn can strengthen the will to live life more fully, one more day.

We sometimes use a different prayer when the directee gives evidence of a negative self-image or depression, a prayer that can lead to a more positive self-image, and to feelings of acceptance and self-love. This prayer too comes from the section of prayers known as the Morning Blessings. "Elohai neshamah sh'natatah bi . . . My God, the soul that you have given me, it is pure," it begins. This first line alone is sufficient to shift someone's perspective. We invite the directee to become aware of his soul. This is something that most people have never even considered. "Think of your unique essence," we might suggest, "the part of you that is uniquely you." And then we repeat the words of the prayer, and encourage him to become aware, if he is able, of the pureness of his soul. "Separate from the layers of 'stuff' that we accumulate over the course of our lives, which result from our own behaviors or our personality flaws, Judaism teaches us that our soul is pure. And God knows that." The tightness in his body begins to release; there is a letting go, a release. Again, we explain how in Hebrew the word for soul, *neshamah*, and the word for breath, *neshimah*, are related. Our breath connects us to our soul; every time we take a breath, we have the opportunity to remember the pure, precious soul inside us, the soul that also connects us to God. We sit patiently, watching as the directee's breath gradually begins to flow more freely, and as the muscles begin to relax. There is a sense of acceptance and compassion; with these more positive feelings comes a softening of the heart, a release of the physiological tension that often accompanies self-judgment.

Finally, there is another prayer (actually a declaration) that we often draw upon in our work, the Shema. Often translated "Hear O Israel, the Lord is our God, the Lord is One," the Shema, we believe, is a statement of equanimity. It affirms that all—the good, the bad, and the ugly—are a part of the Mystery of Life, a part of the underlying Unity (One, in Hebrew, *Echad*) that is present in all existence. Traditionally Jews recite the Shema morning and evening: when they rise up (*u'vkumecha*) and when they lie down (*uv'shachb'cha*) (Deut. 6:4–9). In the bedtime version of this prayer, there is an additional prayer that can be found only in traditional prayer books; for some unknown reason many liberal prayer books have left it out. In this version, there is a paragraph in which the person reciting it forgives those who have harmed her, and asks forgiveness of anyone whom she has harmed. "Can you imagine saying this at the end of every day?" we ask, knowing what a profound spiritual practice forgiveness can be. The opposite—not forgiving—creates tremendous stress in the body: it leads to repressed anger, guilt, hurt—all of which are emotions that cause restriction, tightness, as opposed to expansiveness, openness. To forgive—even just to make the effort to forgive—makes the heart soften into a more supple state; that suppleness ripples out through the muscles, and stress is reduced. With forgiveness comes a letting go. Affirming the Unity of Life, and letting go of anger and hurt—what more profound spiritual practice could there be?

MEDITATION

Meditation in Jewish tradition takes many forms. In our work as Spiritual Directors, we have found several meditative practices to be particularly helpful in creating a more expansive consciousness, a deeper sense of peace and equanimity. Many people come to Spiritual Direction with an expressed desire to feel a connection to God more often throughout their daily lives, not only during the time in the morning or evening when they are engaged in some sort of spiritual practice. When we meet with them, we often explain the age-old practice of meditating on a verse, particularly the verse from the book of Psalms: *Shi'vi'ti HaShem L'negdi Tamid.* "I place the Eternal before me always" (Psalms 16:8). Some do this by sitting in front of a wall hanging, known as a *Shi'vi'ti*, a traditional wall card, poster, or plaque with the verse from Psalms on it. Some of these wall hangings are elaborate works of art, with beautiful illustrations and other scriptural verses surrounding Psalms 16:8. The Hebrew letters of God's name (YHVH) are often arranged vertically; they become the focus for visual meditation. Various teachings throughout the ages describe this practice: "Many people write the name YHVH on a piece of parchment . . . and keep it in front of them while they pray, according to the way of 'I have placed the Lord before me always.' And this brings awe of God into their heart and clarifies your soul to purity."[10] They then strive to keep the image of God's name before them throughout the day, without any external visual aids. Visualizing God's name encourages one to be aware of God's Presence—in every action, in every interaction. One delightful folktale tells of the holy Rabbi Yaakov Koppel Hasid of Kolomaya, the disciple of the Baal Shem Tov (the founder of Hasidism), who would repeat the line from Psalms at all hours of the day, nonstop. He would even repeat it during the hours of work and business. It is said that even the gentiles called him "The Shvittinik [the Shiviti person]."[10] In our work with individuals, we might make a copy of a *Shi'vi'ti* that can be found in certain prayer books; we suggest they experiment with the practice of meditating on God's Divine name as a means to remind them to strive to be aware of God's Presence at all times.

Of course, one can enter into a meditative state without focusing on a particular verse, but rather, simply by immersing oneself in a consciousness of God's presence or existence in the universe. Various great teachers from Jewish tradition spoke of this practice, known as *hitbonenut*. Following is one teaching of Moses Maimonides, the great thirteenth-century physician and philosopher:

> What is the way to love and fear G-d? When a person contemplates (*hitbonen*) His great, wondrous deeds and creations, seeing through them His boundless, infinite wisdom, he immediately loves, exults, and is ecstatic with a passion to know the great Name. This is, what King David meant when he said, "My soul thirsts for G-d, for the living Deity." (Psalms 42:3)
>
> When one thinks about these things, he immediately becomes awed and abashed. He realizes that he is but an infinitesimal creature, lowly and unenlightened, standing with his diminutive, deficient mind before the Perfect Mind. David thus said, "When I see Your heavens, the work of Your fingers . . . what is man that You consider him?" (Psalms 8:4–5)[11]

In other words, Maimonides suggests, by pausing and seeing *beyond* what appears on the surface a person can become aware of the various ways that God is or might be present: in any created object, in an event, in any experience of life. When he is able to do this, he will be filled with an awareness of God, and will realize his own minuteness relative to the magnificence of the Great Mystery of the Divine. His sense of self will recede, and his awareness of God will move to the forefront.

To help them imagine this state of consciousness, we might invite our directees to close their eyes and see themselves against the backdrop of the mystery of all life. We might ask if they are aware of God's role in that mystery, as well as their own place in it. Often they sink into silence, and we sit quietly together, humbly aware of the Mystery of Life of which they, and we, are a part.

Kevin Masters writes "persons who during their prayers felt they were experiencing an interaction with God or had feelings of increased peace were also the ones more likely to report greater levels of well being."[5] Indeed, we have found that from the meditative state that is achieved, whether through visualizing God's name and becoming increasingly aware of God's Presence, or sitting against the backdrop of the mystery of life, there often emerges a deep sense of calm and tranquility. With that sense of calm and tranquility often comes a letting go of the obsessive concern with things that in our day-to-day lives seem so important.

SABBATH TIME

As noted earlier, the theological basis for Sabbath observance is found in Genesis: "The heaven and the earth were finished, and all their array. On the seventh day God finished the work that He had been doing, and He ceased on the seventh day from all work that he had done. And God blessed the seventh day and declared it holy, because on it God ceased from all the work of creation that He had done" (Genesis 2:1–3). This understanding has led Jews over the ages to emulate the Divine pattern and to abstain from all work from nightfall on Friday evening to nightfall on Saturday (the Jewish day begins at sunset). The English word "Sabbath" is a direct translation of the Hebrew "*Shabbat*," which means "rest."

Over the centuries there has been much discussion and debate about this apparently simple prescription. What exactly is meant by work, and what is meant by rest? Does work refer simply or primarily to physical exertion, or perhaps to paid labor? What about intellectual work? Does rest refer to the abstention from effort, or to leisure activities? And what exactly is the purpose of the Sabbath? While it would carry us too far afield to discuss these points now, it is worth pointing to one traditional answer to the last of these questions. The intent behind Sabbath observance, the ancient rabbis suggested, is to celebrate Creation. Jews, they argued, were to abstain from creative acts in order to savor and appreciate the created world—to enjoy it, as the following description points out:

> Work can make man free, but one can also be a slave to work.
> When God created heaven and earth, says the Talmud, they went

on unreeling endlessly, "like two bobbins of thread," until their Creator called out to them, "Enough!" (Talmud Chagigah 12a). God's creative activity was followed by the Sabbath, when He deliberately ceased from His creative work. . . . It is thus not "work," but "ceasing from work" which God chose as the sign of His free creation of the world. By ceasing from work every Sabbath, in the manner prescribed by the Torah, the Jew bears witness to the creative power of God. He also reveals Man's true greatness. The stars and the planets, having once started on their eternal rounds, go on blindly, ceaselessly, driven by nature's law of cause and effect. Man, however, by an act of faith, can put a limit to his labor, so that it will not degenerate into purposeless drudgery. By keeping Sabbath the Jew becomes, as our Sages say, *domeh l'Yotzero*—"like his Creator." He is, like God, work's master, not its slave.[12]

One of the prayers from the Sabbath liturgy expresses this sentiment well: "Those who keep Shabbat by calling it a delight will rejoice in Your realm. The people that hallows Shabbat will delight in Your goodness. For, being pleased with the Seventh Day, You hallowed it as the most precious of days, drawing our attention to the work of Creation."[13]

Here then is an understanding, and a practice, that speaks to the stress of living in both the ancient and the modern world. For surely the working day in all cultures, past and present, has been filled with the stress of physical and mental labor: continuously engaging in acts of creation and productivity, continually striving for achievement. The Sabbath is conceived as a day to let go of the willful striving for productivity; it is instead a day to appreciate the simple experience of being alive, to feel gratitude for the marvels and mysteries of the created world. Abraham Joshua Heschel's well-known passage speaks to this understanding: "He who wants to enter the holiness of the day must first lay down the profanity of clattering commerce, of being yoked to toil. . . . He must say farewell to manual work and learn to understand that the world has already been created and will survive without the help of man. Six days a week we wrestle with the world, wringing profit from the earth; on the Sabbath we especially care for the seed of eternity planted in the soul. . . . Six days a week we seek to dominate the world, on the seventh day we try to dominate the self."[14]

In our work as Spiritual Directors and teachers, we have found some of the traditional practices and customs of Shabbat to be a valuable starting place for helping to create islands of calm in the otherwise hectic and hurried lives of our directees. Here are three simple practices that can be used to create a few moments, an hour, or a full day of Sabbath time.

One custom practiced by more observant Jews entails going to a mikveh, a natural or artificial body of water in which one fully immerses, in preparation for the Sabbath. Short of going to a mikveh, one can simply wash in hot water. The following description, based on various traditional teachings, helps explain the benefits—not only physical, but spiritual as well—of this practice:

> It is a traditional practice to wash in hot water before Shabbat. The hot water will change your body-feeling, removing any negativity and the weekday "set," and ready you for the renewal that comes with Shabbat. Bodily cleanliness also has a spiritual effect. It is hard to feel spiritually pure when you are physically unclean; conversely, being clean in body natural conduces to a feeling of spiritual cleanliness.[10]

For those who hope to incorporate some sort of Sabbath time into their lives, we might suggest that they prepare by taking a hot bath, allowing themselves to linger in the water for a while. As is reflected in the above teaching, water—particularly hot water—can have healing and transformative qualities. As they relax in the water, preparing themselves physically, spiritually, and emotionally for the sacred time they are about to observe, their muscles relax, and stress is released.

Alternately, for a shorter period, they might simply do a ritual hand washing, to delineate sacred time from ordinary time. Even symbolically, pouring water over one's hands can suggest a release from negativity or a sense of letting go of the past (stress) and opening to the future (a new way of being). We might suggest singing a lovely melody set to a verse from the Prophet Isaiah: "Draw water in joy, from the living well. Mayyim Chayyim. Waters of Life. Shalom."

The second suggestion is based on the traditional practice of welcoming the Sabbath by lighting candles. The flame of a candle is a universal symbol of God's Presence, as well as of the soul and the spiritual; indeed, there is something transformative that can happen when one lights candles, demarcating one period of time from another. One teaching, for example, says "On the holy Sabbath, whose inner meaning is the spiritual elevation of all the worlds ... the

Sabbath candles serves to symbolize the elevation of the soul and of holiness."[10] We might suggest then, that to begin a period of sacred time, whether an hour or a day, our directees light a candle and sit in front of it for at least a few moments, meditating on the flame, opening to God's Presence, or simply sitting quietly.

Finally, the third practice comes out of the traditional understanding of the Sabbath as a time to abstain from working. Over the centuries, to decide what was permitted and what was prohibited on the Sabbath, the ancient rabbis had to grapple with what exactly constituted work (the word for work in Hebrew is *melakhah*). While the details of their understanding is mainly relevant for Jews who fully observe a traditional Sabbath, the underlying principle they came up with is more broadly applicable: on the Sabbath, Jews are to abstain from the ordinary, task-oriented practices of the workweek in order to remember and feel gratitude for the gift of God's creation. Thus Grunfeld, referencing the writings of Rabbi Samson Raphael Hirsch, one of the foremost Jewish thinkers of the nineteenth century, writes, "Man . . . is engaged in a constant struggle to gain mastery over God's creation, to bring nature under his control. By the use of his God-given intelligence, skills and energy, he has in large measure succeeded in this. He is thus constantly in danger of forgetting his own creaturehood—his utter and complete dependence on the Lord of all things. He tends to forget that the very powers he uses in his conquest of nature are derived from his Creator, in Whose service his life and work should be conducted."[12]

Taking this principle into our work with directees, we may suggest that they create sacred time by unplugging for a period of time from all their devices: BlackBerry, computer, telephone, etc. For many this is a radical notion and takes some getting used to; it makes them realize that they do have some choice in whether they are always "on" or sometimes "off," and forces them to confront their own addictions and attachments to these tools. We have found that for some, the practice of unplugging is liberating, providing periods of quiet and calm.

THEORETICAL AND EMPIRICAL LITERATURE

There is an extensive and growing literature on the value of Buddhist meditation as a source of stress reduction and general wellness (see elsewhere in this volume). There is also an active literature that explores the efficacy of prayer, both from a specifically Christian and from a multidenominational perspective. Yet as far as we know, there are no scientific studies that have addressed specific Jewish practices of the form we have been discussing here.

A considerable amount of work, however, has been done over the last decade or two on the topic of healing from a Jewish perspective. This body of work may have some relevance for the subject of spiritual practice and well-being; as far as we know, however, scholarly studies have not yet been conducted. This would be an area that would be fruitful for further research and exploration.

APPLICATIONS

Our experience suggests that it is a select group of people who are drawn to a more contemplative approach to Jewish practice. But there are limited opportunities within the mainstream Jewish community for such people to study and experiment more deeply. Some more spiritually oriented retreat centers do exist, and in addition to three or four programs training Jews in Spiritual Direction, there is also now an Institute for Jewish Spirituality, which introduces Jewish professionals (rabbis and cantors), and more recently, laypeople, to a more contemplative approach to Judaism. This program is growing in popularity, and satellite programs are being offered at various places around the country.

It is currently hard to know to what extent this approach might be of interest to the majority of the Jewish population if it were to be more widely available. For such people, we would hope, there may be value in creating opportunities for ongoing learning and experimentation, as well as additional resources, such as this collection, for study.

CONCLUSION

The Jewish practices we have described in this chapter—prayer, meditation, and Sabbath time—are rich and multifaceted. While each of them clearly has correspondences in other traditions, the specifically Jewish manifestations we have discussed here have deep roots in Jewish history, texts, and culture. A Jewish person searching for solace, comfort, and healing may well find it in non-Jewish practices; indeed, it is well known that many Western Jews now fill Buddhist and Hindu meditation halls well out of proportion to their representation in the larger culture. But there is a kind of healing that we have both experienced and witnessed that occurs when one makes peace with one's own tradition and is able to find sustenance through it. It is the rare individual who, when looking for peace and stress reduction, is likely to embrace a full Jewish life. It is much more likely that such an individual may adopt one or more of the practices discussed here, and gain some of what she is looking for not only through the techniques themselves but through the power of their connection to a vast and life-giving tradition.

REFERENCES

1. Schur, T. G. (1993). *Illness and crisis: Coping the Jewish way*. New York: National Conference of Synagogue Youth, 79.

2. Plante, T. G., & Thoresen, C. E. (Eds.). (2007). *Spirit, science, and health: How the spiritual mind fuels physical wellness* (p. 6). Westport, CT: Praeger.

3. Muller, W. (1999). *Sabbath: Finding rest, renewal, and delight in our busy lives*. New York: Bantam Books.

4. Shapiro, S. L., & Walsh, R. (2007). Meditation: Exploring the farther reaches. In T. G. Plante & C. E. Thoresen (Eds.), *Spirit, science, and health: How the spiritual mind fuels physical wellness* (pp. 57–69). Westport, CT: Praeger. See p. 60.

5. Masters, K. S. (2007). Prayer and health. In T. G. Plante & C. E. Thoresen (Eds.), *Spirit, science, and health: How the spiritual mind fuels physical wellness* (pp. 11–24). Westport, CT: Praeger.

6. Benson, H. (1975). *The relaxation response*. New York: Avon Books.

7. Jantos, M., & Kiat, H. (2007). Prayer as medicine: How much have we learned? *Medical Journal of Australia, 186*(10 Suppl.), S51–S53.

8. McCullough, M. E. (1995). Prayer and health: Conceptual issues, research review, and research agenda. *Journal of Psychology and Theology, 23*, 15–29.

9. Pert, C. B. (1999). *Molecules of emotion: The science behind mind-body medicine*. New York: Touchstone.

10. Buxbaum, Y. (1990). *Jewish spiritual practices*. Northvale, NJ: Jason Aronson.

11. Kaplan, A. (1978). *Meditation and the Bible*. New York: Samuel Weiser, 132–138.

12. Grunfeld, D. D. I. (2003). *The Sabbath: A guide to its understanding and observance*. Jerusalem: Feldheim, 16–17.

13. *Mishkan T'filah: A Reform Siddur* (2007). New York: Central Conference of American Rabbis.

14. Heschel, A. J. (1985). *The Sabbath: Its meaning for modern man*. New York: Farrar, Straus and Young, 13.

CHAPTER 8

A Comprehensive Contemplative Approach from the Islamic Tradition

Aisha Hamdan

Islam is more than simply an organized religion; it is a way of life that penetrates every thought, emotion, and action of its adherents. Comprehensive guidance is provided for even the most mundane aspects of life and encompasses the religious, spiritual, psychological, physical, social, political, and economic. Foundational to this system is the development of human potential and purification of the soul. This is achieved through complete submission and obedience to Allah, our Creator. Through this process, the human being experiences inner peace, contentment, and bliss, the elusive elements that humans have strived to attain since the beginning of their existence. The soul is provided with the food that it longs for through prayer, supplication, reading of the Holy Qur'an, remembrance of Allah, etc. In times of adversity and tribulation, the believer calls upon Allah, relies upon Him, and seeks refuge in Him, only to find the pressure of life washed away like dust on a rainy day.

The Arabic word for contemplation and reflection is *tafakkur*. The ability to reflect, to contemplate, and to understand is one of the greatest blessings that Allah has bestowed upon humans.[1] Through proper use of this ability, the human should easily find the truth of Allah's Oneness and Uniqueness and develop a keen desire to worship Him. This understanding frees him from the traps of Satan and engagement in mindless and useless pursuits. It inspires him to prepare for the Hereafter and focus on the important things in life, which, in turn, leads to inner peace, contentment, and general well-being. In the Islamic framework, contemplation is generally thought to be a specific form of remembrance. For purposes of this chapter, I will broaden the definition to encompass other traditional practices and attitudes.

Islam offers a comprehensive system of contemplative practices primarily for preventive purposes. This chapter will introduce the primary contemplative practices within traditional Sunni Islam. The foundation of contemplation is the five daily prayers through which the believer is consistently linked to his Creator. This is supported by other contemplative practices such as remembrance of Allah, reading of Qur'an, supplication, and specific contemplation. The specific description and details of these practices are elucidated in the Qur'an and the *Sunnah* (practices or way) of the Prophet Muhammad (peace and blessings be upon him), and can even be traced back to previous Prophets (peace be upon all of them). Focusing on the spiritual modeling of the Prophet (peace and blessings be upon him), the essential components of these contemplative practices will be presented with an emphasis on the nurturing of attitudes and beliefs and the resultant benefits for devotees. The empirical literature related to the practices will be reviewed as well as current or potential applications in various settings. Finally, suggestions for future research will be addressed, highlighting the need to explicate the mechanisms of action in the religiosity/spirituality and mental health link.

CONTEXT

The formal prayers in Islam are the main source of contemplative practice for Muslims. All of the previous prophets sent by the Creator of the heavens and the earth were commanded to perform the prayers and the movements in the prayers were common among them.[2] After Abraham (peace be upon him) built the Ka'bah in Makkah (present-day Saudi Arabia), he said, as mentioned in the Qur'an, "O Lord, I have settled some of my descendents in an uncultivated valley near Your sacred House, our Lord, that they may establish prayer."[3] Abraham also said, "My Lord, make me an establisher of prayer, and [many] from my descendents. Our Lord, and accept my supplication."[3]

While referring to the Prophets Abraham, Isaac, and Jacob (peace be upon them), the Qur'an says: "And We made them leaders guiding

[men] by Our command, and We inspired to them the doing of good deeds, establishment of prayer and giving of zakah (alms-giving)."[3] Allah revealed to Moses (peace be upon him), "Indeed, I am Allah. There is no deity except Me, so worship Me and establish prayer for my remembrance."[3] Jesus (peace be upon him) said, "Indeed, I am the servant of Allah. He has given me the Scripture and made me a Prophet. And He has made me blessed wherever I am and enjoined upon me prayer and zakah (alms-giving) as long as I remain alive."[3]

After the testimony of faith, formal prayer was the first religious duty made obligatory upon the Muslim community, three years before the emigration of the Prophet and a group of believers from Makkah to Madinah. The significance of the prayer is supported by the fact that its obligation was ordered in heaven by Allah Himself during the Prophet's night journey from Makkah to Jerusalem and then into the heavens (*Israa'* and *Mi'raaj*).[4] Initially Allah ordered 50 prayers per day, but these were reduced several times (on the recommendation of Prophet Moses) until they were 5. The Prophet (peace and blessings be upon him) then said that Allah proclaimed, "These are five prayers and they are all (equal to) fifty (in reward) for My Word does not change."[5]

Prayer is one of the pillars of Islam, a basic foundation upon which other aspects are built. Most scholars agree that not praying and denying its obligation is disbelief and takes the person outside the folds of Islam. Millions of Muslims around the world regularly complete their five daily prayers. In fact, throughout the world, at any one time, there are Muslims praying. There may be variations due to culture or religious sect, but the *Sunnah* (practices or way) of the Prophet Muhammad (peace and blessings be upon him) is clear, detailed (see discussion below), and should be followed. Regarding the more informal practices of supplications, remembrance of Allah, and specific contemplation, many Muslims regularly engage in these practices, again with variations that may or not reflect the practices of the Prophet (peace and blessings be upon him).

DIMENSIONS OF THE PRACTICE

This section will first provide detailed instructions regarding the formal practice of the five daily prayers in Islam. This will be followed by a discussion of the more informal practices including remembrance of Allah, supplication, and specific contemplation.

Formal Practice—Obligatory Prayers

The five formal, daily prayers are an obligation for each Muslim who is mature and sane. They are completed in a structured format in the Arabic language and at specific times throughout the day. The decree for prayer is mentioned several times in the Qur'an: "Indeed, prayer has been decreed upon the believers a decree of specified times."[3] "Maintain with care the [obligatory] prayers and [in particular] the middle [i.e., 'asr] prayer and stand before Allah, devoutly obedient."[3] "He has certainly succeeded who purifies himself and mentions the Name of his Lord and prays."[3]

Prayer is a fundamental practice in Islam and it indicates the human's intention and desire to submit to and worship Allah. It frees the individual from associating partners with Allah and is essential for purification of the soul. Allah mentions, "You can only warn those who fear their Lord unseen and have established prayer. And whoever purifies himself only purifies himself for [the benefit of] his soul. And to Allah is the [final] destination."[3] Prayer provides the believer with a continuous source of strength, protects and purifies him from sinful behavior, develops his character and conduct, instills self-discipline and perseverance, and leads to feelings of peace and contentment.

It is not only a matter of praying, but rather "establishing the prayer," which entails performing the prayer according to the guidelines of the Qur'an and *Sunnah* (in terms of manner, time of prayers, and attention during prayer). Devotion to prayer is a characteristic of the true believer. In describing the believers, Allah states, "They are humbly submissive in their prayers";[3] "And who (strictly) guard their prayers";[3] and "Those who believe in the Hereafter believe in it [the Qur'an], and they are maintaining their prayers."[3] The Prophet Muhammad (peace and blessings be upon him) also described the prayer in its proper time as being the best deed. Abdullah ibn Masood, one of his companions, said, "I asked the Prophet (peace and blessings be upon him), 'Which deed is most beloved to Allah?' He replied, 'The prayer in its proper time.' "[5]

Sulaiman Nadwi describes the prayer in the following way: "What is Salat (Prayer)? It is the expression of devotedness by the created to his Creator with his whole being, i.e., heart, tongue, feet and hands; it is the remembrance of the Most Merciful and the Most Gracious; it is the thanksgiving for His limitless favors; it is the praise and adoration for the eternal beauty of His creation and acknowledgement of His Unity and Greatness; it is the communication of soul with the Beloved Lord; it is the complete obeisance by body and soul to the Master; it is the dedication of one's internal feelings; it is the natural music of one's heart-string; it is the tie of relationship between the Creator and the created and the latter's strong bond of devoutness; it is the comfort for the agitated and uneasy mind; it is the solace for the restless soul; it is the remedy for the hopeless heart; it is the natural internal call of a receptive and sensitive mind; it is the purpose of life and the essence of existence."[2]

Times of the Prescribed Prayers

The following are the specific times for the prayers:

Dawn (*Fajr*): from the first light appearing in the sky until sunrise

Noon (*Thuhr*): from the decline of the sun (about 20 minutes after it has reached its zenith) until *'asr*

Afternoon (*'Asr*): from mid-afternoon (when the length of a shadow is equal to the length of its object) until *maghrib*

Sunset (*Maghrib*): from the disappearance of the sun until "*isha*"

Night ("*Isha*"): from the disappearance of the red glow in the sky (about one and a quarter hours after sunset) until midnight (halfway between *maghrib* and *fajr*)[4]

Conditions of Prayer

Certain conditions or prerequisites are required before beginning the prayer:

1. Knowledge that the time for prayer has arrived.
2. Ablution (*wudhu'*)—see description below.
3. Cleanliness of body, clothing, and place of prayer (free from blood, vomit, urine, excrement).
4. Proper covering of the body—men must cover from the navel to (and including) the knees as a minimum; women must cover all of the body except the face and hands.
5. Facing the direction of the *qiblah* (the *Ka'bah* in Makkah).
6. Intention in the heart to perform a particular prayer.[4]

Ablution

Prior to the formal prayer, the person must perform *wudu* or ablution. Prayer, in fact, is invalid without proper ablution. Ablution involves washing several body parts as described below:

1. Having the intention in the heart to purify oneself for prayer.
2. Saying "In the name of Allah, the Entirely Merciful, the Especially Merciful."
3. Washing the hands three times.
4. Rinsing the mouth and nostrils three times.
5. Washing the face three times.
6. Washing the right forearm including the elbow three times, followed by the left forearm.
7. With water on the hands, wiping over the head and hair once, then the ears with the thumbs and index fingers.
8. Washing the right foot including the ankle three times, followed by the left foot.
   Note: In some cases, a person must complete *ghusl* or a full bath. This would be required for the following: (1) ejaculation of sperm due to sexual desire, (2) contact between genitalia of husband and wife, (3) completion of woman's menstruation, (4) completion of postpartum bleeding, and (5) upon converting to Islam.

Components of the Prayer

The following are the components of the daily prayer:[6]

1. Turn one's face and whole body toward the *Qiblah* (Ka'bah in Makkah), intending by the heart to perform the prayer that he wants to fulfill, whether it is an obligatory prayer or a supererogatory prayer. He should make a *sutra* (i.e., a barrier in front of the worshipper).
2. Say "*Allahu Akbar*" (Allah is the Greatest) and look downward to the place of prostration. While saying this, the worshipper should raise his hands to the level of the shoulders or near to the lobes of the ears.
3. Put the right hand over the left hand and left wrist, and put them both over the chest.

4. It is recommended that the worshipper recite this opening supplication, saying: "Praise and glory be to Allah. Blessed be Your
   Name, exalted be Your Majesty and Glory. There is no god but
   You." He may say any other supplications that the Prophet (peace
   and blessings of Allah be on him) used to say in his prayers.

5. The worshipper then says "I seek protection of Allah against the
   accursed Satan, In the name of Allah, the Entirely Merciful, the
   Especially Merciful," and recites al-Fatihah (opening chapter of
   the Qur'an): "[All] praise is [due] to Allah, Lord of the worlds—
   the Entirely Merciful, the Especially Merciful, Sovereign of the
   Day of Recompense. It is You Alone we worship and You Alone
   we ask for help. Guide us to the straight path—the path of
   those upon whom You have bestowed favor, not of those who have
   evoked [Your] anger or of those who are astray."

6. The worshipper bows in "*ruku*," raising his hands up to the level
   of his shoulders or ears while saying "Allahu Akbar," then bends
   down, making his head and back on one level and putting his
   hands with the fingers spread on his knees. He should say thrice
   at least: "Glory be to my Lord, the Almighty." It is advisable to
   say in addition to that, while bowing: "Glory be to Thee, O Allah,
   and I praise Thee, forgive me my sins."

7. To raise the head up from bowing, raise the hands to the level of
   the shoulders or ears, saying "Allah listens to him who praises
   Him." While resuming the standing position, say: "Our Lord,
   praise be for Thee only, praises plentiful and blessed as to fill
   the heavens, the earth, what in between, and fill that which will
   please Thee besides them." The worshipper is advised to put
   his hands on his chest, as he had done before he bowed.

8. To prostrate saying "Allahu Akbar," the worshipper should touch
   the ground with his hands before touching it with his knees, if
   that is possible for him. His fingers and toes should be directed
   toward the *Qiblah*, and his hands should be stretched, the fingers
   close together and not separated. In prostration, the worshipper
   should make sure that these seven parts touch the ground: the
   forehead, the nose, both hands, both knees, and the internal parts
   of the toes. Then the worshipper should say thrice or more:
   "Glorified is my Lord, the Exalted."

   It is recommended for the worshipper to increase supplications
   during prostration because the Prophet (peace and blessings be
   upon him) said: "As for bowing you should glorify your Lord

during performing it, as for prostration, you should do your best to supplicate and ask for more from Him, because your supplications during prostration are more worthy to be accepted."

9. He should raise his head from prostration saying "Allahu Akbar," then lay his left foot flat on the ground and sit upon it, keeping his right foot erected, his hands on his thighs and knees, and say "O my Lord, forgive me, have mercy on me, guide me, provide me with your blessings and console me."

10. To prostrate again saying "Allahu Akbar," repeat during the prostration what was done and said in the first prostration.

11. Then the worshipper raises his head saying "Allahu Akbar," taking a pause similar to the pause between the two prostrations; this is called "the pause for rest." Then the worshipper rises up and stands, reads al-Fatihah and some other verses of the Qur'an, and does just as he did in the first unit of prayer.

12. If the prayer consists of two units of prayer (i.e., morning prayer), the worshipper sits after the second prostration, with his right foot erect, sitting on his left foot laid down, putting his right hand on his right thigh, all his fingers close-fisted save the index finger (or keeping both the little and ring fingers closed, while rounding his thumb and middle finger in a ring shape), which he uses to point out as a sign for his monotheistic belief, and his left hand is put on his left thigh. The worshipper recites the following: "Greetings, prayers and the good things of life belong to Allah. Peace, mercy and blessing of Allah be on you, O Prophet. May peace be upon us and on the devout slaves of Allah. I testify that there is no god but Allah and I testify that Mohammed is His slave and messenger. O Allah, bless Mohammed and his family as You blessed Ibrahim and his family. You are the Most-Praised, the Most-Glorious. O Allah, bestow Your grace on Mohammed and his family as You bestowed it on Ibrahim and his family. You are the Most-Praised, The Most-Glorious."

13. The worshipper then asks Allah's protection from four evils, saying "My Lord, I ask your protection from torment of the Hell, torment of the grave the trials in life-time and after death, and from the impostor Antichrist." He may supplicate to Allah at this time.

14. The worshipper terminates his prayer by turning his face to the right, and then the left, saying "Peace and mercy of Allah be on you" each time.

15. In case of a three-unit prayer (i.e., evening) or a four-unit prayer (i.e., noon prayer, late afternoon prayer) the worshipper stands up after reciting the *Tashahud* according to the manner stated before, and raises his hands up to the level of his shoulders saying "Allahu Akbar." The worshipper puts his hands over his chest as it has been explained before, and recites only al-Fatihah. He then completes the prayer as described above.

NONOBLIGATORY PRAYERS

In addition to the five obligatory prayers, there are nonobligatory, optional prayers that the worshipper may engage in during specific times or situations. They have generally been legislated to make up for any deficiencies in the performance of obligatory prayers. There are several prayers in this category, but the primary ones include the following:

1. *Sunnah* prayers (regular practice of the Prophet) before or after the formal prayers (two units before *fajr*, four units before *dhuhr* and two or four after it; two units after *maghrib*, two units after "*isha*").

2. Night prayers (*tahajjud*)—includes 11 or 13 units of prayer usually done after one has slept and best during the last part of the night; *taraweeh* are prayers performed at night in congregation or individually during the month of Ramadan.

3. *Witr* prayer—final prayer of the night, which concludes the voluntary night prayers so that they become an odd number.

4. Mid-morning prayer (*duha*)—two to eight units from when the sun is about a spear's length above the horizon continuing until the sun reaches its meridian.

5. Friday prayer (*Jumu'ah*)—congregational prayer that is obligatory for men (women and children may attend, but are not required to do so); consists of two units replacing the four units of *dhuhr* prayer, which is preceded by a sermon given by the *imam* (religious leader).

6. Holiday (*Eid*) prayers—following the month of fasting of Ramadan and on the tenth day of *Hajj* (pilgrimage); special congregational prayer of two units held after sunrise followed by a speech by the *imam*.

INFORMAL PRACTICES

In addition to the regular obligatory prayers mentioned above, there are several other more informal tools the worshipper may utilize to maintain serenity throughout the day. These include remembrance of Allah (*dhikr*), supplication (*du'a*), and specific contemplation and reflection.

Remembrance of Allah (*dhikr*)

Believers are encouraged to remember Allah throughout the day. Allah says, "O you who have believed, remember Allah with much remembrance and exalt Him morning and afternoon. It is He who confers blessing upon you, and His angels [ask Him to do so] that He may bring you out from darknesses into the light. And ever is He, to the believers, Merciful."[3] "And when the prayer has been concluded, disperse within the land and seek from the bounty of Allah, and remember Allah often that you may succeed."[3] "Those who have believed and whose hearts are assured by the remembrance of Allah. Unquestionably, by the remembrance of Allah hearts are assured."

The Prophet Muhammad (peace and blessings be upon him) said, "Shall I inform you of the best of your deeds, the one that raises you most in rank, most purifying to your Lord, which is better for you than giving gold and silver and better for you than meeting your enemy and striking their necks and them striking your necks?" They said, "Certainly, [tell us]." He said, "It is the remembrance of Allah, the Exalted."[1] He (peace and blessings be upon him) also said, "The similitude of the one who remembers his Lord and the one who does not remember his Lord is like the similitude of death and life."[5]

There are two different types of *dhikr* or remembrance of Allah. The first is the more formal or ritualized form wherein the individual remembers Allah at specific times and occasions throughout the day, using the precise words as they were transmitted by Prophet Muhammad (peace and blessings be upon him). The prayer itself as mentioned above is the most important of the formal type of remembrance of Allah.[1] Allah says, "Indeed, I am Allah. There is no deity except Me, so worship Me and establish prayer for My remembrance."[3] Other times of formalized *dhikr* include following each of the five daily prayers, in the morning and evening, before and after eating, upon entering or leaving the house, upon entering or leaving the mosque, upon entering or leaving the bathroom, after sneezing, etc.

It is important to mention that one must do one's best to use the exact wording of the Prophet (peace and blessings be upon him) and to avoid innovation (e.g., repeating the word Allah or one of Allah's Names), which was not done by the Prophet (peace and blessings be upon him) himself.

The other type of remembrance of Allah is the constant, unwavering form in which the individual is continuously mindful of Allah as he conducts his daily routine and activities. This entails a higher level of spiritual development and is achieved by dutifully and devotedly practicing the first type of *dhikr*. It can also be achieved by remembering the true purpose of life and our ultimate goal, which is the Hereafter.

Supplication (*du'a*)

Allah says, "And when My slaves ask you (O Muhammad) concerning Me, then (answer them): I am indeed near. I respond to the invocations of the supplicant when he calls on Me."[3] Supplication is another form of worship that is beneficial for purification of the soul and for overcoming any tribulation that an individual may face. Supplication demonstrates the worshipper's sense of humility, powerlessness, and weakness while affirming Allah's Power and Ability to respond and carry out His decree. If the supplication is made with sincere intention, it can relieve worry and distress, and bring a sense of peacefulness. Allah responds to each supplication and may fulfill the person's hopes by executing that which is requested; if not, He will give something better. The Messenger (peace and blessings be upon him) said, "There is no Muslim who supplicates Allah with a supplication that does not contain anything sinful or asks for the ties of kinship to be broken save that Allah gives him one of three things: either He will give him what he asks for soon, or He will delay it for him for the Hereafter or He will keep a similar evil away from him."[1]

There are many types and examples of supplications used by the Prophet Muhammad (peace and blessings be upon him). Anas reported, "The most frequent invocation of the Prophet (peace and blessings be upon him) was: 'O Allah! Give us in this world that which is good and in the Hereafter that which is good, and save us from the torment of the Fire.'"[7] To relieve anxiety and distress, he would say, "There is no-one who is afflicted by distress and grief, and says, 'O Allah, I am Your slave, son of Your slave, son of Your maidservant; my forelock is in Your hand, Your command over me is forever executed and Your decree over me is just. I ask You by every name belonging to You which You have named Yourself with, or revealed in Your Book, or taught to any of Your creation, or You have preserved in the knowledge of the Unseen with You, that You make the Qur'an the life of my heart and the light of my breast, and a departure for my sorrow and a release for my anxiety,' but Allah will take away his distress and grief, and replace it with joy."[8]

Supplication is also beneficial as a form of protection. The supplicant may pray to Allah for refuge from distress, heading it off before it occurs. For example, the Prophet Muhammad would say, "O Allah, I seek refuge with You from grief and worry, from incapacity and laziness, from cowardice and miserliness, from being heavily in debt and from being overpowered by men."[7] Several of the remembrances that are prescribed for Muslims throughout the day are supplications and may include this preventive aspect.

Specific Contemplation and Reflection

This is the category that is generally considered when discussing contemplation. An important type of specific contemplation is reflecting upon Allah's creation in nature. This is mentioned many times in the Qur'an. "Indeed, in the creation of the heavens and the earth and the alternation of the night and the day are signs for those of understanding—who remember Allah while standing or sitting or [lying] on their sides and give thought to the creation of the heavens and the earth saying, 'Our Lord, You did not create this aimlessly; exalted are You [above such a thing]; then protect us from the punishment of the fire."[3] Through contemplation of nature, the believer draws closer to Allah in awe of His strength and power to create such amazing beauty. It increases his faith, love, and gratitude for the many bounties that he has received from Allah. It should also make one aware of how dependent he is upon the Creator for everything and reduce any tendency for arrogance.

The believer is also encouraged to contemplate death and what will happen to him in the grave, on the Day of Resurrection, and in the Hereafter. The Prophet (peace and blessings be upon him) said, "Increase your remembrance of the destroyer of pleasures: death. No one thinks about it during times of straitened circumstances except that it makes it easier upon him. And no one thinks about it during times of ease except that it constrains it upon him."[1] This type of contemplation reminds the individual that he will not live forever, but that he will move on to another life. He will then work hard to prepare for that Day by engaging in more good deeds and avoiding sinful behavior.

Related to remembrance of death is the realization of the true nature of existence in this worldly life. Life is only a transient phase that is filled with various diversions and fleeting pleasures. Allah says, "And the worldly life is not but amusement and diversion; but the home of the Hereafter is best for those who fear Allah, so will you not reason?"[3] and "And present to them the example of the life of this world, [its being] like rain which We send down from the sky, and the vegetation of the earth mingles with it and [then] it becomes dry remnants, scattered by the winds. And Allah is every, over all things, Perfect in Ability. Wealth and children are [but] adornment of the worldly life. But the enduring good deeds are better to your Lord for reward and better for [one's] hope."[3] Having the realization of the fleeting nature of this world leads the believer to become detached from it and to deal and cope with it in the appropriate manner.[1]

CULTIVATION OF ATTITUDES

From the perspective of Islam, Allah created humans with the potential for both good and evil. The test for every human being is to choose which of these characteristics he will support and develop and which he will attempt to control or eliminate.[1] Allah says in the Qur'an, "And [by] the soul and He who proportioned it and inspired it [with discernment of] its wickedness and its righteousness. He has succeeded who purifies it, and he has failed who instills it [with corruption]."[3] The choices that he makes will be reflected in his behaviors, thoughts, and emotions.

In order to support the contemplative practices mentioned above, it is important for the believer to follow the guidance of Allah in all areas of life and work on developing noble and virtuous characteristics. The character traits that one should strive to develop include humility, honesty, patience, trustworthiness, gentleness, justice, etc. This is the path of purification of the soul and the path of moderation and balance. As the human would be fulfilling his natural inclination to worship Allah, there will be no conflict in his personality or distress. Good mental and emotional health can also be attained by restraining the negative attributes of the self (i.e., jealousy, greed, anger, etc).

Purification of the soul and subsequent personality/character development occurs by bringing out what is best in the soul and minimizing or completely eradicating its evils.[1] The soul can be purified through performance of acts of worship such as prayer, fasting, charity, etc. Purification is also achieved by obeying the commands of Allah, avoiding the prohibited, and being conscious of Allah at all times. Islam offers a comprehensive model of living that encompasses the psychological, physical, social, political, and economic, and thus guidance is provided for every area of life. The guidance comes from the Qur'an and the *Sunnah* of Prophet Muhammad (peace and blessings be upon him).

SPIRITUAL MODELS

The Prophet Muhammad (peace and blessings be upon him) provides not only the ideal model to achieve inner serenity and well-being through the contemplative practices described above but also an overall philosophy and approach to life. Prophet Muhammad (peace and blessings be upon him) was conferred the status as a final and universal role model for Muslims until the end of time. His example is one of exceptional morality, righteous behavior and character, and outstanding skills, all of which are characteristics that reflect his position as a Prophet.[9] The Holy Qur'an refers literally to the status of Prophet Muhammad (peace and blessings be upon him) as a role model: "There has certainly been for you in the Messenger of Allah an excellent pattern for anyone whose hope is in Allah and the Last Day and [who] remembers Allah often."[3] The Arabic word *uswa* in the verse means example or model that should be obeyed and followed. A person who follows another imitates their behavior, attitude, and style. This verse shows the importance of Prophet Muhammad's *Sunnah* (way or path) in the lives of Muslims who practice his way in almost every aspect of life.

Following the Prophet's *Sunnah* is a form of obedience to Allah. Allah says, "Whoever obeys the Messenger verily obeys Allah; but if any turn away, We have not sent you to watch over their (evil deeds)."[3] Any knowledge that came from the Messenger actually originated with Allah. Several verses in the Qur'an order the Muslims to follow and obey the Prophet (peace and blessings be upon him). For example, Allah says, "Say, Obey Allah and obey the Messenger. But if you turn away, he is only responsible for the duty placed on him and you for that placed on you. If you obey him, you shall be on right guidance. The Messenger's duty is only to preach the clear (message)."[3] This verse indicates that the person who obeys the Prophet (peace and blessings be upon him) will be on right guidance.

The *Sunnah* of the Prophet (peace and blessings be upon him) is reported through the *Ahadith*, and consists of his sayings, actions, and silent approvals. These are considered inspiration from Allah and are second only to the Qur'an in terms of significance and evidence. The Prophet's *Sunnah* has been preserved in books, the most famous of which are *Sahih al-Bukhari* and *Sahih Muslim*. The Prophet's Companions recorded or memorized his statements and actions, which were transmitted from generation to generation by scholars. A strict methodology of *Ahadith* was developed to determine authentic (*sahih*) *Ahadith* from those that were weak or fabricated.

REVIEW OF THE THEORETICAL AND EMPIRICAL LITERATURE

The main area of empirical literature in relation to Muslims and the religiosity and practice of Muslims pertains to mental health. There is limited information related to physical health, although several articles focus on fasting during Ramadan and various health outcomes.

RELIGIOSITY AND MENTAL HEALTH

Researchers investigating the relationship between religiosity and mental health in Muslim populations have focused on several variables, primarily religious coping, well-being, happiness, life satisfaction, marital satisfaction, anxiety, and depression. Several researchers have also looked at death anxiety and suicidal thoughts/behaviors, antisocial behavior, and alcohol use/abuse. Researchers of religious coping have found that Muslims commonly engage in religious coping when faced with challenges or traumas in life.[10] In their study of 38 parents of children diagnosed with cancer in the United Arab Emirates, Eapan and Revesz found that 100 percent of the participants relied upon religion to cope with the experience.[11] Religious coping would obviously involve some of the contemplative practices discussed above.

Several researchers have reported a positive association between Islamic religiosity and well-being, happiness, life satisfaction, overall mental health, and marital satisfaction.[12–14] Some of these have used single-item, self-ratings of level of religiosity, but others have utilized religiosity scales that encompass beliefs alone or beliefs and practices. For example, in a cross-sectional study of 1,000 Pakistanis ranging in age from 16 to 80 using a religiosity scale (beliefs and practices), Suhail and Chaudhry found a positive relationship between religiosity and well-being.[13]

Some of the above-mentioned researchers as well as others have reported a negative association between Islamic religiosity and depression and anxiety, in general,[15,16] as well as between religiosity and stress, death anxiety, suicide, alcohol use/abuse/dependence, and antisocial behavior/delinquency.[17–19] These associations remained even after controlling for such variables as gender, age, social class, marital status and ethnicity. The results are similar to those reported with non-Muslim populations.

RELIGIOUS PSYCHOTHERAPY WITH MUSLIMS

At least four studies have found that a form of religious psychotherapy may be effective with Muslim clients who suffer from anxiety, depression, and bereavement.[20–23] Participants in the religious psychotherapy groups in each of these studies responded significantly faster than those receiving standard treatment. For several of the studies, the positive outcomes were maintained at six months follow-up.

Razali, Hasanah, Aminah, and Subramaniam studied the effectiveness of religious-sociocultural components in the treatment of Muslim patients with generalized anxiety disorders and major depression.[23] Negative or maladaptive thoughts of participants were identified and altered to correspond with traditional Islamic beliefs derived from the Qur'an and *hadith* (sayings and customs of the Prophet Muhammad [peace and blessings be upon him]). Discussions regarding other religious issues and cultural beliefs related to the illness were conducted, and advice was provided to change behavior to correspond with the customs of Prophet Muhammad (peace and blessings be upon him). Contemplative practices such as prayer, reading of Qur'an, and remembrance of Allah were also generally encouraged. Patients receiving additional religious psychotherapy showed significantly more rapid improvement in anxiety or depressive symptoms than patients in the control group at 4 and 12 weeks.

Azhar and Varma randomly assigned patients ($n = 64$) to either a religious psychotherapy group or to standard psychotherapy without religious content.[20] Both of the groups were given weekly psychotherapy and mild doses of antidepressant medications. The study group was given additional religious psychotherapy each week (15–20 sessions). After one month and three months of therapy, patients receiving religious psychotherapy showed significantly more improvement than the control group on depressive symptoms (Hamilton Rating Scale for Depression). At the end of six months, this difference became nonsignificant.

Azhar and Varma conducted a similar experiment to the one mentioned above, but with 62 patients with generalized anxiety disorder.[21] After three months of treatment, the study group had significantly better improvement than the control group, indicating that they responded faster to religious psychotherapy. At six months, no significant difference was found between the groups.

The same authors carried out a similar study with 30 patients experiencing bereavement.[22] There was significant improvement in depressive symptoms (using the Hamilton Depression Scale) in the study group as compared with the control group on day 30, 90, and 180. The authors concluded that patients responded faster to religious psychotherapy than conventional psychotherapy.

In summary, the evidence indicates that being religious and engaging in religious practices, such as the contemplative practices mentioned above, has a beneficial effect upon the psychological and emotional health of Muslim adherents.

APPLICATIONS/INTERVENTIONS

Due to the religious nature of these practices, application would be limited to Muslim clients or patients, rather than being used for the general public. For this reason, the most appropriate settings for integration would be medical, psychological, or pastoral care. Examples of religious psychotherapy with Muslim patients have already been described in the empirical section. These therapeutic strategies could readily be integrated into standard psychotherapy to enhance treatment outcomes or to speed the process of recovery.

In health care settings, physicians, nurses, and other health care professionals may support patients who wish to include contemplative practices in their daily routines. This would initially require completing a brief spiritual history with the patient to gather information regarding the importance of religion in his or her life. It may be appropriate to refer some patients to an *imam*, Muslim chaplain, or community resources for assistance and guidance in carrying out their religious practices. Being a medical patient often poses special challenges, leading to questions regarding acceptable choices and behaviors.

For example, there are special rulings regarding formal prayer that may apply to the medically ill patient. He must do every obligatory aspect of the prayer to the extent possible. In cases of difficulty or hardship, the prayer may be revised according to the following:

1. The sick person must perform the obligatory prayers standing even if bending or leaning against something (i.e., a wall or stick).

2. If he is unable to stand, then he may pray sitting (sit cross-legged during standing and bowing positions).

3. If he is unable to pray sitting, then he should pray on his right side, facing the *Qiblah*. If he is unable to face the *Qiblah*, he may pray in any direction he is facing.

4. If he is unable to pray on his side, then he may pray on his back, with his feet toward the *Qiblah*, attempting to raise his head in that direction. If he is unable to direct his feet toward the *Qiblah*, then he may pray in the direction he is facing.

5. The sick person should bow and prostrate in prayer, but if he is unable to, he should indicate by inclining his head, making the prostration lower than the bowing.

6. If he is unable to incline his head in bowing and prostration, he should indicate with his eyes, closing them a little for bowing and closing them more tightly for the prostration.

7. If he is unable to incline his head or indicate with his eyes, he should pray with his heart (intentions), reciting and intending the bowing and prostrating in his heart.

8. The sick person must offer each prayer at its stated time. If it is difficult for him, then he may combine the *dhuhr* and *'asr* prayers as well as the *maghrib* and *"isha"* prayers.[24]

Special supplications are also available for those who have medical or mental health problems, such as the following: "O Allah, Lord of the people, take away the disease and cure me; You are the One Who cures and there is no cure except Your Cure—a cure that leaves no disease," or "O the Lord of Glory and Honor, O Ever Living One, O Eternal One, I seek help through Your mercy."

NEW RESEARCH DIRECTIONS

It is important to note that the Muslim believer/worshipper is in no need of scientific evidence to demonstrate the efficacy of these beliefs and practices. It is sufficient that it is mentioned in the Holy Qur'an and that he feels it in his life. For those interested in research outcomes, it would be beneficial to conduct further research in the area of mechanisms of action.

Park, for example, suggests that one way to study the influence of religiosity/spirituality on health is to focus on "the role of the explicit and implicit health-related influences that various traditions and ways of being religious or spiritual impart to global meaning systems, and thus, indirectly, to health."[25]

The theodicies of various traditions are suggested to have an impact upon beliefs, goals, and values, which may then influence mental health on multiple levels and through multiple pathways. Some examples of possible influences might include methods of dealing with stressors, general orientation toward life, and explanations for tribulations and sufferings. The theodicy of Islam is rich in this regard as it provides a comprehensive guide to life. Further research and investigation would elucidate the specific components and mechanisms by which Islamic beliefs and practices impact upon both the mental health of its adherents. This may include such components as understanding the nature of this life, reliance upon Allah, hopefulness, understanding the purpose of afflictions, remembering the Hereafter and the rewards that will be obtained for patience, etc.

CONCLUSION

Islam offers a comprehensive system of contemplation that guides the individual to the straight path that results in tranquility and happiness in this life, and will lead him to Paradise in the Hereafter. The most fundamental aspect of contemplation in this framework is the five daily, obligatory prayers. These are enriched by various other practices including nonobligatory prayers, remembrance of Allah, supplication, specific contemplation and reflection, and following the teachings of the Qur'an and *Sunnah*, as modeled by Prophet Muhammad (peace and blessings be upon him). The ultimate purpose of these acts of worship is the realization of *tawheed* or belief in and worship of one true God, Allah. The individual who implements these practices is submitting to Allah and thus fulfilling his true purpose in life. The spiritual and psychological contentment that is experienced is beyond description and has the capability to prevent or alleviate any type of mental disorder or suffering.

REFERENCES

1. Zarabozo, J. (2002). *Purification of the soul: Concept, process, and means.* Denver, CO: Al-Basheer.

2. Nadwi, S. (1994). *Worship in Islam.* Karachi: Darul Ishaat.

3. Saheeh International. (1997). *The Holy Qur'an: Arabic text with corresponding English meanings.* Jeddah, Saudi Arabia: Abul-Qasim.

4. Umm Muhammad. (1994). *The path to prayer with a description of the Prophet's prayer.* Jeddah, Saudi Arabia: Abul-Qasim.

5. Az-Zubaidi, Z. A. A. (Compiler). (1996). *Summarized Sahih Al-Bukhari.* Saudi Arabia: Darussalam.

6. Ibn Baz, A. A. (1992). *Prophet Muhammad's manner of performing prayers.* Riyadh, Saudi Arabia: Presidency of Islamic Researchers IFTA and Propagation. Available at http://www.themodernreligion.com/prophet/prophet_prayer.htm.

7. Al-Mundhiri, Z. A. (Compiler). (2000). *Summarized Sahih Muslim.* Saudi Arabia: Darussalam.

8. Al-Munajjid, M. S. (1999). *Islam's treatment for anxiety and stress.* Riyadh, Saudi Arabia: International Islamic.

9. Al-Mubarakpuri, S. (1996). *The sealed nectar: Biography of the Noble Prophet.* Riyadh, Saudi Arabia: Dar-us-Salam.

10. Ai, A. L., Peterson, C., & Huang, B. (2003). The effect of religious-spiritual coping on positive attitudes of adult Muslim refugees from Kosovo and Bosnia. *International Journal for the Psychology of Religion, 13*(1), 29–47.

11. Eapen, V., & Revesz, T. (2003). Psychosocial correlates of pediatric cancer in the United Arab Emirates. *Supportive Care in Cancer, 11*(3), 185–189.

12. Abdel-Khalek, A. M. (2006). Happiness, health, and religiosity: Significant relations. *Mental Health, Religion & Culture, 9*(1), 85–97.

13. Hunler, O. S., & Gencoz, T. (2005). The effect of religiousness on marital satisfaction: Testing the mediator role of marital problem solving between religiousness and marital satisfaction relationship. *Contemporary Family Therapy: An International Journal, 27*(1), 123–136.

14. Suhail, K., & Chaudhry, H. R. (2004). Predictors of subjective well-being in an Eastern Muslim culture. *Journal of Social and Clinical Psychology, 23*(3), 359–376.

15. Amer, M. M., & Hovey, J. D. (2007). Socio-demographic differences in acculturation and mental health for a sample of 2nd generation/early immigrant Arab Americans. *Journal of Immigrant Minority Health, 9,* 335–347.

16. Lopes Cardozo, B., Bilukha, O. O., Gotway Crawford, C. A., Shaikh, I., Wolfe, M. I., Gerber, M. O., & Anderson, M. (2004). Mental health, social functioning, and disability in postwar Afghanistan. *Journal of the American Medical Association, 292*(5), 575–584.

17. French, D. C., Eisenbery, N., Vaughan, J., Purwono, U., & Suryanti, T. A. (2008). Religious involvement and the social competence and adjustment of Indonesian Muslim adolescents. *Developmental Psychology, 44*(2), 597–611.

18. Jahangir, F., & ur Rehman, H. (1998). Degree of religiosity and vulnerability to suicidal attempt/plans in depressive patients among Afghan refugees. *International Journal for the Psychology of Religion, 8*(4), 265–269.

19. Karam, E. G., Maalouf, W. E., & Ghandour, L. A. (2004). Alcohol use among university students in Lebanon: Prevalence, trends and covariates: The IDRAC University Substance Use Monitoring Study (1991 and 1999). *Drug and Alcohol Dependence, 76*(3), 273–286.

20. Azhar, M. Z., & Varma, S. L. (1995a). Religious psychotherapy in depressive patients. *Psychotherapy and Psychosomatics, 63*, 65–168.

21. Azhar, M. Z., & Varma, S. L. (1995b). Religious psychotherapy as management of bereavement. *Acta Psychiatrica Scandinavica, 91*(4), 233–235.

22. Azhar, M. Z., Varma, S. L., & Dharap, A. S. (1994). Religious psychotherapy in anxiety disorder patients. *Acta Psychiatrica Scandinavica, 90*(1), 1–3.

23. Razali, S. M., Hasanah, C. I., Aminah, K., & Subramaniam, M. (1998). Religious-sociocultural psychotherapy in patients with anxiety and depression. *Australian and New Zealand Journal of Psychiatry, 32*(6), 867–872.

24. ar-Rumaikhaan, A. S. (Compiler). (2004). *Guidelines and fataawa related to sickness and medical practice.* London: Invitation to Islam.

25. Park, C. L. (2007). Religiousness/spirituality and health: A meaning systems perspective. *Journal of Behavioral Medicine, 30*, 319–328.

CHAPTER 9
The Path of Yoga

T. Anne Richards

Yoga is a friend to those who embrace it sincerely and totally.
It lifts its practitioners from the clutches of pain and sorrow,
and enables them to live fully, taking a delight in life.

—B. K. S. Iyengar, *Light on the Yoga Sutras of Patanjali*

Yoga, meaning union, is a system of Indian thought that stems from the
Vedas (1700–900 BCE), the oldest record of Indian culture.[1] It was
systemized by Patanjali (200 BCE) in the Yoga Sutras, 195 aphorisms
that map the philosophy and practice of yoga as a system intended to
cease the fluctuations of the mind, bring peace to the experiences of
daily life, and ultimately bring the individual spirit (Atman) into union
with the Universal Spirit (Brahman).[2] Yoga as a contemplative practice
is undertaken through the combination of asanas (physical postures),
breathing (pranayama and yogic breath in asana practice), and study
and application of the spiritual and philosophical principles set forth in
the Yoga Sutras. Other ancient texts did follow Patanjali's work but
the Yoga Sutras are the foundation.

The philosophy of yoga embraces a view of health and well-being as
a state that arises from the quality and balance of mental, physical,
emotional, and spiritual conditions.[3] The benefits of yoga have been
researched for close to a century in Indian research institutes. As yoga
grew in popularity in the West, scientific interest and research into
yoga as therapy has grown as well.[4] Studies have been conducted

documenting the effects of yogic practice on a number of psychological, emotional, and physical health challenges including depression, anxiety, eating disorders, cardiovascular problems, asthma, diabetes, cancer, and rheumatoid and osteoarthritis.[4,5] Medical and psychological studies have yet to explore the transformative spiritual potential of yoga among longtime practitioners and how yoga may change their approach to and experience of living.

I became interested in the philosophy and cleansing techniques of yoga in the early 1970s and began an active asana practice in 1984, which has continued, with degrees of ebb and flow, to date. Yoga has been a resource for creating calm in my body, focus in my mind, and greater peace in my heart. It was my engagement in a three-year advanced-studies program at the Yoga Room in Berkeley, California, that not only certified me as a teacher, but brought me deeply into yoga as a contemplative practice, for which I am profoundly grateful. I have also used yogic practice as a means of managing and living with osteoarthritis.

CONTEXT

There are six fundamental systems of Indian thought collectively known as Darsana, meaning "to see," to look inside ourselves, to better observe our self. Yoga is one of these six systems. Fundamental to Darsana is the idea that there is a Supreme Universal Spirit that permeates all that exists, and that the individual is one with the Universal Spirit. Yoga is a path for cultivating individual consciousness in order to experience greater harmony in life and ultimately experience oneness with the Universal Spirit.[1,2,6]

Within Indian philosophy, being consists of five sheaths (koshas), which surround the Higher Self or Soul. The five sheaths of being are the anatomical or physical sheath, the physiological or energetic sheath, the mental sheath, which includes the emotional, the intellectual or sheath of wisdom, and the blissful or the sheath of fulfillment and joy. The practice of yoga aims to create consciousness or awareness and balance in these sheaths, to enable the practitioner to reach the center of being, the Universal Self or Soul. Yoga is a journey of intelligence from the external to the internal, from the internal to the external.[6]

In the Yoga Sutras, Patanjali drew from the principles of the Vedas passed on through oral tradition and provided us with an ancient text that gives the blueprint for yogic practice. Written as a book of aphorisms, the depth and complexity of this text is vast. Because they are aphorisms, the Sutras are open to interpretation by different schools of thought. Contemporary books written on the Yoga Sutras are diverse in the translation and phrasing of the sutras and use a variety of conceptual language in interpreting them. However, the essential principles hold firm through the various lenses.

The Sutras are divided into four chapters (padas). The first chapter addresses contemplation and consciousness (Samadhi pada). Yoga is defined in relationship to moving away from identification with the individual self, also called the ego or sense of "I," and moving into recognition or realization of being part of the Universal Self, also called the Soul. Through the disciplines of yogic practice, consciousness is reshaped and refined so that the mind moves toward identification with the Universal Spirit and suffering and confusion, which comes from identification with the ego (individual self), recedes, giving the practitioner better capacity to see and interact with life with greater clarity and joy.

Chapter 2 (Sadhana pada) outlines the discipline of practice (kriyayoga) as the path of action in pursuit of Self-Realization. Here the dimensions of the practice are laid out through the eightfold path or eight limbs of yoga, which is the path toward physical, mental, and emotional stability and well-being. This chapter describes how awareness shifts through practice and qualities are developed within the body and mind that cause the practitioner to thrive.

In Chapter 3 (Vibhuti pada) Patanjali described the capacities and powers of the focused mind free from distraction that can be achieved through ardent practice. Concentration opens the way of meditation and meditation opens the way to a sense of oneness, the experience of merging with the Universal Spirit or Soul. By focusing attention through concentration and meditation, the sense of the individual self or ego can be transcended and an expanded awareness of one's place in the wholeness of life is available.

The final chapter (Kaivalya pada) is concerned with transformation and the ultimate freedom from the bondage of "incorrect comprehension" or ignorance (Avidya). Preoccupation with the concerns and enjoyments of daily life are lifted, control over the mind is gained, and it becomes a servant rather than master. A state of tranquility and steadfast wisdom is maintained when one is freed from the constraints of incorrect comprehension of self and how the world is constructed.[1,2,6]

Although in Indian mythology it is said that Lord Shiva's consort, Parvati, was the first to be taught yoga by Lord Shiva, in its early history, yoga was an esoteric practice, undertaken by unmarried men (nonhouseholders) who lived the life of an ascetic. This gradually changed to include men who were householders, and women.

There are several schools of yoga including Raja (royal union or classical yoga), Mantra (chanting or "seed sound"), Jnana (path of wisdom, study of sacred scriptures), Karma (path of action, adherence to duty), Kundalini (prana, energy complexes within the body), and Bhakti (devotional, relationship with God). Because the Yoga Sutras are so complex, the different schools that have evolved can be viewed as different doorways onto the same path. While all of these disciplines are available in the West, Hatha yoga, which is an aspect of the Raja tradition, has become mainstream. Hatha yoga is focused on asana (physical postures) and pranayama (breathing) and is considered to be a beginning phase for disciplining the body in preparation for long periods of meditation.

Hatha yoga requires no particular belief system and can be practiced by anyone regardless of religious affiliation. Most commonly yoga is practiced by those who seek to improve their physical, psychological, and emotional health and reduce the impact of contemporary stresses. Yoga is also practiced in athletics for its strengthening, stretching, and balancing aspects. It is also beneficial to those coping with serious health challenges such as cancer and heart disease. Yoga is sometimes used as a management tool for those with muscular-skeletal problems such as arthritis, chronic fatigue syndrome, and fibromyalgia. It is now one of the most prescribed and investigated modalities in complementary and alternative medicine.[7] As a contemplative practice, people who have maintain asana and pranayama practices for an extended period of time are those oriented toward deepen their meditation practice as they are drawn toward the state of Oneness. Some who seek a spiritual path undertake Bhakti, Jnana, or Kundalini yoga and pursue their practice under the tutelage of a spiritual master or his or her followers, often through an ashram. In Hatha yoga practices, it is often the case that teachers and their lineage of teachers become role models or spiritual models for students. Any school of Hatha-based practices provides the practical discipline that is the foundation of spiritual development.

DIMENSIONS OF THE PRACTICE

How does one begin yoga as a contemplative practice? Desikachar[1] believes it doesn't matter whether yoga is entered through asana, pranayama, or study of the Yoga Sutras. He has stated that once the process is begun, the practitioner will find his or her way to the other aspects of practice. This is often the case for those who undertake a longer, more dedicated course of practice. The eight limbs of yoga from the Yoga Sutras lay out the dimensions of yogic practice and provide guidance for constructing a yogic practice.[2,6,8] Practice is intended to lead the practitioner into self-observation, looking at attitudes and behaviors and their consequences. The first two limbs of yoga, yama and niyama, provide moral and ethical guidance. Yama is concerned with how we direct ourselves outwardly in the world, and niyama are principles for our personal spiritual development and our personal habits and self-discipline. The five yamas in the Yoga Sutras are nonviolence (ahsima), truthfulness (satya), nonstealing (asteya), control of sensual pleasure (brahmacharya), and nonavariciousness (aparigrha). The five niyamas are cleanliness (saucha), contentment (samtosa), austerity or burning desire (tapas), study of the sacred scriptures and of one's self (svadhyaya), and surrender to God (isvara pranidhana).

Asana (postures) is the third limb and is the physical practice of the yoga postures that disciplines the body. Asana opens the body and gives the practitioner an experience of more space and lightness physically. Asana maintains the strength and health of the body. Movement, stillness, focused attention, and breath awareness are all within asana whether it is the simplest or most advanced of postures. It is in asana practice that the individual can observe and explore yama and niyama as they exist within his or her self and how they carry out the poses. Then it is possible for the observance within the practice to lead to the vision of how the contradictions of yama and niyama exist in daily living, where it is more difficult to observe these shortcomings and how to overcome them.[8]

The fourth limb, pranayama, is the yogic art of breathing. Prana is vital energy that permeates all that exists. In pranayama, the breath is intentionally moved rhythmically through the body with attention to the inflow of air, how it moves and infuses the various organs and parts of the body, and how the breath leaves the body. Pranayama practice uses specific techniques for lengthening the intake, the retention, and the exhalation of the breath. It is practiced either in supported reclining positions (often better for beginning practitioners) or in seated positions. Learning and practicing these techniques calms the emotions, focuses the mind, and enhances breath awareness and rhythmic breathing within asana practice.[9] "Pranayama is prayer and not a mere physical breathing exercise."[10]

The fifth limb (pratyahara) is sensory withdrawal or control of the senses. In yoga this means moving awareness from the physical to the silent, spacious interior core of being. Asana and pranayama practices lead practitioners to this state moving through the sheaths of the body inward toward the Self. This inward movement is the process of freeing one's self from the control of the desires of the senses so that their gratification ceases to be a constant distraction. The more a person practices asana and pranayama, the more he or she cultivates an experience of this internal place of reference that can then influence self-understanding and how he or she responds to the circumstances of living.

The fourth and fifth limbs (pranayama and sensory withdrawal) are the inner quests, distinguished from the first three limbs, which are the outer quests. Pranayama or the practice of rhythmic breathing draws the practitioner inward furthering the capacity for withdrawing the senses, moving from outward directed consciousness to inner awareness and a deeper sense of the spiritual within. The first five limbs create the fertile ground for cultivating the final three limbs.[2,8]

Concentration or complete attention (dharana) is the sixth limb and is the idea of holding focused attention in one direction for a sustained period of time. This provides the necessary condition or vessel for the seventh limb, meditation on the Divine. Uninterrupted concentration allows the practitioner to sustain communion so that "his body, breath, senses, mind, reason and ego are all integrated in the object of his contemplation—the Universal Spirit."[2] The final limb is the end of the quest, union with the Divine (samadhi). In this state the illusion of separation is dispelled; oneness with the Universal Self is experienced with pure joy.

Yoga is a practical discipline. It often engages the practitioner who is initially drawn to it and then, as in my own experience, has an ebb and flow of engagement over the course of time due to other life circumstances. But experienced practitioners tend to agree that yoga never leaves the body, mind, or spirit, and at the time of reengagement, after a hiatus, they reenter practice from the internal point where they left off. The following case study provides some insight as to the place of yoga in the life of a woman who practiced for 30 years.

"Linda" came to yoga in her late 20s while in graduate school. She was very flexible and was drawn to the stretching aspect and to "invoking through physical intelligence, through awareness, [the ability] to more fully inhabit the body." She had a tendency to turn her very active emotionality and intense cognitive capacity into anxiety, so yoga provided for her a "grounding" allowing her to "move energy in a different way." In her early 30's she was exposed to fairly sophisticated, knowledgeable senior teachers in the Iyengar yoga tradition. Then life turned and she was working and raising children. Linda stopped attending classes but maintain a personal home practice. As her children grew older she went back to classes and engaged in advanced studies.

> "If you take a class without practice [on your own] you never ground it because you don't have the opportunity to create your own dialogue with yourself about refinement (what if I did this, what about that)—the real spirit of experimentation and taking the teaching into your body. And if you only have a practice without a teacher it's easy to reinforce the wrong patterns and it is a little more challenging to truly learn things."

Her practice was asana focused through these years. Parallel to her asana practice, Linda was part of a spiritual group and "had a path" that required a commitment of daily sitting meditation practice, meetings one night a week, as well as periodic retreats involving classes, discussions, and meditation. The two practices worked well together for her.

> "It was so helpful in terms of the mental, emotional, nervous wiring. I do think that like water on a rock these practices reshape your consciousness and how energy flows. They reshape, they transform. And for me [yoga] became another place; rather than focusing on 'no thinking' it was focusing on the physical field. That became the field of attention. To bring conscious awareness into different parts of my body—to be able to visualize anatomy and change energy was another way of clearing and quieting and focusing. My yoga practice has always been internally focused. It has not been athletic."

After more than 15 years it became clear she could not commit to both paths and chose yoga because it involved a physical practice but still uses the form of meditation learned in her spiritual group. Linda transferred the humility and "dropping of ego" she had learned in her spiritual practice to her yoga practice.

> "When I walk into a class I literally think about crossing a threshold, a sacred space and I'm not letting my personality into the room. As a student I'm more receptive. As I integrated [the two practices] I think I brought some of the understanding of what

it means to be a seeker into the class. However, there are times when what I need is the sitting. That's a little different than the full body [awareness]."

Linda was introduced to Patanjali's Sutras within the context of her meditation group. They were read in their entirety during a retreat. During the course of her advanced yoga studies, the principles put forth in the yamas and niyamas became relevant in the following way:

"[They] took hold when we would study a yama or niyama and then apply it to our practice and have to write about that. What did it mean to take an idea and apply it and how did it transform your practice of [the asana] triangle pose. So when it was applied and I was asked to write about it—that took hold."

Linda currently maintains a home practice as well as attends classes. At this point yoga for Linda is asana, concentration, focus, and being present, consistent with the developmental path laid out by Patanjali.

As to how her sustained yoga practice relates to her daily life, Linda said:

"In a cumulative way, having a regular practice allows for a cycle of release and new beginning. If on a regular basis you are practicing you are not holding on to a certain level of stress. Not having a residual build up of body tension is, in terms of well being, is really important. I think there is a consolation and confidence that comes from knowing that when you get yourself to the mat and you spend 10 minutes or 15 minutes or 2 hours you will emerge fundamentally different from where you began. And to know that and have that confidence means you know you have a tool. Finally, I think I'm wired for anxiety. Busy mind. It's just how I'm wired. I'm really smart, I think fast. So pervasively it has helped me experience and more skillfully cultivate spaciousness and stillness and silence. And I don't know that would be that available to me if I didn't have a practice. And once you are aware of it, you know how to go back for it."

Linda has used yoga to manage osteoarthritis and asthma. She feels that it has given her "a sense of agency" in managing these disorders. Of yoga in her personal development and learning Linda said:

"I feel so grateful to have it as a companion. I feel like I will have yoga as a companion until my last days. I imagine, like any

companion, the way we are together will change as my body changes but I imagine it is a companion that I will always have. It is so humbling and wonderful to have a practice that if you lived 4 life times you wouldn't know everything or be able to do everything. It's limitless."

REVIEW OF THE THEORETICAL AND EMPIRICAL LITERATURE

Several explanations have been proposed to account for effects of yoga on various physical and psychological conditions. Briefly, yoga practice is considered to modulate the autonomic nervous tone with a decrease in sympathetic activity and an increase in parasympathetic activity. There is a reduction of cognitive and somatic arousal. The limbic system is quieted and the relaxation response in the neuromuscular system increases.[11]

The first studies of yoga began in India in the early twentieth century.[12] Within biomedical and psychological research and practice, yoga is investigated and applied as therapy directed toward specific disorders. Compared to the ancient intent of the practice, the development of higher consciousness, this is a limited approach and has been criticized by some.[13] As research on yoga grew and the number of clinical trials increased, the parameters for investigation became increasingly limited, forcing a narrowing of investigations to the impact of specific poses or breathing practices on isolated diseases or disorders. Khalsa[4] states, "In fact, since the primary goal of yoga practice is spiritual development, beneficial medical consequences of yoga practice can more precisely be described as positive 'side effects.'" However, he also points out that yoga is a healing tradition and, in that broader sense, shares common ground with medical science.

Khalsa's bibliometric review[4] is an excellent resource for understanding the state of medical research into yoga and its psychophysiological effects as documented through early 2004. One hundred and eighty-one clinical trials (controlled and uncontrolled) appearing in 81 journals from 15 countries were gathered into a bibliography. Only studies specific to yoga, not involving a second type of practice (i.e., yoga in combination with vipassana meditation), were reviewed. Studies were taken from both yoga specialty journals and nonyoga research journals. Forty-eight percent of the studies were uncontrolled and 39.8 percent were randomized control trials. The majority of randomized control trials (58% in nonyoga journals) were conducted in India followed by the United States (slightly less than 29%).

Analyses of all studies showed that studies reported in yoga specialty journals were valuable but not as rigorous scientifically as those reported in the nonyoga journals. Twenty-one studies in nonyoga journals examined yoga in relationship to two or more disorders. Studies of the impact of yoga on discreet disorders in nonyoga journals were on asthma (23 studies), hypertension (21 studies), heart disease (18 studies), diabetes (16 studies), depression or dysthymia (14 studies), and anxiety (6 studies). Yoga is considered effective for stress reduction and reducing autonomic arousal, and there is scientific evidence in support of this with the majority of studies focusing on the effects of yogic practice on psychopathologies, cardiovascular disorders, and respiratory disorders. Khalsa asserts that it is unlikely that these discrete disorder investigations will provide consistent or reliable data, and that what should be considered is a meta-analysis evaluating relative effect sizes for yoga interventions across disorders.

Complications in conducting research on yoga as well as interpreting findings across studies were pointed out. There are a variety of types of yoga ascribing to different methods of asana practice, pranayama, and yogic breathing, as well as dietary and "complete yoga lifestyle interventions." There is not a standardized yoga practice format, which complicates scientific investigations. Yoga, as originally intended, is a multidisciplinary system for self-transformation, and therefore a fit between the limitations of the scientific method and this ancient art and science is difficult.

Another article, by da Silva, Ravindran, and Ravindran,[5] provides a review of literature specific to the effects of yoga on mood and anxiety disorders. Khalsa made the arbitrary decision to examine controlled and uncontrolled studies solely focused on yoga but addressing a full spectrum of disorders. Da Silva et al. limited the studies to mood and anxiety disorders but included all publications up to July 2008 including controlled or uncontrolled trials, case reports, chart reviews, and retrospective analyses utilizing yoga and other forms of treatment including medications. Seventeen studies on the efficacy of yoga practice in relationship to mood disorders and 17 studies on anxiety disorders were reviewed. Studies were summarized in table format categorizing diagnosis, study format, duration of treatment, monotherapy or augmentation to medication, size of intervention groups, and results. Results were evaluated using a standard methodology for strength of evidence for efficacy and tolerability.[14]

Across all studies 11 styles of yoga practice were utilized. In studies on major depression, yoga proved to be beneficial as both a monotherapy and in conjunction with medications in mild, moderate, and severe depression. A form of yoga, Sudarshan Kriya Yoga, which is a controlled breathing practice, had the most evidence for efficacy as a monotherapy with depressive disorders. Iyengar yoga, a form of Hatha yoga, had the next most evidence as a monotherapy for depression and the most evidence for efficacy as an augmentation to medication. Iyengar yoga concentrates on proper alignment in asanas, which are sustained, and attention is focused on alignment and breathing while sustaining the pose.

Studies of yoga and its effects on anxiety attended to generalized anxiety (psychoneurosis or anxiety neurosis), obsessive-compulsive disorder, posttraumatic stress disorder, and performance and test anxiety. Da Silva et al. stated that given the prevalence of generalized anxiety disorders, the number of studies examining yoga in relationship to these disorders was limited. Findings in the area of anxiety disorders were not as clear-cut as those on the effects of yoga on depressive disorders. There was evidence to suggest that yoga may benefit some types of anxiety disorders, but the effects are largely unknown. This further illustrates the comment Khalsa made in his paper regarding the difficulty in assessing the impact of the many variations of yogic practices in relationship to discrete disorders. Perhaps his suggestion of meta-analyses examining the relative effect sizes across discrete disorders is relevant across anxiety disorders.

Included in the da Silva review were 15 randomized control trials and 5 open trials on depressive and anxiety symptoms in the medically ill including breast and ovarian cancer, migraine, irritable bowel syndrome, hypertension, fibromyalgia, diabetes, obesity, asthma, and chronic low back pain. Da Silva et al. state, "Overall, yoga was found to have positive effects on depression and anxiety associated with physical illness" (p. 6). Again, the study of discrete disorders in relationship to yoga shows trends, but stable and consistent conclusions cannot be drawn.

Research on yoga is clearly on the rise. From 1973 to 1989 the number of published randomized control trials in India was 11 and in the United States, 2. From 1990 to 2004 the number of trials increased in India from 11 to 21 and in the United States from 2 to 16.[10] While it is likely that research will continue in the direction of specific yoga interventions for discrete disorders, the need exists for longitudinal research on the effects of yogic practice on integrated body-mind-spiritual health, ethical and compassionate behaviors, and shifts in worldview as to how life is construed. This would better match the model of human-centered strategies of whole-person health care,[15] providing new evidence for how to think about health, development, and care.

APPLICATIONS/INTERVENTIONS

In the United States, yoga is one of the most widely practiced forms of complementary health care. A report on complementary and alternative medicine released in 2008 stated that according to their surveys, 6.1 percent of the U.S. population practice yoga.[7] There already exist a number of venues for developing yoga practice. Classes are offered in yoga studios, spas, health clubs, and gyms. Weekend and weeklong yoga retreats at vacation destinations around the world are advertised regularly. Work sites that are engaging in work site wellness programs frequently have on-site yoga classes as part of their wellness menu of offerings. There is an increase in advanced-studies programs aimed at bringing experienced yogis and yoginis deeper into their practices. Yoga is frequently offered in meditation retreats. In a recently published book on meditation,[16] meditative practices are categorized as sitting, sounding, and moving. Yoga is presented as one form of moving meditation. There is a gradual shift taking place among the general population's perception and utilization of yoga toward a longer, more engaged course of practice. It may be that there is an increasing understanding of yoga as a path for realization of Self and wholeness that Patanjali laid out thousands of years ago.

One environment ripe for the application of yoga as a contemplative practice is higher education, where there are currently few offerings. Colleges and universities are ideal for introducing yoga as a whole system including the physical, mental, philosophical, and spiritual aspects. Two of the few developed yoga courses within higher education are at DePaul University. One four-credit course taught quarterly titled "Body, Mind, Spirit: Yoga and Meditation" is taught in the School for New Learning to adults returning to school for their bachelor's degree. The other is a two-credit course, also using yoga and meditation, taught to regular undergraduates in the Peace, Justice and Conflict Studies program titled "Peace for Activists." Both courses engage students in asana and pranayama practices, readings on yoga including the Yoga Sutras, and personal reflections.

There are a few principles related to teaching and studying that I believe are important to designing and carrying out university-based courses on yoga. A good structure would be a series of classes over the course of a school year with the each course being prerequisite for the next course. This would provide adequate time for an introduction and beginning exploration of all aspects of the yogic system. If a student lost interest, he or she would simply not sign up for the subsequent course. Study over the course of a year would also give students adequate time to reflect on the changes they may experience in body-mind awareness, personal habits, reactivity in difficult life events, spiritual experiences, and shifts in worldviews.

Alternatively, as in the DePaul model, a course could be situated within another context, such as the Peace, Justice and Conflict Studies program using practice to apply what Patanjali prescribes in the yamas: one's actions in the world; or the niyamas: one's self-attitudes and -disciplines. Classes lasting one and a half hours would well support learning with time for practice as well as time for reflection and discussion.

However the course is constructed, it is vital that the teacher have an extensive personal practice and is well qualified to teach asana and breathing practices, since any course must be experiential as well as conceptual. Both asana and yogic breathing need to be approached slowly with great attention and care. Injuries can occur in asana practice, and breathing practices can have powerful effects. So that students can be well attended to, class size should be limited to 15 students.

As our case study participant pointed out, it is important to both practice with a teacher and practice alone for adequate personal exploration time. A good course of study would include home practice (homework) involving asana, breathing, and applications of the yamas and niyamas. A short essay, a paragraph or two on how a particular yama or niyama came to bear within a given practice, heightens inner reflection, bringing into greater awareness the place that particular principle (contentment, nonviolence, etc) held within the time frame of a single practice.

There is a wealth of excellent books on yoga to draw from for conveying the philosophical and spiritual principles of yoga as well as books guiding asana and breathing practice. The Yoga Sutras should be part of any course.

Meditation is an important aspect of practice, even at the beginning. In an introductory course, meditation is built into the practice by ending each asana session with the pose savasana (corpse pose).

The practitioner lays on the floor, relaxing into the body and the breath. It is in savasana that the practice integrates and sinks into the body. Casting the eyes toward the heart brings thoughts into greater stillness during savasana, aiding in the withdrawal of awareness from the outer body and placing attention and focus on the stillness within, the contemplative space. As practitioners advance, an awareness is developed within each pose. Practitioners can then be directed toward the discovery that there is the work of the pose and then there is stillness in the pose or repose. Finding these still points within an asana then becomes the next level of meditation. Sitting meditation can be introduced at any time as part of asana practice and will deepen as asana and pranayama practices deepen.

NEW RESEARCH DIRECTIONS

Research on how individuals grow, developing awareness and wisdom through a longitudinal course of yogic practice, could provide insight at a number of levels beyond the currently known benefits of practice: self-management through stressful events, self-responsibility for actions in the world, caring and nurturing attitudes toward self and others, development of physical and emotional well-being, the experience of joy, and perceptions of and relationship with the Divinity of life. As the literature review indicates, biomedical research focuses on interventions for discrete illnesses. I am suggesting research focusing on the development of the whole person. Mixed research methodologies of qualitative inquiry and quantitative measures would fit well in this type of research. Keeping in mind the proposition of developing yoga studies in colleges and universities, students within those classes would be ideal for the investigation of the effectiveness of yoga as a contemplative practice.

A three-phase model of effectiveness could be used for this type of examination as suggested to me by S. B. Khalsa in a personal communication. Phase 1 would involve measurement of immediate improvements in the reduction of arousal and stress. Phase 2 would examine the development of body and self-awareness with changes in mind-body activities such as reactivity in stressful situations, flexibility in attitudes or mind-set, and a general feeling of being more comfortable in one's body. The third phase would look for changes in psychological and philosophical perspectives and shifts in worldviews.

CONCLUSION

Yoga is a path for developing consciousness and spiritual awareness through practices that unite body, breath, mind, intelligence, and Spirit. The ultimate aims are the experience of inner peace, outward integrity, and knowing God. Through yoga's eightfold path, living can become more ethical, kind, and enjoyable. Vitality of the body and the mind are supported, and health difficulties, physical and psychological, are better managed. It is a practical discipline that can carry the practitioner through all stages of life. It can be practiced by seniors, adults, teens, and children, and by anyone irrespective of religious, social, and geographical backgrounds.

Yoga is becoming well integrated into the health practices of millions of people within the United States and throughout the world. It has been part of Eastern cultures for centuries and has now taken root in Western cultures. As a therapeutic intervention, yoga is now applied in complementary medicine, and biomedical investigations of yoga are on the increase.

For many, yoga will remain solely a means of decompressing from a stressful day. And this is good, for that alone will change the quality of their lives and the lives of those around them. However, there is a growing recognition that beyond the reduction of stress, this ancient art and science brings practitioners to a fuller understanding of themselves and their connection to life as a whole, provides an expanded capacity for the experience of joy, and is a path for knowing God within.

ACKNOWLEDGMENTS

With gratitude I acknowledge my teachers and their teachers: The Yoga Room in Berkeley, CA; Mary Lou Weprin and Donald Moyer; 4th Street Yoga in Berkeley, CA; the San Francisco Iyengar Institute; B. K. S. Iyengar.

REFERENCES

1. Desikachar, T. K. V. (1999). *The heart of yoga: Developing a personal practice*. Rochester, VT: Inner Traditions International.

2. Iyengar, B. K. S. (2005). *Light on life*. New York: Rodale.

3. Iyengar, B. K. S. (1988). *The tree of yoga*. Boston: Shambhala.

4. Khalsa, S. B. S. (2004). Yoga as a therapeutic intervention: A bibliometric analysis of published research studies. *Indian Journal of Physiology and Pharmacology*, *48*(3), 269–285.

5. Da Silva, T. L., Ravindran, L. N. B., & Ravindran, A. V. (2009). Yoga in the treatment of mood and anxiety disorders: A review. *Asian Journal of Psychiatry*, *2*, 6–16.

6. Iyengar, B. K. S. (1993). *Light on the yoga sutras*. London: Aquarian Press/HarperCollins.

7. Barnes, P. M., & Bloom, B. (2008). Complementary and alternative medicine use among adults: United States, 2007. *National Health Statistics Reports*, *12*, 1–24.

8. Iyengar, B. K. S. (1979). *Light on yoga*. New York: Schocken.

9. Iyengar, B. K. S. (2002). *Light on pranayama*. New York: Crossroads.

10. Iyengar, B. K. S. (2004). Pranic awareness in an asana. *Yoga Rahasya*, *11*(3), 17.

11. Riley, D. (2004). Hatha yoga and the treatment of illness. *Alternative Therapy in Health Medicine*, *10*(2), 20–21.

12. Yogendra, J. (1970). The study of clinical-cum-medical research and yoga. *Journal of the Yoga Institute*, *16*, 3–10.

13. Gharote, M. L. (1991). Analytical survey of research in yoga. *Yoga Mimamsa*, *29*, 53–68.

14. Yatham, L. N., Kennedy, S. H., O'Donovan, C., Parikh, S., MacQueen, G., McIntyre, R., Sharma, V., Silverstone, P., Alda, M., Baruch, P., Beaulier, S., Daigneault, A., Milev, R., Young, T., Ravindran, A., Schaffer, A., Connolly, M., & Gorman, C. P. (2005). Canadian Network for Mood and Anxiety Treatments (CANMAT) guidelines for the management of patients with bipolar disorder: consensus and controversies. *Bipolar Disorder*, *7*(3), 5–69.

15. Serlin, I. A., DiCowden, Rockefeller, K., & Brown, S. (Eds.). (2007). *Whole person health care*. Westport, CT: Praeger.

16. Shapiro, E., & Shapiro, D. (2009). *Be the change: How meditation can transform you and the world*. New York: Sterling.

CHAPTER 10

Zen and the Transformation of Emotional and Physical Stress into Well-Being

Sarita Tamayo-Moraga and Darlene Cohen Roshi

A fierce and terrifying band of samurai was riding through the countryside, bringing fear and harm wherever they went. As they were approaching one particular town, all the monks in the town's monastery fled, except for the abbot. When the band of warriors entered the monastery, they found the abbot sitting at the front of the shrine room in perfect posture. The fierce leader took out his sword and said, "Don't you know who I am? Don't you know that I'm the sort of person who could run you through with my sword without batting an eye?" The Zen master responded, "And I, sir, am the sort of man who could be run through by a sword without batting an eye."[1]

In Zen lore, there are many stories about Zen masters who face disaster and hardship without blinking an eye. Sylvia Boorstein, cofounding teacher of Spirit Rock Meditation Center in Marin County, California, recounts this classic Zen story, "Without Fear" in a talk on fearlessness. Zen masters such as the one in the story have reached an equilibrium that could be described as happiness that is not dependent on external circumstances. This ease is based on fearlessness and a total acceptance of the present moment in which the practitioner is released from attachment to wanting reality to be different from how it is. This deep kind of release means one is less and less controlled by external circumstances. What is unique to Zen is the fact that for Zen, this kind of equilibrium is achieved not by rejecting the world, but instead by completely accepting the world. This complete acceptance of the world is intimately related to how one perceives the world.

This stance is not negative or passive. Instead, it is dynamic and results in emotional well-being that translates into increased physical well-being although it is absolutely not a wonder drug. Zen masters and students get cancer, go through divorces, lose children, etc. They are still human, but the difference is that they accept that reality rather than reject it. Therefore, the way Zen practice transforms suffering and results in well-being is different from what one might accept. It is not a magic wand for getting what you want. Instead, Zen practice slowly wears down the ego and cultivates stability, wisdom, and compassion. The Zen practitioner is less and less controlled by external circumstances.

The medical world has turned its attention to many forms of meditation because of their seeming power to improve mental and physical health. Mindfulness in particular has received increased attention because of its capacity to aid those with mental and physical ailments and enrich lives.[2] Scientific research is now documenting the physiological changes that result from meditation in general and Zen in particular.[3] Neurobiology in particular is the area in which increasing research is being done on how meditation changes the brain. In effect, preliminary research suggests that Zen seems to rewire the brain and the nervous system.[4] Where science, psychology, and Zen seem to be meeting is the changing how one perceives transforms the mind and body. For Zen and psychology what transforms is suffering and for science what transforms is the brain and nervous system.

THE ALLURE OF ZEN "SERENITY"

Zen is now used to sell things. One can buy a "Zen" phone, have a "Zen" spa day, or even buy "Zen" perfume. President Obama is sometimes described as "very Zen" in articles about his calm, unruffled demeanor in the midst of conflict.[5] The power of Zen's promise of tranquility, coolness, and serenity seems to have captured the minds of marketers, advertisers, and journalists. What marketers have tapped into is actually an ancient concept—the *Brahma Vihara* of *upeksha* or "boundless equanimity."[6] The *Brahma Viharas* are the different faces of love in Buddhism. The literal translation of *Brahma Vihara* is boundless abode. The other three are *maitri* or "boundless kindliness," *karuna* or "boundless compassion," and *mudita* or "sympathetic joy," which means happiness for others in their happiness.[7] Zen Master Robert Aitken describes the *Brahma Vihara* of boundless equanimity as a "broad, serene acceptance of self and others" that accepts even their and our own faults.[8] This "broad, serene acceptance" is what people want but cannot figure out how to get. Furthermore, it is at the heart of how and why Zen practice in its ancient and modern manifestations has the potential to transform the suffering of emotional and physical stress into peace, joy, and liberation. The problem is that this equanimity does not look the way people think it should because it is about letting go of how you want things to be in order to make room for what is actually in front of you, your own direct experience of the present moment.

The Vietnamese Zen Master Thich Nhat Hanh describes equanimity in the following way in his book, *Teachings on Love*: "The fourth element of true love is *upeksha*, which means equanimity, nonattachment, nondiscrimination, even-mindedness, or letting go."[9] Thich Nhat Hanh's interpretation of this fourth *Brahma Vihara* expands on Aitken Roshi's understanding because Hanh emphasizes letting go as part of the equanimity. This letting go is incredibly difficult and is why zazen, or Zen sitting meditation, is at the heart of Zen practice and the foundation of all the transformation attributed to Zen. Why is that? Because when you sit zazen, you notice, accept, and let go of everything that arises, no matter what. Shining the light of awareness on more and more of one's life gently transforms you and your life. Off the cushion, the practitioner manifests this process as mindfulness and letting go. Such an approach leads to a life of radical acceptance and oneness with life circumstances. She or he learns how to include more and more of her or his experience. Soto Zen also emphasizes ways in which to get knocked out of concepts into direct experience. Dualistic thinking traps us into rigidity and keeps us from seeing reality as it is. Thus, this kind of practice emphasizes a nondual way of living that is fluid in which concepts are tools rather than prison bars. This fluidity increases the ability to respond instead of react.

The entire point of Zen practice in particular and Buddhist practice in general is to transform suffering into peace, joy, and liberation. Thus, each section on Zen practice and the Buddhist concepts that are at the basis of this practice will aim to explain how it is supposed to transform suffering by changing how one perceives and relates to the world, others, and oneself, how this process of transformation is linked to alleviating stress, and finally, how this transformation actually changes the body itself, in particular the nervous system and the brain. Finally, since both authors are priests in the Soto Zen tradition, and Darlene Cohen is in addition a Roshi or Master in the Soto Zen tradition, the authors will primarily concentrate on Soto Zen when discussing the practice of Zen, rather than its venerable sister tradition, Rinzai Zen.[10]

TRANSFORMING *STRESS* BY CHANGING HOW ONE PERCEIVES THE WORLD

There are many teachings and practices in Zen that relate directly to changing one's perception and how that change results in skillful means, or effective action that transforms suffering. These include not-knowing mind, karma, oneness with one's experience, continuous practice, impermanence, and direct experience. All of these can be summarized as seeing things as they are—just this. Therefore, perception is everything in Zen. Buddhism teaches that how we see the world directly affects how much we suffer. Modern mind-body medicine emphasizes the same point. In this section, we will interweave the work of mindfulness guru Jon Kabat-Zin and ancient Zen Buddhist practices in order to explain how and why this kind of transformation eases suffering in general and the suffering from stress in particular.

Jon Kabat Zin, the scientist who is a pioneer in the use of mindfulness meditation and practices in health care, defines stress in the following way:

> The popular name for the full catastrophe nowadays is *stress* . . . It unifies a vast array of human responses into a single concept with which people strongly identify. . . . stress occurs on a multiplicity of levels and originates from many different sources. . . . Stress can be thought of as acting on different levels, including the physiological level, the psychological level, and the social level . . . In the vast middle range of stressors, where exposure is neither immediately lethal, like bullets or high-level radiation or poison, nor basically benign, like gravity, the general rule for those causing psychological stress is that *how you see things and how you handle them makes all the difference in terms of how much stress you will experience.*[11]

Thus, we see immediately that perception plays a vital role in minimizing reactivity to stressors and in fact in reducing the number of things we might see as stressors. Thus, perception itself can either increase or decrease our level of stress. Since Zen is all about changing one's perception in such a way as to transform suffering, right away we can see the link between Zen and stress reduction.

Kabat-Zin further describes the link between stress and changes in perception in the following way:

> So it can be particularly helpful to keep in mind from moment to moment that it is not so much the stressors in our lives but how we see them and what we do with them that determines how much we are at their mercy. If we can change the way we see, we can change the way we respond.[12]

This process of changing the way we see, which then results in changing the way we respond, summarizes Zen practice. The primary activity for this process is mindfulness. Mindfulness is the bridge between Zen, psychology, and science. In Zen, mindfulness is simply noticing what one is actually doing, thinking, feeling, sensing, perceiving, etc., without trying to change it. Because this task is far more difficult than it appears, Zen practitioners meditate as the core of their practice. Literally, they are learning how to return to the present moment, how to notice what is in the present moment, thus increasing their capacity to notice more and more of their experience, and cultivating the ability to tolerate what they notice without changing it, judging it, pushing it away, or clinging to it. This has the potential to result in a soft, flexible mind that is clear, forgiving, compassionate, and wise.

This retraining of perception that is fundamental to Zen practice intersects with psychology and neurobiology because how we see our circumstances affect our mental and physical health. Kabat-Zin's work on mindfulness and stress relief demonstrates that stress can just as easily arise from a misperception or thought instead of from what is actually there or happening. He describes this process as follows:

> As we have seen, even our thoughts and feelings can act as major stressors if they tax or exceed our ability to respond effectively. This is true even if the thought or feeling has no correspondence with "reality." For example, the mere *thought* that you have a fatal disease can be the cause of considerable stress and could become disabling, even though it may not be true.[13]

Thus, even if one is healthy and well with no sign of disease, the mere thought that one might actually be ill, which is not reality at that time, can cause stress.

This example demonstrates how not seeing what's actually there (health) but instead fearing what might be there (sickness) leads to suffering. One perceives what one imagines instead of what is actually happening and even though it is not happening, one suffers all the same.

If this mode of misperception remained only in the realm of psychology and did not affect the physical body, then perhaps it could be forgotten or dismissed. However, past and current research on the physiological impact of stress shows that this is not the case. The following classic description from Kabat-Zin is that of the fight-or-flight response that occurs when a person perceives a threat to his or her well-being:

> When we feel threatened, the fight-or flight reaction occurs almost instantly. The result is a state of physiological and psychological *hyperarousal*, characterized by a great deal of muscle tension and strong emotions, which may vary from terror, fright, or anxiety to rage and anger. The fight-or-flight reaction involves a very rapid cascade of nervous-system firings and release of stress hormones, the most well known of which is *epinephrine (adrenaline)*, which are unleashed in response to an immediate, acute threat . . . The output of the heart jumps by a factor of four or five by increasing the heart rate and the strength of the heart-muscle contractions (and thereby the blood pressure) so that more blood and therefore more energy can be delivered to the large muscles of the arms and legs, which will be called upon if we are to fight or run.[14]

It does not matter whether there is an actual threat or not; all that is required for the mental and physical response of fight or flight is for the person to *think* there is a threat. Those who are overly stressed then enter a cycle of remaining stuck in this fight-or-flight cycle to the point that they see everything as a stressor and threat. Buddhism teaches that humans tend to categorize the world into that which they desire and that which they wish to avoid. Science and psychology teach us that humans can get stuck in this method of categorization to the point that they see more and more of their life circumstances, the people around them, etc., as a threat to their well-being, even if that is not the case.[15] Thus, most of the suffering that arises from stress comes from getting stuck in a mode of perception that keeps inspiring the physiological fight or flight.

What is it about Zen that provides this mechanism of change in perception? One primary mechanisms is the not-knowing mind, as described by Mu Soeng:

> The Zen tradition has tried to comprehend this wisdom through the now formalized teaching of not-knowing. Not-knowing is the intuitive wisdom where one understands information to be just that—mere information—and tries to penetrate to the heart of the mystery that language and information are trying to convey. All we have in, in normal human conditioning is second-, third-, or fourthhand information. In our ignorance, we treat these units of information as self-evident truths and fail to investigate our own experience directly. The not-knowing approach is not a philosophical or intellectual entertainment; it is a doorway to liberation.[16]

Zen provides a way to see the world and oneself as only information. This neutral way of seeing removes the charge of seeing something as a threat or as a support to be chased and held onto. It circumvents the fight or flight reaction and thus the physiological cascade of events that stress initiates in the body.

How is this related to happiness that is not dependent on external circumstances? Because when one sees external circumstances just as information, then one is no longer controlled by them. The clarity that comes in the wake of not being controlled enhances one's ability to respond instead of react. Thus, Zen and mindfulness actually change the body, especially the brain and the nervous system. These changes will be explicitly linked to neurobiological changes in a later section.

So how does Zen practice help us see things as information rather than something to run toward or away from? Zen teaches us that one can have a painful experience or loss without stress. One simply has the experience. Thus, Zen is not about getting rid of feelings of any kind, but is instead about living life in a way that leaves "no trace." Thus, your feelings, thoughts, emotions, and perceptions come and go and you experience them, but when they are gone they leave no trace because you have fully experienced them, fully accepted them, and fully let them go.

The next Zen story is often used to exemplify how "no trace" or oneness with circumstances is about fully and completely having one's experience. Francis Cook used this story in his commentary on Soto Zen's founder Dogen's essay on karma:

A young monk was disillusioned with Zen when he heard his revered master scream in pain and fear as he was being murdered by thieves. The young man contemplated leaving Zen training, feeling that if his old master screamed in the face of pain or death, Zen itself must be a fraud. However, before he was able to leave, another teacher taught him something of what Zen is all about and removed his misconceptions. "Fool!" exclaimed the teacher, "the object of Zen is not to kill all feelings and become anesthetized to pain and fear. The object of Zen is to free us to scream loudly and fully when it is time to scream."[17]

This extreme example of oneness with circumstances or one's karma is supposed to wake us up to another facet of equanimity, which is that responding appropriately to circumstances is not about not feeling. Instead, as exemplified by the story, the point of Zen practice is to free us to laugh when we are supposed to laugh, scream when we are supposed to scream. Much of Zen practice is about getting kicked out of concepts and ideas into direct experience where everything is just information. Dwelling in direct experience frees one to respond appropriately. When one unites with the experience or rather just is the experience, then one is free no matter what the circumstances. Zen tends to use extremes to make important points about the transformation of suffering.

One of the reasons that everything does not flow, especially in the face of a crisis, is that instead of having a direct experience of our life, we want a theory about our life that will make our life the way we want it.[18] Then when life does not turn out to match our theory, we suffer in subtle to gross ways. Having plans about what we want in our life and how we want it to be is not the problem. The problem is staying attached to the outcome and our expectations. Thus, believing that a theory about our life is the reality rather than our direct experience of our life sets us up for suffering. Staying stuck to the outcome we want does not enable us to see our life as it is. In fact, we are then controlled by our expectations and thus miss the opportunities that are not part of our plan. Thus, we exist like ghosts, neither here nor there.

ONENESS WITH CIRCUMSTANCES AS A WAY TO TRANSFORM SUFFERING AND STRESS

In Zen, everything is an opportunity for awakening. Therefore, every single event, experience, thought, feeling, etc. is valuable and useful, including suffering. The operative classical teaching we will focus on in this section is oneness with circumstances (acceptance of karma) as a way to be free from circumstances. Directly related to this classical teaching is Kabat-Zin's emphasis on turning toward one's suffering rather than pushing it away or escaping from it. The irony is that one cannot release or transform what one denies or is not aware of. In a classic Zen poem, "Song of the Jewel Mirror Samadhi,"[19] this process of witnessing without acting on aversion or desire is described as "Turning away and touching are both wrong, for it is like a massive fire."[20] Not touching and not turning away in Zen focus on not changing oneself or one's experience, but instead witnessing it.

Again and again, Zen emphasizes that when you impose yourself on what is in front of you, you do not see it as it is. When you impose yourself on yourself, you do not see who you are. Thus, the act of imposing yourself impedes clear perception and encourages reactivity. How then can we allow things to be themselves? We can do this by being as completely present as we can. As we cultivate the ability to include more and more of our experience, we become less reactive and more responsive. This is the transformation that occurs through self-acceptance and letting go, which turns out to be a very effective strategy for dealing with stress.[21] Things become what they are and you become who you are.

In the *Genjo Koan*, Dogen-Zenji, founder of Soto Zen, writes, "Yet in attachment blossoms fall, and in aversion weeds spread."[22] That to which we are attached we see as a flower and yet that flower still falls and decays. That to which we are averse appears to us as a weed and it seems to multiply despite our best efforts to kill it. The way one does not touch or turn away and how one loves one's weeds is exemplified by the next koan (a puzzling question or story that is designed to knock people out of concepts into direct experience), which is exactly about how this activity is manifested as oneness with circumstances. We will see that the essential ingredient is a simultaneous unity with circumstances and freedom from circumstances that stems from constantly returning to one's direct experience. Returning to direct experience is what changes one's perspective—not the other way around.

The following koan from Dogen's essay "Spring and Fall" illustrates how direct experience can cut through categories and alleviate suffering:

A certain monk asked the great master Tung-shan, "When the cold or heat arrives, how can one avoid it?" The master answered,

"Why don't you go to a place where there is no cold or heat?"
"Where is this place where there is neither cold nor heat?" asked
the monk. Said Tung-shan, "When it is cold, the cold kills the
monk; when it is hot, the heat kills the monk."[23]

So—what is the place where there is neither cold nor heat? Direct
experience. Oneness with experience, regardless of what it is. This is
simply being as present as possible to whatever is happening, both
inside and outside oneself. This is not touching, not turning away.
The mystery of Zen is that by doing this, one transforms suffering.
The closest words that get to it is that by doing this, one stops struggling to force things to be different and stops struggling to maintain
comfort and ideal circumstances. Dropping the struggle itself allows
one to rest and creates the possibility of clarity because one's personal
agenda is finally, if not out of the way, at least not the dominant lens
through which the world and self are seen.

But as we all know—it is much harder to get to that place than we
think. And the kind of effort we think it takes is not that at all. It is
actually zazen effort. So, we do not actually work to be free—we work
to notice when we are not free—when we are free—and we sit zazen to
practice not separating from our experience, no matter what it is.
Dogen then continues—"when it is cold, be thoroughly cold, and
when it is hot, be thoroughly hot."[24] By affirming one's conditionedness, one becomes free from one's conditionedness.[25]

So how does one affirm one's very conditionedness? What does Zen
teach about that and how does it happen? It happens because when
you are present to what is in front of you and to yourself, you are
actually affirming it. Being present to our direct experience, especially
in zazen, teaches us that everything changes and that we have no continuous self and that our perspective is limited. Thus, we can then see
the world differently. Scientific research now teaches us that this shift
in perception is also a physiological shift. In the section on Zen and
science, we will see that there are actually pathways in the brain and
nervous system that shift when one's autobiography or personalized
lens on the world drops and one sees what's there without oneself in
the way. The change is physiological because our lens on the world
is actually a pattern in the brain and nervous system.

ZEN AND WELL-BEING FROM A SCIENTIFIC PERSPECTIVE

Now that we have reviewed some ancient practices that Zen teaches and uses in order to achieve well-being, we will move to some current scientific understandings and hypotheses of what is actually changed in the brain and nervous system through these practices and others like them, primarily Zen and its practice of mindfulness. Really what we will be looking at is what could be described as a modern-day, scientific understanding of karma, namely behavioral, perceptual, and emotional patterns that are inscribed in the nervous system and brain from our up-bringing, our social, national, physical, monetary, familial, etc. context. What Zen seems to do is unwrite or at least fade this physically inscribed karma and rewrite a new physical karma that does not necessarily erase the old karmic pattern but instead bypasses it.

How does this relate to the alleviation of stress? Basically, stress responses can inscribe pathways in our brain and nervous system.[26] And if we get stuck in stress reactivity, then the pathway becomes more and more entrenched and harder to change. Therefore, from a neurobiological perspective, Zen practice and mindfulness practices in general, because they are about rewiring us into well-being, can also be directly applied to stress pathways and responses if only because Zen provides a way to build an alternate pathway. The specific rewiring that seems to take place according to current research is that one moves from perceiving the world through one's autobiography to instead perceiving the world through selflessness. This switch has a physiological component, which James Austin, MD, describes as moving from egocentric perception to allocentric (other-centered or self-less) perception, which has literal correlates in the parts of the brain that perceive and then react to that perception.[27] Therefore, in this section, we will focus on how Zen and mindfulness rewire the brain and nervous system in general, with a special focus on how this relates to stress in particular.

James Austin, MD, has made how Zen changes the brain the focus of much of his career, specifically in the books *Zen and the Brain*, *Zen-Brain Reflections*, and *Selfless Insights* in addition to many papers and other research. As a medical doctor, a Zen practitioner of many years, and a neurobiologist, he has a unique perspective from which to uncover much of what happens to the brain in zazen and mindfulness practices. He writes,

> A Zen perspective has been available for centuries. But until recent decades, the scientific community did not understand the message, or it chose to ignore it. How can Zen make its age-old contribution to the study of consciousness? By inviting us to ask the naïve and seemingly incredible question: what is this world *really* like without our intrusive self-referent self in the picture? Putting it another way, let's suppose a brain drops off all its subjective veils of *self*-consciousness. What, then, does the rest of its awareness—and its pure, objective consciousness, perceive?[28]

Where this links back to Zen and the brain is that Zen's focus on bypassing one's personal agenda in order to have a direct experience is just the kind of change that facilitates clear perception as documented in James Austin's books on Zen and the brain. One does not actually have to drop one's personal agenda. Instead, all one has to do is cultivate the ability to return to one's direct experience of the present moment over and over again. Such a cultivation also fosters the ability to include more and more of one's experience. Eventually, one's personal agenda is just one facet of how one perceives the world.

How does this intersect with stress? As seen earlier in this article, stress is an emotional and psychological response to a stressor. However, emotions are hard to change and often not subject to reason. Basically, by turning to the present moment over and over again, we are providing ourselves with an alternate focus while our brain is in tumult, until it calms and we develop new nerve pathways. Science shows us that this shift of focus to the breath and the present moment actually calms the firing of maladaptive neural pathways.[29]

Zen teaches us, as we saw earlier, that the less we see our world just as information, the less effective we will be in it and the more controlled we will be by circumstances. However, what we see here is that we are controlled by external circumstances *precisely because we are controlled by internal circumstances, NOT the other way around.* Thus, if we can change these, we have more of a chance of not being controlled by external circumstances. These internal circumstances are encoded in our brain and nervous system. Since our brains and nervous system are wired to perceive the world in the way that we have been taught and that we remember from past experiences, most of us walk around with a perceptual filter that does not see things as they are. This personalized filter causes us to select and reject material based on our memories and conditioning in terms of what has helped most in the past, or simply what we have learned from our roles models and/or society and/or family. Thus, we're already wired to walk around with a personalized filter. But, in addition to faulty perception, we are also wired emotionally by our own genetics, our environment, our upbringing, etc. This emotional wiring is intimately related to how we perceive. Thus, if what we perceive is already filtered by our wiring, then changing the way we respond or react depends on changing our perception. And yet, these seem to be locked in a mutual embrace calculated to keep us from doing just that. So how is this related to stress, and how is it related to Zen?

Basically, zazen, or sitting meditation, provides a format to watch ourselves react to our own thoughts, perceptions, emotions, and sensations, in a safe, closed loop. Because we are silent and still while we watch the cascade of reactions and thoughts, we eventually see how we are the source of our warped window on the world and that our window might not match what is in front of us, or even match our direct experience. From a neurobiological perspective, what this does is calm the firing of the neurons that access memories.[30] Zen and its practices provide a way to *bypass* our internal circumstances because Zen practice is about just noticing those internal circumstances and not changing them. It turns out that the very act of non-judgmental attention enables those internal circumstances to slowly stop dominating us if only because we finally realize we do not have to act on our thoughts and feelings and we will still survive.

According to Austin, the good news is that the brain is plastic and can change, and new nerve cells and nervous system pathways can be born and old ones can be changed or wither away.[31] The bad news is that experientially, one needs to be able to withstand the pull of the old pathways and habits while building the new ones that are more fruitful and less maladaptive. This requires stability, which comes from regular meditation and mindfulness practices, which is strengthened by sitting with a group and working with a teacher. However, Zen practice and other forms of mindfulness meditation provide a way to change these maladaptive pathways—remember back to earlier in the chapter when we discussed not-thinking and its role in seeing everything as simply information rather than seeing everything only in terms of desire or aversion. It changes the overconditioning of the limbic system if only because we watch everything that pops up while silent and still and we begin to see the web of self and memory that we impose on what is in front of us. These changes happen indirectly in Zen practice.

In particular, preliminary research and speculation upon the research by Austin suggests that the very mechanisms by which Zen for centuries has relied on changing perception in order to transform suffering deactivate an overconditioned limbic system.[32] The research in his three books is extensive, highly technical, and very specific. For that reason, we will be concentrating only on some key aspects that reflect how changes in perception change the brain and nervous system.

First, we will concentrate on the pathways in the brain that have been linked to overwhelming anxiety and fear that then lead to reactivity without choice. The seat of these emotions in the brain seems to be the amygdala in the limbic brain, which is a "gateway" from the limbic brain to the neocortex and other parts of the brain. Austin describes its primary function in the following way:

> It [the amygdala] codes for the potential emotional, social, and survival value of an arousing stimulus, then relays this information elsewhere where it can serve matching responses appropriately and be consolidated into potentially useful memories...
> The amygdala is not activated each time we consciously judge whether an ordinary stimulus is pleasant or unpleasant. However, emotional states of extreme anger or fear almost always activate the normal amygdala. The amygdala also becomes more activated during the readiness to act, psychological conditioning, autonomic arousal, release of "stress" hormones, and when our attention is heightened.[33]

Austin goes on to describe a study in which participants were asked "to maintain their negative emotion *after* they viewed a disturbing 'negative' picture."[34] Activity rose in their amygdala, and those who had reported having a negative worldview had the highest increase of activity in this part of the limbic brain.[35] The amygdala has a strong influence on the neocortex and on our actions and on our responses to stressors. Austin suggests that Zen practice helps loosen the dominance of the amygdala on the neocortex and reactivity in general:

> Unstated in Zen is a major premise of long-range meditative training: diminishing the unfruitful influences that the amygdala

has on other regions, higher and lower (part VII). Yet these personal liberations usually evolve at a glacial pace, much too subtly to seem practical, recognized more in hindsight than at the time. On the background of such incremental change, could a deep crevasse open up suddenly, an event that cuts through every knotted problem in the psyche, from top to bottom?[36]

If Zen practice is to have an influence on an important seat of extreme fear and anxiety and instantaneous reactions to those overwhelming feelings, then the next place to look is at the phenomena of fearlessness and awakening in Zen practice. Austin focuses on kensho, a "seeing into the essence of things, insight-wisdom,"[37] as an experience Zen practitioners have that can point to what happens in the brain. Satori is the term reserved for "a deeper, more advanced state of insight-wisdom."[38] Austin hypothesizes that kensho and satori result in a state in which perception is primarily allocentric and that the fear-based self through which we see the world drops away.[39] If true, such experiences would reduce "the resonances of fear in the amygdala and other limbic and para-limbic regions."[40]

He goes on to hypothesize further that repeated experiences of kensho and satori continue to change the brain. In the brain, there are "other-referential attentional and processing functions" and "pathways that are Self-referential."[41]

Simply stated, his theories based on current research imply that Zen strengthens "other-referential" pathways, or Selfless pathways in the brain rather than "Self-referential" pathways in the brain. Thus, the problems alluded to earlier in the chapter about how to get around perceiving the world through memory and our autobiographical Self now have a tentative answer. He then goes on to explain how mindfulness and bare awareness contribute to a more clear perception of the world:

> Unfortunately, our biases distort perception. They cause us to remember false information ... the more directly we integrate our earliest perceptual messages—the simpler ones that first register *seeing* and *hearing*—with our medial temporal lobe memory functions, the more likely we are to record details accurately and remember an event in ways that consciousness might regard as valid, at least tentatively. Otherwise, greater degrees of uncertainty arise, and will persist.
>
> The world is like a Rorschach ink blot test. We insert the imaginary projections of our subjective Self into everything we

see there. The simplest way to gather valid factual information is by learning to observe the world mindfully, unjudgmentally, clearly, using the other-referential ventral pathways that bypass the intrusive filters of Self.[42]

Returning one's attention to the present moment seems to reinforce allocentric pathways in the brain while continuing to try to force the world to fit into one's veil of memory and autobiography reinforces Self-oriented pathways in the brain. Austin is attempting to explain and understand from a neurobiological standpoint the kind of clarity of perception that was described earlier in this chapter as not-thinking. Although there is not yet a definitive answer from the scientific standpoint, he explains:

> Meditation creates a series of complex psycho-physiological changes. To begin with a loose generalization, one might say that Zen meditation does involve a kind of *not* thinking, *clearly*. And it then proceeds to carry this clear awareness into everyday living ... Zen training is an agency of character change. It's a program designed to point the whole personality in the direction of increasing selflessness and enhanced awareness.[43]

Thus, this ancient combination of Zen practices, which include zazen, mindfulness, and not-thinking (not being trapped by concepts), focused on cultivating awareness and dampening the ego in order to cultivate wisdom and compassion, gently nudges the brain toward the allocentric pathways and not the egocentric pathways.[44]

Another important aspect is the relationship between nuclei of the dorsal thalamus (a part of the limbic brain) and the neocortex. In addition to the influence of the amygdala, these nuclei also send "impulses from the limbic system ... to influence the emotional responses of the cortex."[45] These ripples between the thalamus and the neocortex could serve to reinforce egocentric pathways.[46] Austin theorizes that kensho and satori have the potential to "decrease the functions of ... the dorsal thalamus. These deactivations could cause a significant decrease in the maladaptive influences of the Self."[47]

So how does this relate back to stress and Zen's potential to reduce and alleviate the stress response? Basically, just as stress rewires the brain as mentioned earlier, so can zazen and mindfulness practices undo the harm that stress can cause in the body. In particular, current neurobiological research, hypotheses, and theories about how Zen practice affects the brain imply that Zen practice provides a way to calm and bypass the tyranny of the limbic brain over the neocortex because it provides a way to encourage selflessness as a form of perception. Since the limbic brain is actively involved in the stress response and especially in *hyperarousal* and stress reactivity, the potential of Zen to provide relief is then clear. And finally, since Kabat-Zin's mindfulness-based stress reduction programs focus on changes in perception as the foundation of relief from stress and Zen is an ancient practice for changing perception and cultivating clarity, the potential for Zen to aid in that change in perception is present. Ultimately, the letting go and returning to the present moment of zazen turns out to be a form of control and a way to change one's internal circumstances enough so that one is no longer controlled by external circumstances. This entire chapter has been an explanation of how the ancient concept of *upeksha* or equilibrium could be practiced and how and why it leads to happiness that is not dependent on external circumstances.

PRACTICAL SUGGESTIONS

What are some practical applications of Zen practice to help alleviate stress in daily life? In this last section, we will focus on two practices designed to encourage gently returning to the present moment until you can see clearly what is in front of you. Zazen, as described previously, is the foundation of all of these practices. Other practices that have not been fully described in this chapter include cultivating "Right View." one of the practices of the Eightfold Noble Path in Buddhism, creating and using a personal koan, and breath practice in everyday situations.

Thich Nhat Hanh suggests using the question "Am I sure?" when confronted with something that we think threatens us. Such a practice could be used when faced with a stressor. "Right View" is all about realizing that our perceptions are not reality and in fact can never be reality. In his explanation of "Right View," Thich Nhat Hanh points out that the Buddha said, "Where there is perception, there is deception."[48] According to Hanh, "most of our perceptions are erroneous" and erroneous perceptions lead to suffering.[49] This is similar to Kabat-Zin's emphasis on how the stress response often arises in reaction to "perceived" threats, rather than actual threats. Thus, practicing asking "Am I sure?" or "What is this?" potentially buys you time and allows you to tolerate your reaction until perhaps it can become a response.

Therefore, if possible, keep asking the question until clarity arises. The ancient application of "Right View" through questions such as "Am I sure?" or "What is this?" encourages us to question our own perceptions and regain our sanity.

Cultivating a personal koan is also a way to reappropriate the ancient Zen practice of using an unanswerable question to knock the Zen student out of concepts and into direct experience. When you are faced by a situation that you cannot resolve or that puzzles you, you could develop a question that might help you come up with an answer *indirectly* and *spontaneously*. For example, if you cannot tell the difference between a threat and a mild irritant at work, developing a question about that might help. Cohen Roshi describes this process of developing a personal koan in detail in her book *Turning Suffering Inside Out*.

Creating your own personal koan then would involve reflecting on the seemingly intractable situation and finding a question that could neutrally give you information about the situation. For example, if friends complain that you never listen to them, you might use the question "How do I listen?" as a personal koan and see what happens. From the perspective of Zen practice, asking yourself the question at arbitrary times of day and potentially before speaking with a friend *without expecting an answer* is perhaps the most important part of the practice. Forcing change is not part of Zen practice. The question eventually drops the issue into your subconscious and eventually an answer that you did not develop intellectually might arise. Questions tailored to stressful situations could also be devised.

These are only a few of the practical applications of Zen. Many more exist and can be cultivated. These ancient practices have transformed suffering into peace, joy, and liberation for many over the centuries. Kabat-Zin modified Zen mindfulness practices for a general audience and his programs on mindfulness-based stress reduction have been transforming the suffering caused by stress now for decades. Now, with the advent of nascent neurobiological research on how meditation in general and Zen in particular change the brain, we can finally see that to transform our suffering is to transform our perception, which in turn transforms our body.

NOTES

1. Boorstein, Sylvia (Fall 1999). "The Gesture of Fearlessness and the Armor of Loving-Kindness," http://ecbuddhism.blogspot.com/

2009/04/fear-fearlessness-what-buddhists-teach.html (accessed October 30, 2009).

2. Epel, Elissa, Daubenmier, Jennifer, Moskowitz, Judith Tedlie, Folkman, Susan, & Blackburn, Elizabeth. (2009). "Can meditation slow the rate of cellular aging? Cognitive stress, mindfulness, and telomeres," *Longevity, Regeneration, and Optimal Health, 1172,* 34–53.

3. This article will be using primarily the works of James Austin, MD, in particular, *Zen and the Brain, Zen-Brain Reflections,* and *Selfless Insight.*

4. Austin, *Zen-Brain Reflections,* 138–140.

5. Herbert, Bob. (2009, August 21). "Voices of Anxiety." *The New York Times*; Zeleny, Jeff. (2008, December 24). "Obama's Zen State, Well It's Hawaiian." *The New York Times.*

6. Aitken, *Original Dwelling Place,* 47.

7. Ibid.

8. Ibid., 48–49.

9. Hanh, *Teachings on Love,* 8.

10. A basic difference between Rinzai Zen and Soto Zen is that Rinzai Zen focuses on sudden enlightenment whereas Soto Zen focuses on gradual enlightenment.

11. Kabat-Zin, *Full Catastrophe Living,* 235–238.

12. Ibid., 241.

13. Ibid.

14. Ibid., 251.

15. Jon Kabat Zin's *Full Catastrophe Living* is one example of books on the subject. However, James Austin's books *Zen and the Brain, Zen-Brain Reflections,* and *Selfless Insight* are more recent texts on scientific investigation of the effects of Zen on the body and in particular on the brain.

16. Soeng, *The Diamond Sutra,* 63–64.

17. Cook, "Karma," in *How to Raise an Ox,* 43.

18. Kwang, Dae (Fall 1999). "Mind Placebo," http://www.kwanumzen.org/pzc/newsletter/v11n04-1999-apr.html (accessed October 30, 2009).

19. Austin, *Zen-Brain Reflections,* 472. Samadhi means "an extraordinary alternate state of one-pointed absorption" or sometimes it also means merely a state.

20. http://www.berkeleyzencenter.org/Texts/jewelmirror.shtml (accessed October 30, 2009).

21. Kabat-Zin, *Full Catastrophe Living,* 269–273.

22. Eihei Dogen, *Moon in a Dewdrop,* 69.

23. Eihei Dogen, "Spring and Fall," in *How to Raise an Ox,* 111.

24. Ibid.

25. Cook, 43.

26. Austin, *Zen-Brain Reflections,* 113–114.

27. Austin, *Selfless Insight,* 109.

28. Austin, *Zen-Brain Reflections,* xxv.

29. Austin, *Zen-Brain Reflections*, 59.
30. Ibid., 104.
31. Ibid., 141.
32. Austin, *Selfless Insight*, 92.
33. Austin, *Zen-Brain Reflections*, 86, 90.
34. Ibid., 93.
35. Ibid.
36. James Austin, *Selfless Insight*, 201.
37. Ibid., 271.
38. Ibid., 272.
39. Ibid., 93–94.
40. Ibid., 179–180.
41. Ibid., 187–188.
42. Ibid., 142–143.
43. Austin, *Zen-Brain Reflections*, xxv, xxxvi.
44. Austin, *Selfless Insight*, 188.
45. Ibid., 90.
46. Ibid., 92.
47. Ibid., 93–94.
48. Hanh, *The Heart of the Buddha's Teaching*, 53.
49. Ibid.

REFERENCES

Aitken, R. (1996). *Original dwelling place: Zen Buddhist essays*. Washington, DC: Counterpoint.

Austin, J. (2009). *Selfless insight: Zen and the meditative transformations of consciousness*. Boston: MIT Press.

Austin, J. (1999). *Zen and the brain: Toward an understanding of meditation and consciousness*. Boston: MIT Press.

Austin, J. (2006). *Zen-brain reflections: Reviewing recent developments in meditation and states of consciousness*. Boston: MIT Press.

Cohen, D. (2004a). *The one who is not busy: Connecting with work in a deeply satisfying way*. Layton, UT: Gibbs Smith.

Cohen, D. (2004b). *Turning suffering inside out: A Zen approach to living with physical and emotional pain*. Boston: Shambhala.

Cook, F. (2002). *How to raise an ox: Zen practice as taught in master Dogen's shobogenzo*. Boston: Wisdom.

Dogen, E. (1995). *Moon in a dewdrop: Writings of Zen master Dogen*. K. Tanahashi (Ed.); R. Aitken, E. Brown, K. Tanahashi, et al. (Trans.). New York: North Point Press.

Epel, E., Daubenmier, J., Moskowitz, J. T., Folkman, S., & Blackburn, E. (2009). Can meditation slow the rate of cellular aging? Cognitive stress, mindfulness, and telomeres. *Longevity, Regeneration, and Optimal Health, 1172*, 34–53.

Hanh, T. N. (1999). *The heart of the Buddha's teaching*. New York: Broadway Books.

Hanh, T. N. (1998). *Teachings on love*. Berkeley, CA: Parallax Press.

Kabat-Zin, J. (2009). *Full catastrophe living: Using the wisdom of your body and mind to face stress, pain, and illness*. New York: Bantam Dell.

Soeng, M. (2000). *The diamond sutra: Transforming the way we perceive the world*. Somerville, MA: Wisdom.

Suzuki, S. (2005). *Zen mind, beginner's mind*. Trudy Dixon (Ed.). Boston: Weatherhill.

PART THREE

CONTEMPLATIVE PRACTICES IN ACTION: APPLICATION

PREFACE TO PART THREE

Part Three, *Contemplative Practices in Action: Application*, examines various applications of spiritual and contemplative practices. Delbecq's chapter shows that learning meditation—a well-researched and foundational contemplative practice—can have a powerful impact on business leaders. Next, Wachholtz and Pearce remind us that spiritual traditions contain rousing practices as well as quieting practices, and these arousing practices may be useful for treating chronic pain. Finally, Manuel and Stortz examine the spirituality, health, and solidarity-promotional value of three oft-forgotten practices from Christian tradition: lamentation, intercession, and pilgrimage.

CHAPTER 11

The Impact of Meditation Practices in the Daily Life of Silicon Valley Leaders

Andre L. Delbecq

Earlier chapters focused in detail on specific contemplative practices, elaborating on their spiritual and psychological character as well as impacts on individual growth and functioning. The purpose in this chapter is to share how a group of varied practices become integrated into the lives of business leaders in Silicon Valley.

Silicon Valley has a unique culture familiar to those who read the business press. Fast moving, entrepreneurial, innovation driven, wired, hectic, and internationally linked, it is a frenzied intersection of engineering, science, business acumen, and entrepreneurship. At its best the Valley is a place that unleashes the human spirit through a culture of decentralization and empowerment, enabling creative development of products and services for humankind.[1] At its worst, the Valley can be a destructive stew laced with greed, opportunism, and activism. The Valley can be a dangerous place for the spiritually confused. Without an inner compass, the unaware will lead a life of increasing stress and quite often join the ranks of "burned-out" refugees fleeing in a state of brokenness.[2]

INTRODUCING MEDITATION

In the last decade over 450 working professional MBAs, divided equally between men and women, and 350 senior executives have participated in an elective seminar called Spirituality for Organizational

Leadership at Santa Clara University, a Jesuit and Catholic school located in Silicon Valley in Northern California. The average age is 34. Most are high-achieving engineering, scientific, and functional business managers—knowledge workers in their career prime who drive the core strategic business units in the Valley. A few are entrepreneur-owners. Occasionally a participant is between positions (e.g., has sold a company, has been laid off, or is seeking a job change). Typically two or three consultants and two or three CEOs also join the seminar.[3]

The seminar meets from 8:30 to 2:20 on five Saturdays, so a precious day is sacrificed by highly stressed Valley leaders who otherwise would be available "for catch-up" and attention to personal matters. Yet they fill a classroom each quarter the course is offered, largely through word-of-mouth encouragement from earlier participants. A frequently reported reason is to learn meditation practices.

The participants encompass diverse religious backgrounds. Buddhists, Taoists, Muslims, Jews, a variety of Hindi faiths, Christians, agnostics, and a few self-proclaimed atheists are usually represented. The Christian tradition is embraced by approximately 40 percent of the attendees.

By means of quotations taken from reflection assignments, this chapter provides exemplification of how meditation/contemplative practices reshape consciousness and behavior. It is assumed readers have familiarity with the practices themselves (or similar meditation forms) in order to give attention to context, pedagogy, and the developmental sequence achieved through a combination of practices.

THE OVERALL PEDAGOGY

Each seminar meeting is composed of three modules, two topical lecture modules and one contemplative/meditative practice module. The fourth seminar varies, as it is a 12-hour retreat. The module topics together with the meditation/contemplative practice form central to each are:

1. An overview of the Faith/Spirit at Work movement as a societal trend, and as an interest group within the Academy of Management
   Meditation on being present to the "Now" (guided)
2. Investigating business leadership as a calling within a spiritual journey
   Meditation on light and darkness in organizations (guided)

3. Listening to the voices of future generations impacted by business practices
   Meditation on "Living Voices of Future Generations" (guided)

4. Spiritual/psychological development associated with transformational leadership
   Meditation on personal calling to leadership (guided)

5. Discernment as an overlay on strategic decision making
   Introduction to "Lectio Divina" (thereafter self-directed)

6. Approaches to prayer and meditation in the lives of transformational leaders
   Introduction to the "Examen" (thereafter self-directed)

7. The spiritual challenges of leadership power and potential distortions of hubris
   Introduction to "Apophatic" Meditation (e.g., Zen, Centering Prayer, Mantra Meditation, etc.)

8. The spiritual challenges of wealth creation and the need for poverty of spirit
   "Apophatic" Meditation (self-directed)

9. Contemplative practice in the hectic space of leadership
   "Apophatic" Meditation (self-directed)

10. Group retreat
    "Lectio Divina," Breath Meditation, Walking Meditation, Meditation on Calling (group and self-directed), "Apophatic" Meditation

11. Exploring the mystery of suffering as part of leadership
    "Lectio Divina" with spiritual writings focused on suffering (self-directed), "Tong Len" (self-directed)

12. Summing up

Following each gathering participants are given two assignments. The first is to reflect on the lectures, seminar dialogue, and readings. (The course has an extensive reading list. Participants are allowed to pursue each topic through the lenses of different spiritual traditions.) Participants are asked to indicate how their perspectives have been influenced, and what behavioral changes they have integrated into their leadership within the workplace during the two weeks following the seminar. The primary orientation is "action learning" rather than simply theoretical synthesis.

The second assignment is meditation based. Participants are given forms of meditation to practice each day until the next seminar meeting. Again they are asked to reflect on how their leadership perceptions and behaviors have been influenced during the two weeks as a result of the meditation experience.

Normally assignments when submitted are two to four pages in length. (There are other traditional term paper assignments, but they are not our focus here.)

Space precludes treating in detail all the meditation/contemplative practice forms included over the three months. Here we will describe just two meditation forms together with the topics covered by the lecture to illustrate through quotations how meditation impacts on perceptions of leadership.

PRESENCE MEDITATION

The first module of the seminar deals with definitions of spirituality, the contemporary literature regarding Spirit/Faith at work, motivations for exploring the topic in the context of organizational leadership, and norms of appreciative inquiry in interreligious conversation. The module closes by noting how the "Spirit at Work" movement has grown in North America. It reviews the current manifest interest in the topic by both management scholars and business professionals.[4]

Participants are told that spirituality is about "experience," not simply knowledge. Just as they cannot learn to sail a boat simply by reading about boats and oceans, they cannot enter into the spiritual unless they embrace spiritual disciplines and experience. So in every module participants share a meditation form.

The first meditation focuses on "presence." With music, the professor leads a reflection on the importance of being present to the "*now.*" Asking participants to return to a place and time when they experienced inner peace in their earlier lives, they are encouraged to examine the burdens that have accumulated in mind, heart, and spirit since that time and place, and invited to let go of fears, anxieties, work concerns, frustrations, etc. They are invited to experience the freedom of just "BEing." After this five-minute meditation they are asked to gently return to the seminar and to be completely present to the ensuing lecture and shared dialogue; to step away from multitasking and concern with the past and their future. The implications of why it is important for a leader to be fully present for each subsequent task are then discussed.

For many participants this is already new ground. They readily admit they are often not fully present in the frenzy of daily work.

It is an important lesson they continue to examine while engaging this meditation form during the two weeks before the seminar meets again.

Quotations taken from participants' reflection assignments received two weeks later indicate new perspectives.

> The meditations in class have set me up for a more personal experience of the material than I had expected. I had envisioned a more lecture-based approach instead of the more active experience and participation that is needed for this class. My initial reaction was "this puts me way out of my comfort zone." I don't think I would have been able to jump into the meditation assignments without the practice of the "Now" meditation during the lecture.

> My life is a circle. I run around and around. Each day is the same. Month and years all appear the same. I am in a rut. The first meditation brought something to light inside of me. I discovered life does not begin in the future, but now. I began to think that I can break the circle apart.

> Multi-tasking is something I feel comfortable with; feel like I am good at. I now see it sometimes is getting in the way of my connections to others. Being present to the moment means putting less priority on multi-tasking and paying closer attention to the people with whom I work in order to understand and appreciate them.

> Thomas Merton sums up exactly what I am thinking. I am working on finding my true self, but there are so many distractions at work that I'm not always sure which of my feelings are real. How do you overcome all of the fears, obsessions and addictions in order to find yourself? Part of the answer has to be to be "present" so you can listen to God in the "now."

MEDITATION ON THE ROLE OF CONTEMPORARY ORGANIZATIONS

In the second module, attention turns to the importance of the contemporary organization to modern society and why accepting leadership within these institutions can be an important life calling.[5] We reflect on how the goods and services our neighbors depend on are created within and distributed through organizations. We remind ourselves that religious traditions see meeting the real needs of others (e.g., educational, health, housing, nutritional, transportation, etc.) as important service. However, in modern life, these needs are often met through complex chains of causation enabled by organizations whose ultimate clients are at a distance beyond personal contact. A mystic's eye is required by a leader to understand organizational roles as forms of service so that work is not hallowed of transcendent purpose.

We reflect on how charism/gift/talent is unleashed or inhibited within organizations through appropriate decision processes that support the unfolding of individual creative expression.

We reflect on how the contemporary organization is a central "community" replacing former villages or neighborhoods as the dominant primary group for most of the workweek. We remind ourselves of the role of leadership (formal and informal) in creating nurturing group experiences, and of the high psychological cost of pernicious work settings.

Finally, we examine issues of justice and injustice and the impacts of organizations on broader societal well-being. We examine the obligations of stewardship in global business organizations that sometimes control more wealth than smaller nation-states. We look at wealth creation and how it supports governments, the arts, health, social services, and education.

The dark side of the contemporary global business organization is also discussed; e.g., the distortions of power, greed, employee exploitation, environmental degradation, and negative impacts on indigenous cultures caused by global business practices.[6] We come to an understanding that those who accept organizational leadership are not called to a second-rate spiritual path. We discuss the spiritual writers who admonish us to avoid any false dualism between day-to-day work within organizations and the spiritual journey.

These discussions and readings end with a guided meditation that participants practice each day prior to the next class gathering. It is a "Daily Reflection on Light and Darkness in the Organization in Which I Work." A detailed description of this meditation is provided in the Appendix to give the reader a sense of what is meant by "guided" meditation in the context of the seminar. Participants are asked to spend a few minutes, either seated in their car or on a bench outside their workplace before entering to undertake their daily duties, engaging the meditation. They are also encouraged to practice the "Presence to the Now" meditation after they complete one important leadership activity during the day and before they undertake the next critical meeting or activity.

The following quotations are again taken from students' assignments received two weeks following the first seminar gathering:

My workdays were more productive because I focused my thoughts and tasks for the day toward contributing to organizational light at the very beginning of the work day [*sic*]. I stopped my rush to quickly enter my office without attention to the overall purpose of my organization. With focused thoughts my days were more productive.

It was common when I was growing up to hear people talk about teaching as a vocation, or hear people say about some occupations comments like "that nurse is wonderful, you can see her vocation." I have begun to long for "my vocation." It never really occurred to me that a vocation is both something that is offered and something that is received. I am beginning to see my organizational leadership calls me to serve others both within my company, and by serving my company clients, and that this requires spiritual development. I am very excited to see how this new insight develops in my business life.

I have realized my personal relationship with God has been deteriorating as I consumed myself in daily work. I seem to have entirely separated my spiritual life from my work and it has resulted in an unfulfilling path "on the road to success and career progression." I recognized this only after deep, careful thought stimulated by the meditations following our last seminar gathering.

Starting with the lecture, the idea that really struck me was a note that I wrote down: "If I am going to take that much of myself to work it has to mean something. Is my work worth giving so much of my deep self to? I give myself to my job creatively and intellectually, but I have not given my heart. The meditations then helped me to start to see that I don't dislike my job as much as I thought. I just haven't been looking at it from the perspective on how I impact on my client's [*sic*] lives."

It is true that time pressures at work are extreme. However, this is a problem with respect to my spiritual growth only because I have compartmentalized the spiritual aspect of life into a separate box that needs it's own place and time. I now realize that my spirituality needs to be integrated into everything that I do at work. This especially includes the one component that is demanding the most of my present time—my leadership challenges.

My meditation is teaching me that the problem has not been with my work but rather my approach to work. I have been forcing myself to be someone whom I desperately do not want to be at work by leaving my spirituality at the door before I went into the office building everyday [*sic*]. In essence I have been putting on a mask as soon as I walk in.

Embracing my spirituality as integral to my organizational work is helping me react more positively to different situations. It is helping me view the situation with the greater good in mind, not just to focus on narrow tasks that center around myself. I am reaffirming my respect for my organization that enables technologies by producing the semiconductors that enrich our daily lives.

I have had dreams of a vocation that provides for the common societal good, but felt myself mired in the reality of making a living and trying to find a way to get where I want to go. Now I begin to understand I am sitting on my dream—my biotechnology, scientific and engineering roots *are* embedded in the dream I have been seeking. I just didn't recognize the dream of spiritual fulfillment was hidden within the day to day of my organizational life.

OTHER MEDITATION FORMS IN THE SEMINAR

Space precludes a detailed description of the remaining course content and forms of meditation in order to preserve space for a summation of the overall inner journey participants move through, and a description of how practices are incorporated into the leader's day.

Again, the guided meditations incorporated into the seminar are guided meditations and contemplative practices.

GUIDED MEDITATIONS

Meditation on Being Present to the "Now"

Meditation on Light and Darkness in Contemporary Organizational Life

We have discussed the first two guided meditations—Meditation on Being Present to the "Now," and Meditation on Darkness in Contemporary Organizational Life—and the related seminar topics. The remaining forms are:

Meditation on Impacts of the Organization on Future Generations
Meditation on Personal Calling to Leadership

The *Examen*

Lectio Divina

Tong Len

A quick summary of these additional remaining meditation/contemplative practice forms follows:

The meditation "Impacts on Future Generations" builds on a Lakota Sioux "Circle of Living Voices" asking leaders to consider the meaning of today's decisions for those whose "faces have not yet emerged from the earth, seven generations from now."[7] Participants in the seminar find this reflection a powerful reminder that what is done today in their leadership role has implications for the future that is "veiled" but that a mature leader must take into consideration. In a time of increasing sensitivity to environmental concerns, the meditation resonates with participants.

The meditation on Leadership Calling is a guided meditation wherein participants examine personal gifts, the needs of others whose voices they have become conscious of, and steps that might be taken to deepen a response to the calling (either within a present organization or later in another organization). The emphasis in using the meditation is not to "answer" the questions but rather to allow the questions to flow over one's consciousness in order to become increasingly aware of responses in mind and heart.

The *Examen* is a meditation formulated by the Spanish Mystic Ignatius of Loyola.[8] In the form used in the seminar, it is a mental review at the end of the leadership day, hour by hour, to become aware of blessings/light found in the day expressing gratitude to confront difficulties/darkness that were present and then to commend all of the day to the Mercy of the Spirit that bears a thousand names. Participant reflections indicate that the practice helps to elevate consciousness regarding the day's leadership efforts.

Lectio divina[9] is the ancient monastic practice consisting of four steps: (1) reading out loud a short passage from scripture or a wisdom text, finding in the passage words or a phrase that you are particularly attracted to (*lectio*); (2) reflecting on why that passage has caught your attention, and what lessons might be suggested for your life and leadership (*meditatio*); (3) speaking as inspired to the Mystery that bears a thousand names with complete sincerity (*oratio*); (4) and then entering into silence, simply being present (*meditatio*). Participants particularly like this form of meditation, which provides a different way of connecting their active minds as knowledge workers to spiritual writing that inspires a movement into heart and silence.

Tong Len is a Buddhist practice of compassionate presence in the face of suffering, breathing in the suffering of the other(s) dropping the story line (this isn't fair, shouldn't happen, etc.), and breathing out in compassion on behalf of all sensate beings who share a similar form of suffering.[10] It is used in connection with the module that deals with forms of suffering associated with leadership.

CONTEMPLATIVE PRACTICES

The contemplative practices are:

Centering Prayer

Mantra Prayer

Zen

Walking Meditation

These contemplative practices (*apophatic* forms, i.e., meditation moving away from thought, feelings, and sensation into inner quiet) are introduced midway and become the dominant forms for the remainder of the seminar.[11] Specific instruction is given in Christian Centering Prayer, Zen, and Walking Meditation. If participants already engage another contemplative practice (e.g., Transcendental Meditation, Buddhist Mindfulness, A Vedic Form, Breath Meditation, etc.), they are encouraged to use the practice they have already appropriated. Participants' reflections affirm the frequently reported benefits of this form of practice (e.g., greater ability to listen and be present to others, greater freedom to create and focus, lessened dysfunctions of fear and anxiety, higher perceived quality of life, etc.).

THE UNFOLDING OF THE SPIRITUAL JOURNEY

The spiritual journey in the Christian tradition is often described as encompassing stages or cycles.[12] There is variation in the language, but the following descriptors are representative. (Again, space precludes dealing with parallel conceptualizations in other traditions, though excellent current efforts in this regard are available.)[13]

Conversion—Answering a Call to Spiritual Deepening and Service

Purification—Admission of Brokenness

Illumination—Glimpsing the Presence of the Transcendent in Day-to-Day Life

Unification—Living Continually in the Presence of the Transcendent

However, thinking of these experiences as stages can be misleading so I prefer the term cycle or rhythm. New awareness associated with a particular stage is often not permanent; nor are the cycles perfectly sequential. For example, even the advanced spiritual traveler cannot remain always with the consolation of sensing the presence of Transcendence. Nonetheless, it is helpful as we conclude our discussion of the experiences of seminar participants to group some quotations around these rhythms within the spiritual journey.

Conversion

Many of the quotations already cited are suggestive of conversion, an initial opening to the "Inner Voice" beckoning participants to live in new awareness. Now we turn our attention to participant reflections representative of later cycles.

Purification

Progress in the spiritual journey requires one to be in touch with personal brokenness. We need to acknowledge the messes that entangle our lives. In the Christian tradition, a sense of this "brokenness" and its attendant suffering is often the prelude to a deeper turning toward God. Otherwise, we remain in the delusion that we can resolve our quest for happiness through our own efforts, focused on the needs of the false self.[14]

As we become aware of the suffering in our life, there is a temptation to embrace a false resolution: blaming the problems on the organization and on others. For the most part, participants in the seminar come to confront the darkness in self without seeing themselves as victims of others or as victims of the organization.

The following quotations provide examples:

I feel a sense of guilt for my own insensitivity. It has been a rare thing for me to think of others. My drive toward success has dominated my life. I learned the valuable lesson from my meditation that I could not go on in this manner. I need people in my life, but as a consequence of my self-centeredness I am alone at work. I am in horrible, self-imposed, isolated space, and *I need to change my ways.*

I must confess that my work ethics have been warped during the Internet boom. Prior to the boom, I had a very pure view of my engineering career. *After my meditation I prayed to God for guidance to regain the passion and the purity I once possessed for my engineering work because I want to be performing my work in a way that glorifies Him.*

In my meditation and reflection I felt that I was decaying in my work. I could not see beyond all the immature actions and selfish petty ambitions. As I zoom into the darkest spot within my company, I realize that it is myself that is eating up the light. I have been bitter for the last weeks. . . . The source of darkness that was me is starting to show a glimmer of light. I realized how awful my attitude was, and how much it harmed me and all the people around me. The idea that we should be spiritual at work starts to ring in my mind. *I no longer want to contribute to darkness, but want to be a source of light at work the way I was earlier in my employment.*

In many occasions I have given into anger and loss of control. I realize I have to spend time reflecting on the root cause of my behavior. I need to come to understand the pressures of my work life. *I am coming to the realization that "helping others" rather than devoting my career to just satisfying my own self-interests will be an upheaval in my life.* My preoccupations with presenting myself as a shrewd business player who understands the financial aspects of a business has [*sic*] made me disregard the true intent of this organization.

In another of my meditations on Light and Darkness at work I saw the difference between working out of ego and working out of freedom. I realized that I bring darkness to my organization when I work from ego. *I need to change and bring light to my organization and everyone I come in contact with. I now realize that this is possible when I work from freedom.*

I see work as so busy and boring. My work seems almost the same everyday, yet I know there are many challenges I should open up to. Even though I am doing well and my superiors are satisfied with my work, I don't experience any joy in my career. . . . But now I am beginning to understand I can approach all of this as a relational challenge. *Work can be a place where we can meet friends, communicate, learn and teach.* I myself may be a source of some darkness. I have been complaining with my friends in the company. So my emotion influences others, or may discourage them.

Holding back, procrastinating, daydreaming, avoiding involvement—these are ways I protect myself from the pain of failure. *But of course I am also cutting myself off from the joy of putting my heart into my work.*

These quotations parallel the classic stage of purification. The purpose of the italicized type (added for emphasis) is to make clear that purification does not stop with simply recording, complaining about, or giving into organizational darkness. Rather, the movement has led participants to undertake to change their leadership behavior.

ILLUMINATION

Another cycle in the spiritual journey is characterized by "illumination." In the Christian tradition this cycle is reflected in two movements of The Spirit:[15]

- the ability to see God at work in creation
- movement away from focus on self toward a focus on serving others

The journals show seminar participants experiencing this cycle within the spiritual journey as well:

I was seeing the main office in San Francisco from a bird's eye view, at first focused on the immediate organizational setting like we did in class. But then I started seeing the hundreds, thousands of connections to all the people, other organizations, government offices, planning departments, everywhere influenced by everything our work touches. Not only in the present, but I saw these connections in the past as well. I was almost overwhelmed with the magnitude of our mission, the impacts that we have that I have not been conscious of. Now I have a sense that my work touches hundreds, maybe thousands of people every day. This is a wonderful and empowering feeling. I realized I need this image, this awareness of the bigness of my work, to sustain me through the day to day of what I do.

Clearing my mind before work has been an absolutely enlightening experience. I enter each work-day [*sic*] when I complete the

Light and Darkness meditation with a new sense of purpose. I have changed my outlook on my job. In my heart I am no longer simply a Program Manager, but rather I am an enabler of collaboration and communication. I help others see their place on teams and how valuable they are to the company and how their job helps society as a whole. I have stopped bringing my laptop to meetings and I have tried to attend more meetings in person to let others know I am entirely there. I feel as though people are appreciating the fact that I am giving them the attention they would like. I have also noticed myself listening to people completely rather than formulating my answer or opinions before they have completed what they have said.

With new understanding that work can be spiritual, happiness has settled in my inner self. I could not but reflect that my life is exactly as I need it to be to begin the new "me." One of our clients recently sent us a letter praising our work. In the past I wouldn't have thought about the letter. Now, everyday [sic] I think about that letter when I come into work. My meditation has given me a purpose, a mission possibly. I am exactly where I should be.

I always thought we just made "electronic widgets." Nothing spiritual about that! Now my meditations help me to see that our product is important to medicine, education—practically every important societal sector. I realize that I need to see that we are engaged in a very important service that helps many people.

I now complete my work without complaint, and in a positive manner. I help my work team to become more of a big family. Life is not always filled with champagne and flowers, but I foresee a future at work with greater warmth.

Finally, a litmus test of spiritual growth is growth in humility, which must underpin progress. One sign of humility is that the less glamorous aspects of one's work can be embraced as being equally meaningful as more notable actions. As expressed in the Christian tradition, Mother Teresa of Calcutta speaks of "small actions done with great love." This is likewise an aspect of St. Therese of Lisieux's "little way."[16] So in closing I offer the following ode to humility written by a participant:

With regard to hubris, I find myself trying to contain and dissolve occasions of feeling irritated at little things. I did a direct mail campaign and I have chosen to enter my own data in the database. Humbling I can tell you. I'm learning "garbage in garbage out" and what that statement really means. Before I thought I understood it, but now I realize that I didn't have a clue. I'm put to test about this. I find I want to do it right. I also say a silent prayer asking forgiveness for the times in the past, on other jobs, when I was in charge and expressed irritation to the data entry person while asking "why can't I have this by the end of the day?" Now, with having to put my own "regal" fingers to the keyboard I know why!

INTEGRATING PRACTICES INTO THE LEADERSHIP DAY

The discussion has focused how participants have been exposed to a variety of meditation and contemplative practice forms, and reported changes in consciousness and behavior over the course of the seminar.[17] The chapter will close by sharing how a variety forms become integrated into the leadership day of an average participant following the seminar. Of course there are differences across individuals, and some drift away from any practice. However, many do incorporate continuing practice and a typical description would be as follows.

Following the seminar most participants begin their leadership day with an *apophatic* form of contemplative practice consistent with their (non)religious tradition. Whatever the form (e.g. Breath, Mantra, Zen, Christian Centering Prayer, Hesychia, Kabbala, etc.) participants indicate that since the seminar a morning contemplative practice shapes the rest of the day. These intellectually gifted and action-oriented leaders know that without such a practice, the ego easily leads them into patterns of hubris and hyperactivity. So they see an anchoring contemplative practice as critical.

When arriving at the workplace, before entering, they quickly return their consciousness to the overarching purpose of their organization, the light that is encompassed by their important social institution, and the darkness that must be wrestled with. They recommit to leadership as a form of vocational service within their organization.

Throughout the day before each subsequent critical task, they pause to recenter in order to be fully present to the "now" of the next task and to the next individual or group with whom they will be collaborating. Without this practice, the intense experiences of one task overrides attention on the next task. Since leadership is a constant movement across complex shared problem solving, they find this practice essential.

As the day draws to a close, in their office or as they get into their car to leave work, they replay the day in the spirit of the *Examen* in order to find closure and inner peace. Like oncologists and burn unit personnel, they have discovered that unless they book-end the day with this type of spiritual practice, the stresses of the day will flow over into their return to home, precluding their being fully present to family and the opportunity for rest. They find that some form of practice parallel to the *Examen* allows them to avoid both repression and obsession.

Finally, most participants include a bit of spiritual reading before retiring in the spirit of *Lectio*. They report that this practice helps move them into refreshing sleep.

In all of this, they are not compulsive about a particular form. Who would want to do sitting meditation after hours of business travel? So they might substitute walking meditation after being on an airplane. Who would want to do spiritual reading when one could meditate with nature during a meeting at a beautiful resort? So they make use of nature as a form of *Lectio*.

Thus participants flexibly use of a variety of meditation forms discovered in the seminar (and after the seminar). However, they are aware that unless they build forms of practice into their leadership day the pressures of contemporary organization life can rapidly lead to anxiety, ego–distortion, and decreased spiritual meaning.

CLOSING

Often meditation practice is learned in settings where the primary focus in on the "inner life" of the individual. In this chapter we shared how a variety of meditation/contemplative practice forms have been introduced in the context of workplace leadership challenges. We illustrated how resultant spiritual growth, viewed through the lens of classic stages referenced in the Christian tradition, is enhanced through a combination of practices throughout the day.

Future research might fruitfully explore the motivational power of learning practices contextually in occupational settings. It might also address the advantages of juxtaposing a variety of meditation forms, encouraging individuals to use a form that has a natural resonance with different challenges. The seminar experience reported here suggests that learning a combination of forms has been mutually reinforcing and enriching.

APPENDIX I

Daily Reflection on Light and Darkness in the Organization in Which I Work

Andre L. Delbecq
Santa Clara University
E-mail: adelbecq@scu.edu
© 4/6/03

Place yourself in the presence of "The Light" that enlightens all people.
(the Transcendent Mystery, Spirit, as you understand it)

Spend a moment meditating on the revelation of this Light in the day-to-day of your organization at work. Where do you see the manifestation of Light in your organization?

Let us remind ourselves that without this Light, our organization becomes a cold place, devoid of creative energy, mutual caring, and enduring courage, a place unable to maintain a commitment to noble purpose and service to others.

Express gratitude for the presence of this Light in your organization.

If you have lost the sense of "Light" in your organizational setting, due to darkness in the organization, or darkness in yourself, ask that your sight might be restored. Ask for the blessing to be present to this Light so that at the beginning of each day/each Monday morning, you can enter into your organizational world with a renewed sense of joyful freedom to undertake work that matters within an important contemporary institution.

Spend a moment reflecting on the wholeness of your organization through this Light. Ask for the sight to see the organization in all its dimensions and to witness the presence of Light in each dimension.

Examine the nobility of the mission of the organization in which you work and its creative potential to be a force for good in the world.

— *its centrality in providing an important product or service that truly serves society*

— *its power over resources: financial, time, energy, decision agendas, human talents*

— *its locus as a place that should call on your fullest expression of individual creativity*

— *its influence on the presence (or absence) of community that nourishes your spirit and that of others*

Spend a moment examining the presence of Darkness in yourself and in your organization.

Confront Any Darkness in your organization.

Is there darkness in your organization that diminishes its potential for goodness and service to society?

Who are the "poor" and oppressed in your organizational setting (not necessarily economically only)? Whose gifts are ignored; who cannot be part of the agenda? Who is marginalized in your organizational setting?

Have you personally contributed to organizational darkness?

Have you given undue power to organizational darkness by failing to witness to Light at decisive decision moments?

Are there aspects of the overall organization that you ignore or fail to support because of lack of reflection, fear and anxiety, or preoccupation with a narrow, private agenda?

Is there darkness within yourself, such as concern with self-importance, careerism, ambition, or activity wherein you anxiously depend entirely on yourself, that casts a shadow on your contribution to the organization?

Have you been a source of darkness for others by failing to include, mentor, encourage, or respond to your organizational neighbor?

Spend a moment meditating on the call to "holiness" (Wholeness) through and within the busyness of day-to-day organizational life.

We are told by the spiritual masters we will discover everything we need to know about Light, and have all the experience we need perfect our spiritual journey exactly "where we are today" ... in the "eternal now."

Even in the case where later discernment may suggest that at a future point in time you need to change your organizational setting, it is in today's organizational experience that you must see the Light of the transcendent. Ask for greater openness to this Light.

Expression of Gratitude

Spend several moments in gratitude for all the ways that the Light of insight, truth, wisdom, joy, compassion, and courage reveals itself in the organizational setting in which you work—in the many blessings and opportunities of which you have become aware in your meditation.

Sharing and Comment on Your Meditation Experience

For group reflection, participants may wish to share insights that emerged in their meditation. Members should listen with a spirit of "appreciative inquiry"—openness to the truth within another's experience.

ACKNOWLEDGMENTS

I am grateful to Michael Naughton, Director, the John A. Ryan Center for Catholic Thought, University of St. Thomas, St. Paul, Minnesota, for accepting a first discussion paper on this topic and for allowing me to incorporate here material from this prior essay. Delbecq, A. L. (2003). *Crossing the frontier to vocational awareness.* Fifth International Symposium on Catholic Social Thought and Management Education, Universidad de Deusto, Bilboa, Spain (later included in e-book proceedings, Michael J. Naughton and Stephanie Rumpza, *Business as a Calling: Interdisciplinary Essays on the Meaning of Business from the Catholic Social Tradition,* http://www.stthomas.edu/cathstudies/cst/publications/businessasacalling.html).

NOTES

1. Delbecq, A. L. (1994). Innovation as a Silicon Valley obsession. *Journal of Management Inquiry, 3*(2), 266–275; Delbecq, A. L., & Weiss, J. (2000).

The business culture of Silicon Valley: A turn-of-the-century reflection. *Journal of Management Inquiry, 9*(1), 34–44.

2. Delbecq, A. L., & Friedlander, F. (1995). Strategies for personal and family renewal. *Journal of Management Inquiry, 4*(3), 262–269.

3. Delbecq, A. L. (2000). Spirituality for business leadership: Reporting on a pilot course for MBAs and CEOs. *Journal of Management Inquiry, 9*(2), 117–128.

4. Mitroff, I., & Denton, E. A. (1990). *A spiritual audit of corporate America: Multiple designs for fostering spirituality in the workplace.* San Francisco: Jossey-Bass (Chapters 1 and 2); Delbecq, A. L. (2009). Spirituality and business: One scholar's perspective. *Journal of Management, Spirituality, and Business, 6*(1), 3–13.

5. Weiss, J. W., Skelley, M. F., Haughey, J. C., & Hall, D. T. (2004). Calling, new careers and spirituality: A reflective perspective for organizational leaders and professionals. In M. Pava (Ed.), *Spiritual intelligence at work: Meaning, metaphor and morals: Research in ethical issues* (Vol. 5, pp. 171–201). New York: Elsevier; McGee, J. J., & Delbecq, A. L. (2003). Vocation as a critical factor in a spirituality of executive leadership in business. In O. F. Williams (Ed.), *Business, religion and spirituality* (pp. 94–113). Notre Dame, IN: University of Notre Dame Press.

6. Delbecq, A. L. (2000). Spirituality for business leadership: Reporting on a pilot course for MBAs and CEOs. *Journal of Management Inquiry, 9*(2), 117–128.

7. Aschenbrenner, G. (1972). Consciousness examen. *Review for Religious, 33*, 14–21; Gallagher, T. M. (2006). *The examen prayer: Ignatian wisdom for our lives today.* New York: Crossroad.

8. Loyola, I. (1970). *The Constitutions of the Society of Jesus.* (G.E. Ganss, Trans.). St. Louis, MO: Institute of Jesuit Sources. (Original work published in 1556).

9. Pennington, B. M. (1998). *Lectio divina: Renewing the ancient practice of praying the Scriptures.* New York: Crossroad.

10. Chodron, P. (2001). *The places that scare you: A guide to fearlessness in difficult times.* Boston: Shambhala.

11. Fontana, D. (1999). *The meditator's handbook: A comprehensive guide to Eastern and Western meditation techniques.* Boston: Element.

12. Ware, K. (2002). *The orthodox way.* Crestwood: NY: St. Valdimir's Press, 105–133.

13. Fry, L. W. J., & Kreiger, M. P. (in press). Toward a theory of being-centered leadership: Multiple levels of being as a context for effective leadership. *Human Relations.*

14. Keating, T. (2002). *Open mind, open heart.* New York: Continuum, 127–132; Haughey, J. (2002). *Housing heaven's fire: The challenge of holiness.* Chicago: Loyola Press, 11.

15. Keating, *Open Mind*, 127–132; Ware, *The Orthodox Way*, 105–133.

16. Teresa, M. (1998). *Everything starts with love*. Ashland, OR: White Cloud Press; Gorres, I. F. (1959). *The hidden face: A study of St. Therese of Lisieux*. San Francisco: Ignatius Press.

17. Delbecq, A. L. (2006a). Business executives and prayer: How a core spiritual discipline is expressed in the life of contemporary organizational leaders. *Spirit in Work, 6*, 3–8, and 7, 3–7.

REFERENCES

Aschenbrenner, George. (1972). Consciousness examen. *Review for Religious, 33*, 14–21.

Chodron, Pema. (2001). *The places that scare you: A guide to fearlessness in difficult times*. Boston: Shambhala, 55–60.

Delbecq, Andre L. (1994). Innovation as a Silicon Valley obsession. *Journal of Management Inquiry, 3*(3), 266–275.

Delbecq, Andre L. (2000). Spirituality for business leadership: Reporting on a pilot course for MBAs and CEOs. *Journal of Management Inquiry, 9*(2), 117–128 (provides a description of the overall seminar).

Delbecq, Andre L. (2006a). Business executives and prayer: How a core spiritual discipline is expressed in the life of contemporary organizational leaders. *Spirit in Work, 6*, 3–8, and 7, 3–7 (provides a more detailed description of the daily integration of spiritual practices).

Delbecq, Andre L. (2006b). The spiritual challenge of power: Humility and love as offsets to leadership hubris. *Journal of Management, Spirituality and Religion, 3*(1), 141–154.

Delbecq, Andre L. (2009). Spirituality and business: One scholar's perspective. *Journal of Management, Spirituality and Religion, 6*(1), 3–13.

Delbecq, Andre L., & Friedlander, Frank. (1995). Strategies for personal and family renewal. *Journal of Management Inquiry, 4*(3), 262–269.

Delbecq, Andre L., & Weiss, Joseph. (2000). The business culture of Silicon Valley: A turn-of-the-century reflection. *Journal of Management Inquiry, 9*(1), 34–44.

Fontana, David. (1999). *The meditator's handbook: A comprehensive guide to Eastern and Western meditation techniques*. Boston: Element.

Fry, Louis W., & Kreiger, Mark P. (in press). Toward a theory of being-centered leadership: Multiple levels of being as a context for effective leadership. *Human Relations*.

Gallagher, Timothy M. (2006). *The examen prayer: Ignatian wisdom for our lives today*. New York: Crossroad.

Haughey, John. (2002). *Housing heaven's fire: The challenge of holiness*. Chicago: Loyola Press, 11.

Keating, Thomas. (2002). *Open mind, open heart*. New York: Continuum, 127–132

McGee, James J., & Delbecq, Andre L. (2003). Vocation as a critical factor in a spirituality of executive leadership in business. In O. F. Williams (Ed.), *Business, religion and spirituality* (pp. 94–113). Notre Dame: IN: University of Notre Dame Press.

Mitroff, Ian, & Denton, Elizabeth A. (1990). *A spiritual audit of corporate America: Multiple designs for fostering spirituality in the workplace.* San Francisco: Jossey Bass (Chapters 1 and 2).

Naughton, Michael, & Rumpza, Stephanie Rumpza (Eds.). (2005). *Business as a calling: Interdisciplinary essays on the meaning of business from the Catholic social tradition.* St. Paul, MN: Center for Catholic Studies, St. Thomas University.

Pennington, M. Basil. (1998). *Lectio Divina: Renewing the ancient practice of praying the scriptures.* New York: Crossroad.

Ware, Kallistos. (2002). *The orthodox way.* Crestwood, NY: St. Vladimir's Press, 105–133.

Weiss, Joseph W., Skelley, Michael F., Haughey, John C. Haughey, & Hall, Douglas. (2004). Calling, new careers and spirituality: A reflective perspective for organizational leaders and professionals. In Moses Pava (Ed.), *Spiritual intelligence at work: Meaning, metaphor and morals: Research in ethical issues in organizations* (Vol. 5, pp. 171–201). New York: Elsevier.

CHAPTER 12

"Shaking the Blues Away": Energizing Spiritual Practices for the Treatment of Chronic Pain

Amy B. Wachholtz and Michelle J. Pearce

If you would lose your weary blues Shake 'em away
> —Original words and music by Irving Berlin, 1927;
> revised edition: revived by Ann Miller in *Easter Parade*, 1948

While there is a great deal of research supporting the use of meditation and quieting spiritual practices for the treatment of chronic pain, there has been less mention of those practices that energize and focus the spirit in the effort to decrease pain. In this chapter, we will explore the use of energizing spiritual practices to reduce the experience of chronic pain. This will include a review of multiple religious cultures, including Native American and Pentecostal Christian, which will provide a unique insight into this relatively unexplored area of pain management. We will also briefly discuss how physical activation may positively affect the physiological pain pathways and the perception of pain. Finally, we will discuss how other individuals may begin to integrate these practices into their own pain management techniques.

An unknown author once wrote, "Pain is inevitable; suffering is optional." This inspirational quote suggests that we are able to both influence and transcend our experience of pain. Pain is not a one-to-one relationship between the tissue damage and the pain sensation. Instead, we are active interpreters of our pain sensations. We make these interpretations through the filter of our belief systems, and resulting emotions and behavior. Chronic pain is more than simple tissue damage.

Instead it is a multidimensional experience. Biological, psychological, social, and spiritual factors each affect the individual's interpretation of the pain experience. Chronic pain is a complex disorder that often defies traditional treatments. The ongoing experience of chronic pain can span years of an individual's lifetime and severely impede the quality of life for that individual. While certain pharmacological options can be very effective in treating pain, most often have secondary side effects that patients would rather avoid. Given the intractable nature of chronic pain, patients may choose to take treatment into their own hands by seeking out alternative pain control methods, which may include integrating spiritual beliefs and practices into their pain management regimen. There is a wide range of individual experiences related to chronic pain and the potential harmful interaction between pain and suffering. These complex interactions, the need to better manage negative pain experiences, and the desire to improve treatment for chronically ill populations, makes chronic pain a critical area for further study.

Pain is often best described within the framework of the bio-psycho-social model of disease. This model seeks to understand the impact of chronic pain holistically on individuals via the biological, psychological, and social aspects of their lives. Rather than just focusing on disease, this model advocates treating pain by recognizing complex multifaceted interactions that comprise individuals' experience. These may include interactions with their environment, social interactions among other individuals, biological interactions with nonspecific disease factors, and bidirectional pathways that occur among each aspect of the bio-psycho-social parts that make up individual experience. Specific to the treatment of pain, the bio-psycho-social model may also account for the experience of pain without an identifiable patho-physiological etiology.

Specifically, in the context of the bio-psycho-social model, the gate control/neuromatrix theory of pain identifies a construct that explains how spiritual beliefs and practices influence the pain experience and may contribute to improved pain management by describing the impact of psychological (descending pathways) and moderate biological (ascending pathways) pain factors.[1] It has become widely accepted that the experience of pain is not a simple equation of: X tissue damage = X level of pain. The biochemical transmission of pain cannot fully explain the pain experience for the patient. Instead, these theories identify multiple descending pathways that integrate cognitions, emotions, and behavior, which, in turn, influence the perception and interpretation of pain by modulating (up or down) the individual experience of pain, all of which occurs in real time. The psychological and biological states interact to create the experience of pain. This theory facilitated the discovery of the relationships among psychosocial factors, such as negative emotions, social support, sense of self-efficacy, coping strategies, and reports of pain.[2]

Both of the models described above (gate control/neuromatrix models and the bio-psycho-social model) elucidate the role of the individual as an active interpreter of the pain experience and the immediate and direct impact that psychological states play in mediating the experience of pain. They also provide a framework as to how psychosocial variables may be used to treat chronic-pain conditions. In addition, the bio-psycho-social-spiritual model expands on the original bio-psycho-social model by integrating spiritual and religious variables, and identifying the role that these variables may play in modulating the pain experience. The bio-psycho-social-spiritual model recognizes the disruptive impact that pain can have on biological status, psychological health, interpersonal interactions, and spiritual well-being unique to the individual. Since spirituality is an additional coping resource that may affect some patients' pain experience, integrating spirituality into the gate/neuromatrix model is a natural extension of this model. However, the valence of the spiritual practice may impact the direction of the relationship between spirituality and pain sensitivity/tolerance. In a positive relationship, spirituality may reduce the pain experience because individuals feel support from a higher power (e.g., "God is with me in my struggles"), they may have cognitions that reduce stress (e.g., "God would not give me more than I can handle"), or they may use religious/spiritual practices to distract them from pain or create reduced physiological reactivity to pain (e.g., spiritual meditation), and/or provide social interaction (e.g., attendance at worship services). Negatively, spirituality may increase the pain experience by increasing stress among those who view the experience as a punishment from God/Higher Power, or feel abandoned by God in a time of need.

HISTORICAL AND RELIGIOUS CONTEXT

Multiple cultures throughout history and around the world have used music and dance as integral components of health and healing ceremonies. In this section we will explore only a few examples from around the world, although we would encourage those who are interested in pursuing further information to consider the anthropological literature, which provides rich descriptive detail of how cultures use energetic music and dance rhythms as a source of healing traditions. In the context of this chapter, we define *religion* and *spirituality* as aspects of "ideas, beliefs, groups, or institutions associated with a higher power" (p. 311).[2] We define *dance* as intentional, purposeful, rhythmic movements, outside of typical motor movement, that are designed to express a thought, an emotion, or an experience. Dance may be supplemented by music or drums, but can also stand alone with no other accompaniment.

NATIVE AMERICAN—LAKOTA

Arguably the most famous Native American example of spiritual dance and pain is the Sun Dance. While many of the Native American cultures based in the Great Plains region celebrated variations of the Sun Dance, in this section we will be focusing on the Lakota Sun Dance tradition. Traditionally, the Lakota tribe engaged in the Sun Dance ceremony in conjunction with the annual community-wide buffalo hunt. The annual celebration culminated in the Sun Dance in which the honored dancer(s) was pierced with a stick through small slits in their back or chest. The stick was woven through the slits and a rope tied to each end of the stick. The rope was then attached to a sacred tree. The dancer would proceed to dance around the tree for multiple days. During this time he (although dancers could be male or female, they were generally male) would forsake food and water. The dancer would continue to dance until the skin tore, thereby releasing him from the tree. This ceremony not only caused identifiable tissue damage, but to the outside observer it would also be considered unnecessarily, and perhaps gruesomely, painful. However, to the Lakotan dancers, the pain was welcomed, and many times the dancers reported experiencing no pain at all. They understood that the pain was sacred and necessary to help the dancer reach a holy world, as they believed the dance continued the process of rebirth or regeneration, subsequently ensuring the prosperity of the community.[3] The preceding preparatory celebrations, the context of the pain experience, and the postcommunity celebrations of the dancers, provided an energizing spiritual environment that left little room for the experience of pain.

Pentecostal/Charismatic Christianity

Pentecostalism, often grouped with Charismatic Christianity (Pentecostal/Charismatic or P/C), is the second-largest and fastest-growing Christian group in the world, behind Catholicism. According to the World Christian Database, in 2006 there were 580 million Pentecostals and Charismatics in the world, with much of the growth occurring in the global south. Many point to the 1906 Azusa Street revival in Los Angeles as the start of Pentecostalism. Services at Azusa Street did not resemble the typical Christian religious service: worshipers shouted, danced, fell into trances, wept, spoke in tongues, and gave interpretations of these tongues into English. Ecstatic and paranormal religious experiences were the norm.

Pentecostalism has been described as an experiential religion, one that involves the entire body. It emphasizes feelings and demonstrations of God's power over thought and contemplation, and encourages the loss or yielding of self to God, which is manifested or represented in various somatic forms. It has also been argued that these ecstatic experiences are an important part of evangelic activities that continue to promote church growth.[4] These religious experiences or gifts of the Spirit are believed to be given by God to equip his people for service. Pentecostal ecstatic somatic experiences include glossolalia (speaking in tongues), prophecy, being slain in the Spirit, miracles, deliverance, and divine healing. Although the purpose of these experiences is not the reduction of pain, as we will discuss later in this chapter, individuals often report experiencing no pain when they encounter noxious stimuli in this ecstatic state.

Muslim (Sufi)

Within Islam, dance is a very important spiritual practice—particularly within a branch of Islamic practice called the Sufism. The Sufi movement began shortly after Muhammad's death and focused on the mystical practices and ideas of Islam. Although Sufi was initially a term indicating any mystical practice, it soon became associated with the eschewing of the external world to create growth in the spiritual world.

One specific aspect of these practices is what has become known as the Sema or the "whirling dervish" dance. A Dervish describes an individual who belongs to a sect of Islam called Tariqah, which is known for its extreme ascetic practices. A Dervish is similar to mendicant priests/friars and hermits in Christianity and to sadhus in the Hindu and Buddhist traditions.

Within the Dervish sect exists the Mevlevi order. This is a group of Sufi priests who perform the moving meditation—the whirling dervish dance. The whirling dervish dance originated in Turkey stemming from the songs and teachings of Lord Rumi (1207–1273). Within this form of dance, there are multiple layers of symbolism that represent the rotation of the planets around the sun and the passage of blood flowing from the heart. Even the clothing symbolizes the movement toward spiritual enlightenment and receiving the gifts of God; the dancer's hat is the gravestone of the self or ego, the flowing white skirt symbolizes the shroud of the self, and the black cloak (which is removed prior to dancing) represents the casting off of mourning and the spiritual rebirth of the dancer. Dervish dancers feel that the process of dancing helps them to shed external needs, such as hunger and pain, and become closer to God. The dancers generally move to the music of a reed flute. Fittingly, the flute is a symbol of human pain, indicated by the holes in the flute. However, despite (or because of) the holes in the flute symbolizing pain, the flute makes beautiful music. For the Mevlevi order this provides a powerful metaphor for how pain can be transmuted into something beautiful and a means of growing closer to God.[5]

MIZO—INDIA

Mizo culture refers to a group of people primarily geographically located in northeastern India. In the Mizoram language, the term Mizo means "people of the hill." Their culture is originally based in Mongolian groups who moved into the area in the seventh century. While the Mizo people were originally Buddhist, Christian missions during the eighteenth and nineteenth centuries led to mass conversions, with approximately 87 percent of contemporary Mizos identifying themselves as Christian. Initially, Mizo cultural forms of dancing were banned and related to pagan or animist practices. However, recently the Mizo Christian community has reintegrated the cultural dance practices into their worship services. The contemporary Mizo Christianity is a blended form of worship that includes traditional cultural practices.

According to Dr. Lalrinawmi Ralte, a Mizo Christian apologist and an expert on feminist hermeneutics, Mizo dance is an empowering and leveling experience; especially in the context of a revival ceremony, dance plays a central role.[6] Sacred dance in Mizo culture disregards gender, social status, and age. Everyone in the religious community is involved in the dance, and the dance expresses the community's spirituality. Dance theology in the Mizo culture includes dance as a healing expression within the community. It allows the community to respect the body as a sacred dimension of the individual. It is used as a way to heal or cope with both emotional and physical pain. For example, women dance to celebrate the joy of birth even in the midst of labor pain. Dance is also used as an expression of hope in God to ease the pain of a medical condition. Dance is used in the Mizo Christian community to strengthen the body and the spirit to overcome injury at both the individual and community level to create a healthier, more holistic spiritual healing experience.

CURRENT ENERGIZING SPIRITUAL PRACTICES

CHARISMATIC WORSHIP AND HEALING

The Pentecostal service begins with a lengthy time of singing and music that often follows two stages. During the first stage, called "Praise," the songs are fast-paced, energetic, and function to stir up the congregation. During the second stage, called "Worship," the songs are slow-paced, soft, and function to turn one's attention to God and enter into a state of devotion and openness to "the moving of the Spirit." Some have stated that the goal is to become filled or possessed by the Holy Spirit, which is evidenced by the way they dance, sing, and speak in tongues. It is not uncommon for worshipers to enter an altered state of consciousness during worship, or to fall backward, which is called "being slain in the Spirit," when prayed for by elders of the church. In some Charismatic churches, such as the Toronto Airport Christian Fellowship (TACF), known for the "Toronto Blessing," individuals report experiencing unusual physical phenomena, such as animal-sounding noises, ecstatic states and trances, violent shaking and shuddering, and altered states of consciousness, as well as significant, transformative inner experiences resulting from feeling the intimate love of God.[7]

Pentecostalism has been described as providing a message of hope for those who are ill or in emotional or physical pain. The somatic manifestations are understood as signs that God is healing—spiritually, emotionally, socially, and physically. Emphasis is placed on receiving spiritual healing, which is secondary to emotional and physical healing. Emotional pain and fears are believed to manifest somatically, and thus "inner healing" is believed to often have a beneficial effect on physical health. A study by Poloma and Hoelter[8] among 918 individuals who had visited the TACF revealed that measures of spiritual healing were significantly related to the measures of inner, mental, and physical healing. Interestingly, a significant minority of Americans (10–30%) claim to have experienced a miraculous healing and many of these individuals are part of the Pentecostal/Charismatic tradition of Christianity.[8] Polema[7] has suggested that the time of worship and prayer at TACF releases a natural power (called *chi*, *kundalini*, or *prana* in other cultures), as well as a range of human emotions that influence and promote mental and physical health.

Despite the possible effectiveness of decreasing pain through energetic spiritual practices, it must also be noted that some dangers are also present. A small number of individuals have sued their churches or pastors for "slain in the spirit" injuries, claiming that the worshipper was "slain" and fell with no one to catch them. This has resulted in several individuals falling to the floor, or off of podiums/alters, causing or exacerbating injuries. There is disagreement within various religious circles as to the validity of the spiritual experience if an individual is hurt, stating that if the individual was truly slain in the spirit, they would not have been injured. Regardless of these discussions, it is important to know that during states of hyperarousal and altered consciousness, it may be possible for individuals to injure themselves or exacerbate an existing injury, but not feel this pain until after they have returned to their usual state of consciousness.

SPIRITUAL EDGEWORK: EXTREME RITUAL PERFORMANCES

Many have argued that religion is a socially constructed way for individuals to gain a sense of power and control, including power over pain. Bromley[9] argues that when practitioners engage in a ritual practice that risks physical and emotional injury or death, they experience a sense of empowerment and control because of their believed connection to a source of divine power. Bromley calls these types of rituals "spiritual edgework." Three examples of spiritual edgework rituals that put the practitioner at risk of injury, pain, and death are fire walking, fire handling, and serpent handling.

Fire-handling has a long history dating back to 1200 BCE. In modern times, fire walking has been practiced across the globe: by Native North Americans, shamans of north Asia, mediums among the Bataks of Sumatra, and Haitians in their Voodoo or Santeria ceremonies, to name just a few.[10] Fire walking, as an organized and marketed practice in the United States, began in 1978 by Tolly Burkan, and has increased in popularity in America through the New Age movement. It is used as a means for individuals, generally urban professionals, to overcome fear and experience a sense of empowerment, control, and self-actualization. The working metaphor of fire walking is that if you are able to walk on fire, then you are able to face and overcome any limitation or problem you are experiencing in your life. As such, fire is transformed from being a source of danger and harm to that of a healing force producing wholeness.

Practitioners are instructed to maintain a specific physical state by breathing deeply, walking normally, and clenching their right hand to represent a feeling of power. Tony Robbins, a fire workshop leader, asserts that one must program one's self with positive, overcoming commands and be in a "totally focused state" before stepping on the coals, otherwise one will be burned. The fire walk usually takes only a few seconds and covers 8 to 14 feet of coals. People usually report experiencing no pain and often report feeling ecstatic when they finish.

Recent scientific explorations of fire walking, as well as fun experiments such as those carried out on the *Mythbusters* TV show on the Discovery Channel, have identified the physics and power of belief related to walking across 1,000°F coals. As displayed by *Mythbusters*, after a preparatory class on the physics and a strong trust in the physics behind fire walking, walkers may gain the confidence to walk slowly and evenly so that the pressure on the foot is balanced. If they have the necessary conviction, the walker will not stomp the feet, increase downward pressure on the foot by running, or have a psychosomatic reaction that makes the feet perspire since these actions would enhance heat conductivity and allow the person to be burned. However, individuals who are not given this preparation and confidence, through either spiritual means or physics education, are likely to walk over the coals improperly, frequently resulting in burns. While the physics may prevent the individual from being burned while walking over hot coals, it is the belief that you cannot be burned that allows for the proper technique, and courage, needed for the applied physics to protect the walker.

A small minority of Pentecostal Holiness churches in the South currently practice a ritual called fire handling in the context of their services. Services are usually several hours in length and involve energetic dancing, singing, shouting, speaking in tongues, and prophesying. In a heightened collective emotional state and vigorous motor activity, members light torches and touch the flame to parts of their body and clothing for up to 10–15 seconds.[10] Fire handlers believe that they are able to touch the flames without being burned because of their faith in God and because of the power of God, called the "anointing of God," that comes upon the individual, making them immune to the fire. Worshipers assert that they can apply the fire only to the parts of their body that the Spirit directs them to and only for as long as the Spirit is upon them, otherwise they will be burned. Participants describe the anointed state as feeling numb, feeling cold, experiencing a good cold shower, and having hands like a block of ice. It is likely that participants are in an altered state of consciousness when they are "under the anointing."[10]

Serpent handling commenced in the United States around 1915 in the Church of God, a denomination in the Holiness movement, in the hills of eastern Tennessee. It was primarily practiced by rural Christians of lower socioeconomic status. This practice was popular in the 1920s, but was infrequently practiced by the 1930s. There are a few independent Holiness churches that still practice this ritual. The ritual is also seen as evidence that because of their faith in Jesus Christ, they too will be victorious over death and have eternal life. As with the other types of spiritual edgework, serpent handling promotes a sense of empowerment and control among practitioners.[9]

Much like fire handling, serpent handling occurs in the context of intense singing, shouting, dancing, loud music, prayer, and preaching. Serpent handlers have explained their ability to handle poisonous snakes without injury or death by being protected by an anointing from God to carry out his commands. They believe that the Holy Spirit takes control of them, and report feeling sensations such as, energy, joy, peace, physical numbness, tingling in the hands, and electricity. Handlers speak of the importance of waiting until they feel God's anointing before picking up a snake, and of putting the snake down as soon as they feel the anointing lifting. To do otherwise, they state, is foolish and will result in injury. Injuries are regarded as caused by fear, improper preparation, and ego. It is not uncommon for a handler to be bitten; however, there have been only a small number of injuries and deaths as a result of this practice over the years. Engaging in this practice has been described by practitioners as evidence of their obedience to God, of his favor and blessing, and the truth of the Bible.

CONTEMPORARY ROCK MUSIC

Not all individuals who experience spiritual elevation to escape the impact of pain on the body are members of a group or even use these practices as part of a faith tradition. Arthur Coleman, a psychiatrist, struggled for seven years with chronic back pain. He described how he tried multiple forms of physical treatment, physical therapy, medications, chiropractic manipulation, and massage. Yet despite all of these treatments, his battle with chronic back pain continued. Finally, after an eye-opening experience with his son that emphasized how opioid analgesics were damaging his cognitive and social abilities, he began searching for alternative medicine practices. He began to use "strong rock music" and drumming as a way to override his pain experience.[11] It created a feeling of elation that would disintegrate the back pain and allow him to not only escape the pain temporarily while engaging in his "rock music therapy," but to also provide him with relief after he walked away from the drum set. Only by using the intense practices of rock music and drumming was he able to provide the cognitive distraction, and physiological relaxation that helped him continue to cope with his pain.[11]

PATHWAYS LINKING ENERGIZING SPIRITUAL PRACTICES AND PAIN

Across a number of cultures, music has been used to induce strong emotions, dissociative states, trances, and altered states of consciousness.[12] Uplifting, energizing spiritual music may have a positive impact on the mind, body, and emotions. As we know from the neuromatrix theory of pain, positive changes in any of these domains may effectively decrease a person's experience of pain.

SEROTONIN PATHWAYS

Physiologically, religion and/or spirituality may potentially impact the pain experience through multiple pathways. However, much of the research on pathways has focused on decreasing arousal and quieting the spirit. Specifically, research has identified that serotonin receptor density is correlated to spiritual activities. Since serotonin is related to both mood and pain regulation, if spiritual practices affect serotonin release/uptake, these practices may have a causal relationship to changes in both mood and pain.[13] Negative spiritual thoughts (e.g., "God is abandoning me") can increase pain sensitivity, and negative spiritual practices can increase pain sensitivity, decrease pain tolerance, and create a depressed mood. Since spirituality is an active coping mechanism for both neuroscientific and a psychological models of pain, a greater understanding of how and why individuals use their spirituality to cope with pain could be a critical ingredient in improved treatments for individuals suffering from chronic pain. While the empirical literature validating the use of intense spiritual activity for pain relief is rare to nonexistent, there are a number of biological pathways that support the theory that this form of pain relief not only is possible but can be very effective.

ENDOGENOUS OPIOID PATHWAYS

There is a high density of endogenous opioid receptors in brain areas related to auditory, kinetic, and visual perception. The neuroendocrine opioid system is linked to areas of the CNS that are involved in the transmission, processing, and integration of pain, auditory, and kinetic perception, as well as to areas involved in affective states. The physiological "fight or flight" responses to danger or excitement are converted into endorphins. Endorphins are biochemically very similar to morphine; thus in these situations, the human body essentially releases endogenous morphine. Like morphine, endorphins result in diminished pain and a sense of euphoria. This is similar to the "runner's high," described by distance runners or frequent exercisers. Prince[14] asserts that the vigorous motor activities in dance and the fine tremors that almost always accompany nonhypnotic trance phenomena activate the release of endorphins, which generate and maintain the analgesic effect. This analgesia is then supported by the auditory and visual stimuli and rhythmic sounds that are also associated with trances and reduced pain.

When opioids bind with the mu opioid receptors, a number of neuronal changes occur, which influence pain perception, motor behavior, mood, and autonomic responses. In contrast, kappa opioid receptors are implicated in stress and dysphoria. Thus when an individual is experiencing ongoing stress, such as suffering from chronic pain, they are more likely to have elevated activation of the kappa opioid receptors. Therefore, when the release of endorphins shuts down the kappa opioid receptors and activates the mu opioid receptors, the individual would likely feel an even greater "rush" than an individual not experiencing chronic pain. These endogenous opioids exert their analgesic effect by inhibiting pain impulses at the level of the spinal cord from being transmitted to the brain, where sensory signals are registered as pain. Endogenous opioids can be activated by intense emotional states and vigorous physical activity. They can also relieve psychological pain by inducing euphoria and triggering altered states of consciousness.

HYPERAROUSAL AND ALTERED CONSCIOUSNESS

The praise and worship component of Pentecostal services and other services that have similar characteristics elicits not only a strong emotional experience, but also physiological arousal. The cognitive appraisal of the physical arousal further enhances the subjective experience of the emotion. The energizing religious service includes a number of activities that can lead to hyperarousal and altered states of consciousness—clapping, dancing, swaying, raising arms, singing, glossolalia, jumping, repetitive lyrics, and energetic music—to generate enthusiasm and leads to a greater likelihood of experiencing an altered state.[15] Indeed, research has shown that movement, noise, group setting, sensory overstimulation, repetitive lyrics, and instrumental music have all been used to induce a state of hyperarousal, which leads to altered states of consciousness. Not surprisingly then, when participants have been interviewed about their experience in services they use language related to a trancelike state, such as "feeling light, losing track of time, sensing electricity in their body, numbness, and feeling like one's body was on fire." Interviewees also stressed the importance of focus to achieve a "successful" worship experience, and often prepared themselves for the time of worship by praying or meditating before the service began. The physiological arousal and cognitive reappraisal of their experience can act as a powerful analgesic to motivated participants in these religious worship services.

Altered states of consciousness, whether due to hypnosis, meditation, trance, or religious experience, are the result of similar psychological and neurophysiological factors. Research has shown that a number of conditions may generate an altered state of consciousness: reduction or increase in external stimulation and motor activity, emotional hyper-arousal, rhythmic sensory stimulation, focused hyperalertness, relaxa-tion, and various states such as sleep deprivation and exposure to extreme temperatures. Stress, exertion, hyperventilation, and hypogly-cemia all result in increased adrenaline secretion, and increase one's sus-ceptibility to rhythmic auditory and visual stimulation.[16]

Mock Hyperstress Hypothesis

Prince[14] proposed the mock hyperstress hypothesis, which asserts that artificial threat situations (e.g., nightmares, psychoses, ecstasies, trances), although potentially disturbing, are actually helpful healing states because they generate the release of endorphins. Many times the individual will then experience a deep state of peace and euphoria, commonly interpreted as divine intervention. The hyperstress hypothesis may also help explain the elevated emotionalism observed in energizing religious practices cross-culturally.

Emotionalism is a foundational characteristic of energizing spiritual practices. Indeed, energizing spiritual practices are designed to elicit certain emotional experiences and behaviors. Across the multiple cul-tures that engage in energizing spiritual practices there are a few common themes. All of these practices involve rapid music or drum-ming. Research has consistently demonstrated that music elicits spe-cific physiological changes through activating the nervous system.[17] Extensive research on music has documented that fast-tempo, percus-sive, rhythmic, and loud, dynamic music is arousing and causes increases in heart rate and muscle tension, creating an escalation of activity in the sympathetic nervous system. In contrast, slow-tempo, melodic, legato style, and soft, dynamic music decreases arousal and leads to decreases in heart rate and muscle tension, as well as increases in skin temperature and skin resistance. These characteris-tics are related to parasympathetic nervous system activity, the body system that creates physiological relaxation. Researchers have also suggested that when an individual listens to music, he or she internally mimics the expression, and the physiological feedback induces the same emotion in the listener.

In addition to the activation of endogenous opioids, a physiologically based theory has been offered to explain how fire handlers can hold their hand in the flames, without burning themselves. Ample research has demonstrated that the experience of pain is not a linear function of the objective stimuli or degree of tissue damage (e.g., hypnosis as a substitute for anesthesia, soldiers in war reporting no pain until after the battle, shark attacks during which there is no immediate pain). Psychological factors, such as beliefs, attitudes, expectations, attention, anxiety, and conditioning, play an important role in the perception of pain. Given these findings, it has been asserted that fire walkers and fire handling church members can handle the coals and flames without injury because their beliefs and expectations in the trance state influence their neural activity, initiating the release of neuropeptides, and mobilizing a protective nervous system process.[10] As with Prince's mock hyperstress model, the element of danger causes a release of stress hormones, creating increased muscle tension and resulting in vasoconstriction. The coldness and numbness that the handlers report—which notably is the only place to which they touch the flame—is a result of peripheral vasoconstriction, and is one of the factors that inhibits inflammation and damage.[10]

APPLICATIONS FOR MENTAL AND PHYSICAL HEALTH PRACTITIONERS

While scientific research has largely focused on spiritual practices that calm the spirit, we feel that the concept of energizing spiritual practices has been largely overlooked in both clinical practice and the research literature. Across a number of disciplines, there is early research beginning to show the benefits of energizing practices.

DANCE THERAPY

The value of physically energizing practices to manage chronic pain, which may involve energizing the spirit as well, has begun to receive recognition. For example, research has shown that dance therapy is efficacious for the treatment of rheumatoid arthriti.[18] In this study, "vigor" improved while pain and depression decreased after a 16-week program of "enthusiastic dance-based aerobic exercise" in a program called EDUCIZE. Other research in dance therapy has supported this earlier research by showing positive mental and physical health benefits to patients with chronic pain. While there is currently limited research addressing whether these benefits can be explained solely by increased physical activity, the findings do suggest that increasing physical arousal for short periods over a number of weeks can create a decrease in the pain experience.

Music Therapy

Similar to research emphasizing calming spiritual practices, the majority of music therapy research focuses on decreasing physiological arousal, and emotional reactivity to stress. Calming music therapy has been strongly tied to spiritual experiences in palliative care and pain medicine as means to strengthen the spirit and to enhance spiritual well-being. However, a recent study focused on the physiological arousal related to emotionally powerful music, which was differentiated from loud music and fast music. The emotionally powerful music was shown to increase physiological arousal based on vasoconstriction and skin conductivity biomarkers.[19] In other areas of music therapy, actively participating through the production of music, clapping, drumming, or free body movements to melodic or rhythmic sounds appears to create better physical and emotional outcomes than passive listening to music or standard physical therapy. Even the rapid beating of the drum during periods of intense breakthrough pain can provide a physical release of the pain sensation. Music therapy sessions that involve active participation and emotionally powerful music are similar to the energizing spiritual practices described in previous sections. The emotionally powerful music in worship and healing services engages the listener and may facilitate the psycho-physiological hyperarousal that decreases the experience of pain.

Charismatic Worship and Music

A recent study examined the emotional effects of the P/C style of music and worship. Miller and Strongman[20] found that participants in a P/C church had a significant increase in positive mood directly before the service, which increased during the time of worship. In the second part of their study, they compared a P/C group and a non-P/C group's reactions to religious and secular music. They found that the P/C group had a stronger "energetic" and "awesome" emotional reaction to the religious songs than did the non-P/C group. They concluded that music facilitates an emotional experience in a P/C church through familiarity and associations to music, and that music plays an essential role in shifting the mood of the worshipers.

PSYCHOTHERAPY

In the field of psychotherapy, there are also lessons to be learned from energizing spiritual practices. In both psychotherapy and bio-feedback for chronic pain, increasing patient arousal to states of hyperarousal and the impact of this arousal have been vastly under-studied. Health psychologists specializing in pain management often use calming psycho-spiritual practices to help a person increase their emotional control, improve their feelings of self-efficacy, and decrease their experience of pain. Entire books on topics such as pain management, decreasing stress, and improving mood are focused on decreasing physiological arousal. While these tools are certainly useful, and have been repeatedly empirically validated, it is quite possible that psychotherapists have been missing out on another significant potential resources. It is possible that energizing practices may be efficacious as well. Rather than encouraging decreased arousal, we should once again begin exploring, both clinically and in research, the value of cathartic arousal.

Some support for this assertion has been found in the exercise literature. The aerobic-activity research literature shows that moderate physical activity (and corresponding physiological arousal) is associated with decreased depression and anxiety, both of which impact the experience of pain. While we are limited in the conclusions we can draw, and we cannot identify if there are unique characteristics to encouraging energizing spiritual practices, it appears that it is a topic worth exploring with patients. It may be particularly useful with patients who report feeling bored or frustrated, or have difficulties with those activities that decrease physiological arousal such as meditation.

CONCLUSION

It has been argued that as children we learn when and how to express pain from watching others. We also learn what to do to decrease pain. One may choose to attribute the modification in pain intensity to the power of expectations, otherwise known as the placebo effect. For example, it is possible that observing others overcome painful conditions creates expectancies that participating in these rituals will also provide relief. Or, one may attribute this learned control over pain to cultural factors, consistent with the bio-psycho-social-spiritual model of pain. From the review of literature above, it also appears likely that spiritual factors—both meditative and energizing—play a role in the modification of pain.

However, if an individual feels a relief of chronic pain, is the methodology of that pain relief important? As the famous Buddhist quote states, "There are many paths up the mountain"; and when patients are struggling against the mountain of chronic pain, the more pathways available, the better for the patient. These pathways may include traditional pain medications, or medications affecting pathways we know to be involved in the pain interpretation process. These pathways may also include physical manipulation therapies such as occupational therapy, physical therapy, chiropractics, and massage. The paths also include multiple complementary medicine techniques, such as acupuncture, herbal treatments, and Reiki. However, we cannot neglect the spiritual pathways, including the entire pantheon of both energizing and calming practices. Given what we know about the neuromatrix theory of pain and the downward suppression of pain signals through cognitive, behavioral, and emotional states, it is possible that these highly focused, energizing, and elevated spiritual states also create a physiological pathway that down regulates the pain signals, providing partial or total pain relief.

Moderate physical exercise of various types has been recommended for chronic pain patients as part of a multidisciplinary pain management program. The physiological arousal caused by exercise could be part of the formula that explains the pain benefit of energizing spiritual practices. However, simple movement alone is not likely to explain the overwhelming sensations and altered states of consciousness reported cross-culturally by participants in energizing worship services and spiritual practices. As this chapter demonstrated, there are more questions than answers regarding the role of energizing spiritual practices. But as this field continues to develop and engage new ideas for the treatment of chronic pain, it will be exciting, and dare we say energizing, to empirically discover the answers to these questions.

REFERENCES

1. Melzack, R. (1999). From the gate to the neuromatrix. *Pain*, *6*(S1), S121–S126.

2. Wachholtz, A. B., Pearce, M. J., & Koenig, H. G. (2007). Exploring the relationship between spirituality, coping, and pain. *Journal of Behavioral Medicine, 30*(4), 311–318.

3. Andersson, R. H. (2008). *The Lakota Ghost Dance of 1890.* Lincoln: University of Nebraska Press.

4. Poloma, M. M, & Pendleton, B. F. (1989). Religious experiences, evangelism, and institutional grown within the assemblies of God. *Journal for the Scientific Study of Religion, 28*(4), 415–431.

5. Owen, C. (2008). Whirling dervish dance: Where the dance comes from and what it means, http://worlddance.suite101.com/article.cfm/whirling _dervish_dance#ixzz0Cs8L5eLp (accessed April 16, 2009).

6. Ralte, L. (2006). Dance theology in Mizo tradition, http://www .mizobooks.com/dance_theology.htm, (accessed April 29, 2009).

7. Poloma, M. M. (1997). The "Toronto blessing": Charisma, institutionalization, and revival. *Journal for the Scientific Study of Religion, 2*(36), 257–271.

8. Poloma, M. M, & Hoelter, L. F. (1998). The "Toronto" blessing: A holistic model of healing. *Journal for the Scientific Study of Religion, 37*(2), 257–272.

9. Bromley, D. G. (2007). On spiritual edgework: The logic of extreme ritual performances. *Journal for the Scientific Study of Religion, 46*(3), 287–303.

10. Kane, S. M. (1982). Holiness ritual fire handling: Ethnographic and psychophysiological considerations. *Ethos, 10*(4), 369–384.

11. Colman, A. D. (1997). Pain and surgery: The Shamanic experience. In D. Sandner & S. H. Wong (Eds.), *The sacred heritage.* New York: Routledge; : 125–137.

12. Price, C. A., & Snow, M. S. (1998). Ceremonial dissociation in American Protestant worship. *Journal of Psychology and Christianity, 17*(3), 257–265.

13. Borg, J., Andree, B., Soderstrom, H., & Farde, L. (2003). The serotonin system and spiritual experiences. *American Journal of Psychiatry, 160*(11), 1965–1969.

14. Prince, R. (1982). The endorphins: A review for psychological anthropologists. *Ethos, 10*(4), 303–316.

15. Shumaker, J. F. (1995). *The corruption of reality: A unified theory of religion, hypnosis, and psychopathology.* Amherst, NY: Prometheus Books.

16. Neher, A. (1961). Auditory driving observed with scalp electrodes in normal subjects. *EEG and Clinical Neurophysiology, 13,* 449–451.

17. Krumhansl, C. L. (1997). An exploratory study of musical emotions and psychophysiology. *Canadian Journal of Experimental Psychology, 51*(4), 336–352.

18. Perlman, S. G, Connell, K. J, Clark, A., et al. (1990). Dance-based aerobic exercise for rheumatoid arthritis. *Arthritis & Rheumatism.* ;*3*(1), 29–35.

19. Rickard, N. S. (2004). Intense emotional responses to music: A test of the physiological arousal hypothesis. *Psychology of Music, 32*(4), 371–388.

20. Miller, M. M., & Strongman K. T. (2002). The emotional effects of music on religious experience: A study of the Pentecostal-Charismatic style of music and worship. *Psychology of Music, A30*(1), 8–27.

CHAPTER 13

A Pilgrimage from Suffering to Solidarity: Walking the Path of Contemplative Practices

Gerdenio Manuel, SJ, and Martha E. Stortz

This final contribution serves as a kind of paradigm case in two ways. First, it treats a specific form of stress, suffering, and it addresses three common characteristics of people facing loss: denial, isolation, and the need for control. Second, it reaches deep within a particular tradition, Christianity, for practices that address these characteristics: lamentation, intercession, and pilgrimage. While some of the practices in this book fall into the category of "calming" practices (Centering Prayer, mantram repetition, the Eight-Point Program), these practices are "expressive," more like the "energizing" practices discussed in Amy Wachholz's contribution. These practices handle negative emotions, which have an important place in psychic and spiritual health for individuals and communities.

Indeed, these practices have not just an inner dimension but a social dimension. Advocacy emerges as the outer dimension of lamentation, as those who mourn give voice to the sufferings of others. Accompaniment stands as the outer dimension of intercession, a focused solidarity with the suffering of another person or community. Finally, immersion, the ability to simply be present for and with others without judgment or distance, remedy or analysis, comes as the outer dimension of pilgrimage. In their inner and outer dimensions, these practices offer a powerful example of what Ignatius Loyola called "contemplation in action."

INTRODUCTION

The loss of a partner, the death of a child, an unexpected diagnosis, a job terminated, the devastating breakup, the experience of marginalization: suddenly and irrevocably the landscape of the familiar alters. People find themselves lost in the terrain of suffering. They seek solace; yet, denial, isolation, and need for control block the path.

Suffering fragments the soul, whether the soul of a person, a relationship, or a people. What was once integral implodes, and the pieces scatter from a center that no longer holds. Philosopher Simone Weil (1977) identified physical, social, and spiritual dimensions of suffering: physical pain, social degradation, and distress of the soul.[1] Coping with suffering requires "re-membering," literally, forging these scattered fragments into a new whole.

Contemplative practices point the way, for the journey from suffering to solidarity is a spiritual one. They reveal a path from denial to acceptance, from isolation to communion; and finally, from the need to control to surrender. Contemplation aims at union with God, "a long loving look at what is real."[2] Suffering makes God seem distant, remote, even cruel. Suffering blocks union with God, and the psalmist shouts in despair: "My God, my God, why have you forsaken me?" (Psalm 22:1).

Those words were also on the lips of Jesus, who is for Christians the human face of God (Mark 15:34). Through Jesus's life and death, God experienced the full range of human suffering. Through incarnation God comes into the midst of human suffering.

This contribution examines concrete contemplative practices that invite encounter with the suffering God. *Lamentation* encourages people to claim suffering, rather than cutting it out with the razor of denial. *Intercession* opens victims to those around them, who then become fellow travelers. Finally, *pilgrimage* places people on a path where the journey supplants the destination, pointing to the mystery of a suffering God.

Too often contemplative practices are prescribed as the remedy for individual suffering. We argue that they also point to solidarity with others. We met people whose hard-won compassion opened them to the suffering of others. These practices have then an outer as well as an inner dimension, creating solidarity even as they console. Speaking out for those whom affliction has silenced, *advocacy* becomes the outer dimension of lamentation. A focused solidarity with the suffering of others, *accompaniment* stands as the outer dimension of intercession. Finally, in its diffuse availability to the suffering of the world, *immersion* is the outer dimension of pilgrimage.

In their inner and outer dimensions, these contemplative practices connect personal suffering to communal and global realities. They knit together the personal and the social, offering a powerful example of what Ignatius Loyola (1556) called "contemplation in action."[3] In so doing, they carve a path from being a victim to becoming a survivor to acting for change in the world. This volume's title captures the impulse to solidarity: *Contemplative Practices in Action*.

We bring to this project our own experience of suffering, and we remain marked by the suffering of loved ones. As teachers and ministers, we have witnessed the suffering of near and distant neighbors. Finally, as citizens of the world, we have witnessed the genocides of Serbia and Croatia, Darfur and Rwanda, the killing fields of Cambodia, the prisons of Abu Ghraib, Guantanamo, and Tehran's Evin. We see the daily insult of poverty and disease. Suffering people seek the solace contemplative practices offer; they are aroused to action by the solidarity contemplative practices invite.

At the outset, we identify three concrete contemplative practices: lamentation, which moves people from denial to assent; intercession, which points from isolation toward communion; and pilgrimage, which liberates people from the need to control to surrender. In each section, we begin with experience, then examine the specific practice, concluding with its outer dimension. In this we hope to highlight the difference contemplative practices make, not simply for the one suffering, but for a broken world.

LAMENTATION: FROM DENIAL TO ASSENT TO ADVOCACY

In its inability to acknowledge what is real, denial is a first protest against suffering. Denial wants the world to be what it was before. Buttressed by excuses, fortified by fantasy, driven by dissociation, and quick to blame, denial takes work. Finally, it wears people out and wears them down.[4]

Moving out of denial takes work as well. Four stages capture the movement:

1. "This isn't happening!"

He was shocked. He had always known his wife drank a lot, sometimes to excess—but she was not an alcoholic! All she drank was wine and occasionally a little too much. He made excuses for her;

he believed her own excuses, telling himself she was just "coming down with something." When the children were younger and their mom was moody and lethargic, they believed him too. Now they were older. He felt under siege, on one hand from his wife's anger, on the other from their children's exasperation with them both. He talked to her about drinking, and he believed her repeated promises to cut back.

Then, one day when their mother was not home, the children confronted him.

They showed him all of her secret stashes of alcohol—including hard liquor. He felt tricked; he needed to talk. He had needed to talk for years.

This man faces multiple losses: the loss of a fantasy, a partner, his children's respect, confidence in his own judgment. If he is ready to talk, he is ready to move out of denial. That means leaving behind a pattern of behavior characteristic of denial: *making excuses* and *living a fantasy*.

2. "This isn't happening to me!"

For years he prided himself on not needing doctors. Regular exercise kept him lean. He looked good; he felt good; he convinced himself he was invincible. He had experienced some discomfort after eating for years but never believed it to be anything an antacid tablet could not relieve. Gradually, he lost his usual energy. When night sweats broke out, his wife marched him to the doctor, who had ordered preliminary tests for colon cancer, the disease that claimed his father. Now the doctor walked into the examining room looking worried: "Let's just hope we can stop it from progressing to the other organs."

This man felt he could be an exception, denying medical data that he had actually known, but somehow did not think applied to him. He ignored family pressure to be tested regularly; he had even ignored his own body's complaints. Moving out of denial means leaving behind an ingrained pattern of behavior: *dissociation* from information, from family, even from his own body.

3. "This *is* happening—let's find out who's to blame!"

When President Clinton read Philip Gourevitch's exposé on the Rwandan genocide, he angrily forwarded a marked copy to national security advisor Sandy Berger. "Is what he's saying true?" "How did this happen?" "I want to get to the bottom of this!" When news of mass slaughter first surfaced, Clinton had shown no interest. Once the story hit the media, however, he resorted to an excuse the German people used after the Holocaust: "How come we didn't know what was going on?" It was the same move President George W. Bush would make a decade later on Darfur.[5]

Rwanda was set on the administration's back burner until the pot boiled over. When the situation became too blatant to ignore, someone else was at fault. The fact that Clinton responded to Gourevitch's article so passionately indicates a readiness to acknowledge the slaughter, but an unwillingness to take responsibility. To do so, though, he has to abandon another pattern of behavior associated with denial: *the need to blame someone else.*

4. "I can embrace this."

In the immediate aftermath of her stroke, the woman woke every morning thinking it had all just been a bad dream. When she opened her eyes, she was in an unfamiliar room. Nurses helped her into a chair for breakfast. "A stroke paralyzed my left side," she repeated. As she improved, she recovered a sense of agency, and her mantra changed: "I'm using the purple tie-dyed cane my granddaughter gave me." She hobbled out of the skilled-nursing facility on her purple cane. Months later, she returned to the facility to thank her caregivers—and give them her cane: "Someone else may need it more than I do."

Denial is not reserved for addiction or willful ignorance. It is also used by people who have found their lives altered by forces beyond their control. Ambushed by her own circulatory system, this woman fantasizes the stroke was just a "bad dream." When she opens her eyes each morning, she can no longer maintain that fiction. Initially, she sees herself as a victim. Her early response represents a rudimentary lament: "A stroke paralyzed *me.*" She narrates her story as a victim of circumstance. Repetition forces her to listen. Gradually she claims her loss, asserting agency. She becomes a survivor: "*I* use a cane." As she heals, she becomes an advocate: she donates the cane to someone else. This woman has embraced her loss. She not only has let her loss "bless her," she ensures that her loss will bless someone else.[6]

This woman's story captures the clinical distinction between passive *suffering* and active *coping*. *Suffering* is something that happens to people, bearing down on them like a train with failed brakes. People who suffer refer to themselves in accusative case: "The stroke weakened *me*." *Active coping* is different. Picking up the pieces of loss, coping uses nominative case: "*I* use a cane to get my balance." Coping takes charge of suffering.[7] Beyond coping is *advocacy*: this woman gave her cane to someone else.

DEALING WITH DENIAL: THE PRACTICE OF LAMENTATION

The practice of lamentation moves people from suffering to assent to advocacy. Lamentation invites people to speak the unspeakable. As they put words around their suffering, they begin to cope, claiming an agency that has been trampled by silence. In finding a language for their suffering, they give voice to others, who find words to express their own afflictions. Lamentation gives public voice to pain, and in so doing it creates a space of resistance, even hope.

The psalms of the Hebrew Bible stand as classic expressions of personal and social loss. Almost a third are psalms of lament, signaling to worshipers that "authentic worship" emerges only when people bring their deepest pain and most flagrant examples of injustice before God. The God of the Hebrew Scriptures wants people to wail. Loss should not be left outside the synagogue: it belongs inside public worship. Otherwise, worship remains "a shallow affair."[8]

These laments address God directly, demanding response. The language is that of command. Over and over again, the psalmist orders God to "Listen up!" "Hear my prayer!" "Hearken to me!" (Psalms 5:1; 55:2–3; 86:1). At other times, the psalmist begs for compassion: "Have mercy on me!" (51:3; 56:2; 57:2). When God seems distant or remote, the psalmist wails even louder: "Don't rebuke me in your anger!" (6:2). "Don't be silent!" (109:1). The psalms of lament offer evidence that people suffering get to protest—long and loudly.

In these lamentations, the agency of the one suffering shifts fluidly between being a victim and being a survivor, between accusative and nominative cases. Lament itself invites a kind of agency. People still suffer—but they get to protest. That protest takes on a fourfold form. First, lamentation invites people to name the particularity of their suffering: "All your waves and your billows have gone over me" (Psalm 42:7). This graphic image carries the pain of suffering. Second, lament projects the very real presence of an enemy: "Many bulls encircle me ...

they open wide their mouths at me, like a ravening and roaring lion" (Psalm 22:12–13). Lamentation invites vivid descriptions of danger. Third, the psalmist wrestles with depression: "I am poured out like water, and all my bones are out of joint" (Psalm 22:14). Often, to calm an inquiet soul, the psalmist calls happier times to mind: "By the rivers of Babylon—there we sat down and there we wept, when we remembered Zion" (Psalm 137:1). Finally, the presence of God is as real as the presence of the enemy. Psalms begin in direct address, boldly addressing God as "You." In spite of everything, there is someone listening. Indeed, lament reinforces the sense that all suffering happens within the divine embrace. Lament joins with praise as part of a system of respiration that lives in God. Lament invites people into the divine mystery. St. Augustine observes: "If your love is without ceasing, you are crying out always; if you always cry out, you are always desiring; and if you desire, you are calling to mind your eternal rest in the Lord. . . . If the desire is there, then the groaning is there as well. Even if people fail to hear it, it never ceases to sound in the hearing of God."[9]

A survivor of 9/11 made it out of the collapsing towers alive, but many of his colleagues did not. He made a habit of heading to the ocean and yelling into the crashing surf: "How could you do this to us?" The practice consoled him. In the midst of aching loss, there was someone to yell at, someone listening. The psalms of lament tell us that the practice is deeply traditioned.

Having given voice to longing and despair, the survivor leaves words that someone else can use. Jesus reportedly died with the psalmist's lament on his lips: "My God, my God, why have you forsaken me!" (Mark 15:34). He could find no language to express his own pain, so he borrowed the words of Psalm 22. Someone else had been in that place, and their words became his.

The practice of lamentation invites people out of denial, urging them to voice their pains and express their loss in all its awful particularity. Lament leaves a language for others to draw upon, as they search for words that speak the unspeakable. Finally, advocacy is *speaking for* others, who may not have words of their own.

INTERCESSION: FROM ISOLATION TO COMMUNITY TO ACCOMPANIMENT

Suffering grinds people down. It is hard to experience anything but pain; it is hard for others to share that experience. The contemplative practice of intercession invites people to ask for what they need, for themselves and for others. It follows from the practice of lamentation: having found a voice in lament, intercession encourages people to use it. The outer dimension of intercession is accompaniment, which incarnates its prayer.

1. *Noli tangere!* Don't touch!

In the weeks after her husband died, the woman remembered grocery shopping at 5 a.m. She was awake anyway—but that was not the only reason. The truth was she could not stand to see anyone she knew. Their expressions of sympathy felt like body blows. When she had to go out later in the day, she wore sunglasses. In time, she noticed people giving her a wide berth: they nodded, but did not approach. That did not feel right either. She hated being alone.

From ancient times lepers were banished to the outskirts of villages and towns. In the Hawaiian chain, Molokai became an island leper colony. Anyone who had the disease was sent there with a one-way ticket. Suffering isolates people. They lose friends on top of everything else. While some can stand with them, others drop off the radar screen entirely. "It's as if this were contagious," the woman above observed. "If they get too close, they'll lose their partners too." The people she thought would be there couldn't—and people she hadn't even thought of turned up in their place.

People experiencing loss also isolate themselves, like the woman in this story. They exasperate friends who are able to be there. One of the woman's friends—it was not one of her "best" friends either—finally got so frustrated, she phoned the house and simply started talking to the answering machine: "I'm going to talk until you pick up the phone. I'm worried about you. We all are. We can't figure out how to help. You have to tell us what you need." Only then did the woman answer. Often people experiencing loss create what they most fear: isolation. Suffering imposes isolation; it takes a lot of determination on all sides to break through to connection.

2. Ask for what you need.

The adult children watched their parents diminish with growing concern. They still lived in the family home. But when the parents became too scattered to drive, the kids took away the car keys. Eventually, they even had to forbid their father to walk to the market, because he could not get across the street before the light changed.

When a crisis forced the children to deal with their mother's gathering dementia, they had to find a nursing home that would accept Alzheimer's patients. After intensive networking, interviews—and prayer, a bed opened in a nearby facility. "This is a godsend!" the eldest son exclaimed.

Crisis often clarifies need. Before their mother left a burner on all day, her six adult children had seven different opinions about what should happen. Then suddenly they knew what they needed. Finding the right facility took a lot of legwork, but for this particular family, it also took prayer. They asked for God's help, confident that the Creator of the universe would also be interested in finding the right place for their mother. After all, they had been raised in a tradition that taught them to "Ask, and it will be given you" (Matthew 7:7). They believed that God hears prayer. That did not mean getting what they had wanted all the time, but it did mean living in relationship with a God who responded, not always on demand, but in mysterious, even inscrutable ways.

3. It is important simply to ask.

The delegation from Santa Clara University had lunch at a tiny restaurant in the highlands of Guatemala. The only other customers were a group of dirty, sweaty people who ate quickly and left in flatbed trucks with blue tarps lashed over the tops. Later that afternoon, they visited a village that was the site of a mass grave. As the villagers told the stories of the civil war, one of them mentioned that a team of forensic scientists had been there that morning, exhuming bodies for identification. The group quickly realized they had dined alongside the scientists earlier that day. Stunned, a delegate asked: "What do you need?" There was a ready answer, and they heard it through the translator: "Pray for us. Go back to your own country and tell our stories."

Often what is needed is not as concrete as a care facility, a job, or a peace treaty. What comfort could this delegation offer a village ravaged by war? The villagers asked simply for their presence, their ability to be with them in their suffering. They asked for their voice, telling the delegates to share their stories. Finally, they asked for accompaniment in their struggle. Members of the delegation took accompaniment seriously, remembering the villagers' stories in their presentations and their prayers back in El Norte. "Those people are still with me," said a woman, "even after all these years." Intercession reminded her that people depended on her to bear their pain.

She carried those people—and they carried her. When suffering pushes people beyond the limits of human effort, there is nothing to do but be with people in their suffering.

BREAKING THROUGH ISOLATION TO CONNECTION: THE PRACTICE OF INTERCESSION

The practice of intercessory prayer opens people to connection with God, to their own needs, and to the needs of others. It frees people to be present to the mystery of divine compassion, and it frees them to be compassionate with one another. In its dimensions of address, praise, and petition, intercession leads necessarily to accompaniment.

Intercession begins in *address*; petitioners name the mystery to whom they pray. As the chapters in this volume show, religious traditions exercise great care in naming the one to whom they pray, because address simultaneously identifies both the speaker and the one spoken to. Historically, Jews refused to utter the name of God aloud, writing it as the unpronounceable YHWH. Human speech was inadequate. Muslims recognize the limits of language differently. According to a Sufi proverb, there are a hundred names of God. Humans know 99; only the camel knows the hundredth. The camel's knowledge preserves a space of unknowing. Mosques often display the names of God in gold-lettered calligraphy around the dome, so that believers literally can stand in the presence of the many names of Allah. Christians gather in the name of a Triune God. During the course of a worship service, that name is spoken over and over again. Often it is a signal for believers to cross themselves, as if to inscribe that name on their bodies. Repetition of the name recognizes that there are a lot of other gods out there, each eager to stake its claim. Like a licked stamp waiting for an envelope, the human heart stands ready to adhere to all manner of unlikely gods. This first part of intercessory prayer reminds believers of the reality that claims them.

Naming God simultaneously identifies the speaker. Addressing God as "Father or Mother" identifies the speaker as "child." Addressing God as "Creator" states the creature's derivative status. Addressing God as "Shepherd" claims the role of sheep, the chief characteristic of which is dithering. Whatever the name, intercession begins with address, and that address places the one praying in a certain posture before the mystery. Intercession invites connection.

After address comes *praise*, and praise both remembers and gives thanks. Praise flows naturally from address, for each of the names telegraphs a story. For example, "Creator" plays back to the story of creation; "Deliverer" remembers Exodus; "Father" or "Mother" recalls Jesus's unique and familiar way of addressing a sometimes distant God. Praise fleshes out the connection that naming identifies, reminding us to whom we pray and recalling a history of relationship.

Praise not only recounts the past; it *minds* believers toward a shared future. Like a magnet dragged through a pile of filings, praise orients them, turning toward connection. Parents train their children to "mind" them, so they do not have to watch the child's every move. In time, children internalize parental instruction. They learn to act in any given situation as their parents might expect. They have been "minded." The apostle Paul calls on this natural pattern, as he urges the community at Philippi to "mind" Christ: "be of the same mind, having the same love, being in full accord and of one mind.... Let the same mind be in you that was in Christ Jesus" (Philippians 2:2, 5). Praise places people in the posture of "minding" the God to whom they pray.

Address and praise ground petition, for petition presumes the connection that address and petition create. Petition may be the hardest part of intercession. In part, a culture that values independence stumbles over suffering. But in part, wants always get confused with needs. Actress Judi Dench recalls a holiday in Spain, where she sighted a pair of expensive shoes. She wanted those shoes with all the yearning of a 15-year-old girl. Her father suggested they consider the purchase over lunch. At a seafood buffet, shrimp caught her eye, and she wound up ordering the most expensive item on the menu. At the end of the meal, her father observed: "You've just eaten your shoes." Wants take people everywhere, now to shoes, now to shrimp. What do we really need?

A woman whose partner was dying confided: "I don't know what to ask for." As she sorted wants and needs, she realized she could always ask for prayer. Like the villagers, she knew she was surrounded by people who would carry her. All she had to do was let them. She discovered a prayer for such situations: "Behold and bless." It was the prayer she finally offered for her dying partner; it was the prayer people offered for her.

Intercession works to connect. It first establishes a connection with a God "in whom we live and move and have our being" (Acts 17:28). In connecting to this God, people find themselves drawn into the whole of creation. The member of the Santa Clara delegation put it well: "They are still with me." Intercession bears one another's burdens, accompanying people in their suffering.

> I am that child
> with a round face and dirty
> who on every corner bothers you with his
> "can you spare a quarter?"

> I am that child with the dirty face certainly unwanted
> that from far away contemplates coaches,
> where other children emit laughter and jump up and down
> considerably. . . .

> I am that repulsive child that improvises a bed
> out of an old cardboard box and waits,
> certain that you will accompany me.[10]

PILGRIMAGE: FROM CONTROL TO SURRENDER TO IMMERSION

Suffering means loss, whether of one's abilities, one's relationships, one's homeland, one's sense of security. Whatever the tragedy, loss introduces the element of contingency. Nothing can be taken for granted; everything could change in a moment. Finally, all loss is a loss of control that defies competence and remedy, diplomacy and persuasion. The responses to sudden helplessness range from paralysis to manipulation to resignation.

1. "We admitted we were powerless."

He sat glumly in the meeting, listening intermittently to the speaker's story. He did not want to be here, and the precipitating events were a blur. Then, words his wife shouted last night in the midst of a lot of yelling floated to the surface: "You're out of control!" She'd threatened to leave if he did not come, and now he was part of a whole new family: the family of Alcoholics. That's how everyone introduced themselves. As the meeting closed, everyone read the 12 Steps, and the first step echoed his wife's words: "We admitted we were powerless."

If he sticks it out, this man will learn a valuable lesson: he is not in control. For years, alcohol controlled his life, and his resulting behavior has controlled his family. If he stops drinking, they have all got to change. His addiction was a center of gravity for the whole family; no one can imagine what recovery looks like. But no one will get there without taking a first step.

2. From grief to?

She lost her husband of 25 years just 25 months ago, she thought ruefully. Despite the age difference, they had been a great match, sharing professional interests like business, personal hobbies like golf and hiking. Now he was gone. Initially, she had been devastated, losing weight even as she lost herself in work. Now she just felt an aching loneliness, grief in a different key. People were beginning to "set her up" with people or opportunity or even travel. She turned everything aside that felt like going backward. She knew that after 25 months people expected some kind of plan of where she was going. She had none. All she knew was to keep going forward, destination unknown.

Popular literature reminds people that "grief is like a fingerprint": everyone's experience is distinctive. Yet there are some commonalities, and this woman's story displays them. Early grief feels like shattered glass. Gradually, time rounds the rough edges. A lot of people grieve the acute pain of early grief: it makes them feel somehow closer to the one they mourn. Yet, the physical and emotional intensity of early grief is hard to maintain over time. Even if they do not know where they are going, people move forward. Sometimes they fast-forward to a "New Normal," catapulting themselves into a new relationship or situation. Addiction literature calls this "doing a geographic"; inevitably, unresolved grief catches up. A better strategy is to limp ahead, without knowing exactly where the path leads. Often, as in this case, the only direction available is the certain knowledge that there is no going back.

3. "Core of love"

"She had four children in five years. The most significant thing that happened to her in her life, she told us, was losing one of those children to cancer when he was five years old. 'I don't talk about this very easily,' she said, looking down and speaking very quietly, 'but it was pivotal for me. It changed my life—jelled it in a profound way. I have an image that comes to mind about that time. It's of a white fire roaring through my life and burning out what was superficial, frivolous or unimportant and leaving a core of ... I don't think there's any other word for it than love. A core of love. It's hard to convey what that means.' "[11]

The loss of a child ranks as one of the cruelest, and this woman puts it graphically. Yet, the "huge fire" she describes could have left a lot of things in its aftermath: rage, bitterness, despair, or simply black ashes. How did she find herself in this space of love? Love symbolizes ultimate connection between two people. It is a delicate balance between enmeshment, where one self dissolves into another, and narcissism, where every other self functions as nothing more than a mirror.

THE PATH FROM CONTROL TO SURRENDER: THE PRACTICE OF PILGRIMAGE

What points the path from control to surrender? The ancient religious practice of pilgrimage offers a compass. Understood as "a transformative journey to a sacred center,"[12] pilgrimage may take people to sites *held* holy by a religious tradition, Mecca or Jerusalem. Or pilgrimage may take them to sites *made* holy by intense struggle or bloodshed, like Auschwitz, the killing fields in Cambodia, the battlefields at Gettysburg or the beaches of Normandy. Pilgrimage can also be more personal. People use the term to describe visits to the residences of authors or statesmen or even celebrities. Indeed, the homes of Emily Dickinson or Jane Austen attract a kind of reverence usually seen in places of worship. Finally, whether it floats to consciousness or not, people who visit gravesites are on pilgrimage.

Whatever the destination, pilgrimage involves a journey, with the planning travel requires and the dislocation it brings. Further, pilgrimage involves some kind of physical effort, often walking, whether on a trail, through a graveyard, or from room to room. Even journeys described as "inner pilgrimages" employ some regular physical practice, like mantram repetition, yoga, or Centering Prayer.[13] As is the case with all spiritual practices, pilgrimage invites "the body to mentor the soul."[14]

Many world religions look on pilgrimage as a spiritual practice, and Islam recommends that every pious Muslim make the *hajj* at least once a lifetime. Medieval Christians made their way to Rome or Jerusalem or Santiago de Compostela. They walked to do penance, seek healing, visit holy sites or the relics of saints. Their journals recount stories and companions along the way. At the outset, the point of pilgrimage seemed to be reaching the destination. Along the way, though, the journey became an end in itself. Wherever its destination, pilgrimage taught believers to travel light, be receptive, and rest.

Since pilgrims carry everything they need on their backs, they find out very quickly to *travel light*. Pilgrims physically feel the weight of their possessions, and as they plod along they may well begin to ponder how their possessions in fact possess them. Everything borne on the back registers on the feet. In a spirit of surrender, pilgrims learn to let go of all but the essentials.

Like pilgrimage, loss strips everything away. The mother above remembers that the death of a child hollowed her out. It cleared away everything "superfluous, frivolous, or unimportant," leaving behind only emptiness. Janis Joplin (1970) put it more bluntly: "Freedom is just another word for nothin' left to lose."[15]

The experience of loss creates a terrible freedom. Just as the pilgrim chooses what she will carry, one whom suffering has hollowed out chooses what will fill the emptiness. That is the freedom. The danger is that anything can fill that hollowed space: love, peace, bitterness, despair. That is the terror.

It is not clear that Bill W., founder of Alcoholics Anonymous, studied pilgrimage, but he certainly understood emptiness. Alcoholics Anonymous speaks of that "God-shaped hole" in every person. Twelve Step programs encourage people in recovery to fill that hole with spirit and not spirits, with divine mystery and not substances: "Let go and let God." Alcoholics Anonymous also picks up on another dimension of pilgrimage: *receptivity*.

Because they carry so little, pilgrims learn to receive. Dependent on others for food, for shelter, for companionship, pilgrims relinquish control over their surroundings. Wrestling with pain and fatigue, they relinquish control over their own bodies. Whatever the weather and whomever the company, pilgrims move forward into a space of surrender. On the way, they discover the daily graces. Grace comes incarnate in the person of shopkeepers and concierges, hospitalers and fellow travelers. Unbidden and unmerited, the kindness of strangers sustains pilgrims along their way: a sign of divine compassion.

Physically and spiritually, walking is work, and pilgrims relish reaching the day's destination. *Rest* becomes a mini-sabbath, and pilgrims learn to honor it. Tutoring people in rest and sabbath, pilgrimage emphasizes *being* rather than *doing*. Pilgrims are not *doing* anything. They may begin by thinking they will *achieve* their goal of making it to Mecca or Jerusalem, but it does not take long to be disabused of that idea. The point is as much making the journey as reaching the destination.

A woman who climbed Kilimanjaro put it this way: "The other members of our party spoke of *conquering* the mountain, I think the mountain *let itself be climbed*. I understood 'majesty' after that climb." Only in retrospect did she identify the climb as pilgrimage, but she put its sense of sabbath into words. Just as she leaned into the mountain, pilgrims lean into the holy.

Together traveling light, learning to receive, and honoring rest: these aspects of pilgrimage cultivate a spirit of surrender that is at the heart of pilgrimage. Surrender works to unclench the grip of control, acknowledge life's contingency, giving thanks for what has been and being hopeful for what lies ahead. In these three aspects of letting go, receptivity, and rest, pilgrimage is similar to Centering Prayer, itself an inner pilgrimage. Jane Ferguson's chapter in this volume suggests striking similarities.

Pilgrimage extends outwardly into immersion. Many colleges and universities offer opportunities for "immersion experiences," which take students abroad for an in-depth encounter with another culture. Minneapolis's Center for Global Education offers immersion experiences to interested adults, and Director Orval Gingerich is quick to distinguish them from mission trips or service learning projects: "We encourage people to go as receivers. We want to disabuse them of the idea that they have something to offer. We want them simply to receive" (O. Gingerich, personal communication, July 10, 2009). The Ignatian Colleagues Program runs a curriculum for college and university administrators, part of which involves a 10-day immersion in a Third World country. Director Edward Peck calls this part of the program "pilgrimage," and he reminds participants: "You're not there to give; you're there to receive" (E. Peck, personal communication, July 7, 2009).[16]

Why do this? Immersion affords a kind of deep knowing of something else, and that knowledge has a double edge. It opens both to beauty and to pain. Describing a sport he loves, long-distance runner Richard Askwith (2008) captures that double-edged knowing: "The man who is truly at home in the mountains . . . enters into an intimate relationship with them is so deeply in touch with himself."[17] Such intimacy bears pain as well as beauty. Askwith claims it is crucial to get "cold, or wet, or lost, or exhausted, or bruised by rocks or covered in mud. . . . The point is not the exertion involved, it's the degree of involvement, or immersion, in the landscape. You need to feel it; to interact with it, to be in it, not just looking from outside. You need to lose yourself—for it is then you are most human."[17]

Immersion returns to incarnation, for this athlete gives a luminous description of the divine immersion in humanity, living deeply into the beauty of being human—but also into the suffering. Through Jesus Christ, the divine-human, God became one of us, even to the point of death. Jesus laments, and he draws on the psalms to give voice to his suffering. Jesus asks for his own suffering to be lifted, interceding with the divine parent for his burden to be lifted. Then, as he dies, he intercedes for the very people who put him to death, asking his divine parent to forgive them. Finally, his entire life on earth was a pilgrimage. Some would say it led only to Jerusalem and his death. We argue that it led deeper and deeper into the human soul. God knows suffering, because God has been there. In these contemplative practices we walk in the steps of an incarnate God, a God who suffers with us. This was how God came to know the beauty and pain of being human.

CONCLUSION

Retrospectively, we recognize that the entire journey from suffering to solidarity with others and with God has been a pilgrimage. These contemplative practices invite us to follow in the footsteps of Jesus, who leads us deeper into the mystery of being human. At the same time, as they did for Jesus, they take us further into solidarity with the suffering of all people. Poet, essayist, and farmer Wendell Berry has a beautiful poem that ends with the counsel to "practice resurrection." These contemplative practices invite us to "practice incarnation."[18]

REFERENCES

1. Weil, S. (1977). The love of God and affliction. In G. A. Panichas (Ed.), *The Simone Weil reader* (p. 440). Mt. Kisco, NY: Moyer Bell.

2. Burghardt, W. (2008). Contemplation: A long loving look at the real. In G. W. Traub (Ed.), *An Ignatian spirituality reader* (p. 93). Chicago: Loyola Press.

3. Loyola, I. (1970). *The constitutions of the Society of Jesus* (G. E. Ganss, Trans.). St. Louis, MO: Institute of Jesuit Sources. (Original work published in 1556)

    4. Kubler-Ross, E. (1997). *On death and dying*. New York,: Simon & Schuster.

    5. Gourevitch, P. (2006). *Just watching*. *The New Yorker*. http://www .newyorker.com/archive/2006/06/12/060612ta_talk_gourevitch (accessed August 5, 1009).

    6. Rolheiser, R. (1999). *The holy longing: The search for a Christian spirituality*. New York: Doubleday.

    7. Anderson, H. (1993). What consoles? *Sewanee Theological Review*, *36*(3), 374–384.

    8. Pleins, J. D. (1993). *The Psalms: Songs of tragedy, hope, and justice* (p. 15). Maryknoll, NY: Orbis Press.

    9. Augustine. (1975). In Psalmo 37:13–14. In *The liturgy of the hours* (p. 303). New York: Catholic Book.

    10. Schnabel, J. (Director). (2000). *Before Night Falls* [Film]. New York: Fine Line Features.

    11. Ray, P. H., & Anderson, S. R. (2000). *The cultural creatives*. New York: Three Rivers Press/Random House.

    12. Cousineau, P. (1998). *The art of pilgrimage: The seeker's guide to making travel sacred* (p. xxiii). San Francisco: Conari Press.

    13. Several chapters in this volume emphasize the importance of specific physical disciplines: rhythmic breathing (e.g., T. Anne Richards, "The Path of Yoga"), silence (e.g., Jane Ferguson, "Centering Prayer"), or the repetition of a word or phrase (e.g., Jill Bormann, "Mantram Repetition," Tim Flinders et al., "The Eight-Point Program of Passage Meditation"), or even repetitive motion (e.g., Amy Wachholz, "Shaking the Blues Away").

    14. Brown, P. (1988). *The body and society: Men, women, and sexual renunciation in early Christianity*. New York: Columbia University Press.

    15. Kristofferson, K., & Foster, F. (1970). *Me and Bobby McGee* [Janis Joplin]. On Pearl [CD], New York: Columbia (1971).

    16. For more information on the Center for Global Education, see http:// www.centerforglobaleducation.org. For more information on The Ignatian Colleagues, see http://www.ignatiancolleagues.org.

    17. Coffey, M. (2008). *Explorers of the infinite*. New York: Penguin.

    18. Berry, W. (1994). Manifesto: The mad farmer liberation front. In *Collected Poems: 1957–1982* (pp. 151–152). San Francisco: North Point Press.

CHAPTER 14

Contemplative Practices in Action: Now What?

Thomas G. Plante and Adi Raz

This book has attempted to bring together many different and thoughtful voices among professionals who specialize in the integration of spiritual and religious contemplative practices and apply these practices to the development of a higher quality life by enhancing well-being, stress management, wholeness, and healing of body, mind, and spirit. They come from Eastern and Western traditions as well as the integration of the two. They represent Jewish, Muslim, Christian, Hindi, Buddhist, Zen, and other approaches. To our knowledge, no other book has offered this integrative and multitradition approach to applied contemplative practices in both a scholarly and practical way.

The various religious and spiritual traditions all have something important to offer us in terms of contemplative practices. While there are only so many voices that can be heard in one volume, it is clear that there are several unified factors or commonalities present among the traditions. Oman well articulated four similar functions that are elemental in many of the contemplative systems discussed in this book. Most approaches involve setting aside time for practices that reshape and train attention; most also include strategies for centering oneself throughout the day, cultivating personal character strengths, and drawing inspiration and guidance from spiritual exemplars or models. Many of these contemplative practices are more similar than different in terms of their approach and outcomes, while language, culture, and history make each unique and special, perhaps suitable for some people more than others.

Too often we hear in the news and in professional circles that there is a great deal of misunderstanding and often tremendous conflict among and between the religious and spiritual traditions. Many professionals are also not well versed in spiritual and religious matters including contemplative practices.[1] In this project, we brought together Jewish, Muslim, Christian, Hindi, Buddhist, Zen, and others for thoughtful, reflective, and productive collaboration. Some of the contributors include members of the clergy as well (e.g., a rabbi, a Catholic priest, a Zen priest) and several colleagues who are very closely identified with their religious and spiritual tradition and who are devout. Throughout the process of developing this book, including an all-day conference in late 2009, the contributors openly discussed their chapter ideas and learned from each other in a welcoming, honest, and thoughtful manner. They each read and commented on various drafts along the way as well. Everyone had the opportunity to provide feedback for each chapter on multiple occasions. Thus, the efforts of each chapter contributor were informed by careful and thoughtful feedback from all of the other contributors, and the project was therefore truly collaborative in every way.

This book project represents the third edited book that our team at the Spirituality and Health Institute at Santa Clara University have now published that bring together experts and students from the various spiritual and religious traditions in psychology, religious studies, public health, nursing, science, literature, and several other fields.[2,3] Our institute includes quarterly extended lunch meetings to discuss a wide variety of multidisciplinary and multifaith research, teaching, conference, and book projects as well as collaboration on many other related topics as they arise. We fondly begin our meetings with the question, "Where might the spirit lead us this time?" We are never disappointed at the end of our discussions. Our lunch table includes clergy, professors from many academic disciplines (e.g., psychology, religious studies, biostatistics, public health, engineering, philosophy, English literature), students from a variety of disciplines, and community leaders in faith-based, nonprofit, social service agencies. Perhaps this institute and current book project could serve as a model of what could be done elsewhere in both professional and lay circles. We do a lot on a little lunch money.

The religious and spiritual traditions offer much. There is much to learn and celebrate when thoughtful and well-meaning people with skills and perspectives that are informed by their spiritual and religious traditions come together and learn from each other with an open, caring, and respectful manner. Having table fellowship around meals helps to enhance the working and personal relationships as well. We hope that our book project will be a contribution in the right direction for interfaith understanding and benefits, and might stimulate further reflection, research, and application and in doing so, make the world a better place.

Since this volume was not able to address all of the contemplative approaches from the spiritual and religious traditions, future books are clearly needed in our view. Future projects might continue to examine how these and other contemplative approaches can be best understood and used in health promotion broadly defined. Further research may wish to expand in both the empirical and theoretical direction. Empirical research might examine how contemplative practices are most effective with certain populations as well as what role belief in and practice of contemplative practices might play in obtaining the greatest desired effect. Future research may also investigate the effectiveness of these practices from a cultural, socioeconomic, or religion of origin lens in order to determine how these factors might influence their effectiveness in daily life. As we could offer only but a taste of what the world's religions and spiritual traditions have to offer in regards to contemplative practices, future volumes may wish to examine traditions not represented in this book (e.g., Sikhism, Jainism, Taoism, Confucianism, Shamanism, Paganism). Furthermore, many additional contemplative practices within the major traditions presented in this book could be discussed in more detail in future volumes. For example, the Christian tradition includes many different contemplative approaches from various Roman Catholic religious orders and traditions as well as many Protestant groups. Future research may also further investigate other contemplative mind-body connections, discussing the myriad ways in which, for example, exercise from hiking in nature to dance can be both contemplative and healing within a particular contemplative practice system. A further look at the use of nature or dreams in contemplative practices may also be warranted in subsequent volumes as well.

It is apparent that there are many options for individuals to choose when using contemplative practices to make the lifestyle change from mindlessness to mindfulness. The various chapters in this volume address using contemplative practices to better manage the many challenges that arise in daily life. It is our hope that this book will serve as an enlightening and thought-provoking guide to those searching for a more thoughtful, mindful, spiritual, and contemplative path to healing, stress relief, and overall well-being, perhaps for themselves and for others with whom they work. We hope that this book has brought forth a way for individuals to experience a new tradition or provided some insight into how their own tradition approaches the contemplative path. Contemplative practices in action can be both wide and deep with many roads to follow. Perhaps all lead to a better quality of life when used thoughtfully and sincerely.

REFERENCES

1. Plante, T. G. (2009). *Spiritual practices in psychotherapy: Thirteen tools for enhancing psychological health*. Washington, DC: American Psychological Association.

2. Plante, T. G., & Thoresen, C. E. (Eds.) (2007). *Spirit, science and health: How the spiritual mind fuels physical wellness*. Westport, CT: Praeger/Greenwood.

3. Plante, T. G., & Sherman, A. S. (Eds.) (2001). *Faith and health: Psychological perspectives*. New York: Guilford.

Index

About the Editor and Contributors

The Editor

THOMAS G. PLANTE, PhD, ABPP, is professor of psychology at Santa Clara University and adjunct clinical professor of psychiatry and behavioral sciences at Stanford University School of Medicine. He directs the Spirituality and Health Institute at Santa Clara University and currently serves as vice-chair of the National Review Board for the Protection of Children for the U.S. Council of Catholic Bishops. He is president-elect of the Psychology and Religion Division (Division 36) of the American Psychological Association. He has authored or edited 12 books including, most recently, *Spiritual Practices in Psychotherapy: Thirteen Tools for Enhancing Psychological Health* (2009, American Psychological Association) and *Spirit, Science and Health: How the Spiritual Mind Fuels Physical Wellness* (with Carl Thoresen; 2007, Greenwood), as well as published over 150 scholarly professional journal articles and book chapters. Through his private practice he has evaluated or treated more than 600 priests and applicants to the Roman Catholic and Episcopalian priesthood and diaconate and has served as a consultant for a number of Roman Catholic dioceses and religious orders.

The Contributors

JILL E. BORMANN, PhD, RN, is a research nurse scientist at the VA San Diego Healthcare System and an adjunct associate professor at San Diego State University School of Nursing. She conducts a program of research on the health benefits of a mantram repetition intervention in both veteran and nonveteran groups.

DARLENE COHEN ROSHI, MA, is a Zen priest and Dharma heir in the Suzuki-roshi lineage, trained at the San Francisco Zen Center. She is conducting a National Science Foundation–funded study on the relationship between Zen and stress reduction in the workplace entitled "A Study in Contemplative Multi-Tasking," which is based on her book *The One Who Is Not Busy*.

ANDRE L. DELBECQ, PhD, is the J. Thomas and Kathleen McCarthy University Professor at Santa Clara University, where he served as dean of the Leavey School of Business from 1979 to 1989. His research and scholarship have focused on executive decision making, managing innovation in rapid-change environments, and organizational spirituality. He is the eighth dean of Fellows of the Academy of Management. He currently directs the Institute for Spirituality of Organizational Leadership at Santa Clara University, which conducts dialogues between theologians, management scholars, and executives.

DIANE DREHER, PhD, is a professor of English at Santa Clara University. Her most recent book is *Your Personal Renaissance: 12 Steps to Finding Your Life's True Calling* (Perseus).

JANE K. FERGUSON, DMin, is Parish Partnerships Director for Catholic Charities CYO in San Francisco.

CAROL FLINDERS, PhD, has taught courses on mysticism at the University of California–Berkeley, and the Graduate Theological Union–Berkeley. Her most recent book is *Enduring Lives: Portraits of Women of Faith and Action* (Tarcher/Putnam).

TIM FLINDERS, MA, is the author of *The Rise Response: Illness, Wellness & Spirituality*, and coauthor of *The Making of a Teacher*. He teaches courses on contemplative spirituality at the Sophia Center for Culture and Spirituality, Holy Names University, Oakland, California.

AISHA HAMDAN, PhD, is an assistant professor of behavioral sciences in the College of Medicine at the University of Sharjah, United Arab Emirates. She has authored over 100 international magazine articles, several journal articles, and two books related to Islam:

Nurturing Emaan in Children and *Psychology from an Islamic Perspective* (forthcoming from International Islamic Publishing House).

HOORIA JAZAIERI, BS, is a graduate student in counseling psychology at Santa Clara University and is a research assistant at Stanford University.

DAVID LEVY, PhD, is a professor in the Information School at the University of Washington and has focused on bringing mindfulness training and other contemplative practices to address problems of information overload and acceleration.

GERDENIO MANUEL, SJ, PhD, is an associate professor of psychology and rector of the Santa Clara University Jesuit Community. He has published articles on coping with stress and traumatic life events, and the relationship of psychology, faith, and religious life. He is a Jesuit priest as well as a clinical psychologist.

DOUG OMAN, PhD, is adjunct assistant professor in the School of Public Health, University of California–Berkeley. His research focuses on psychosocial factors in health, especially spirituality and religion. A major current interest is applications to spirituality of Albert Bandura's social cognitive and self-efficacy theories. Oman's research publications have explored how longevity is affected by religious involvement, how to conceptualize and measure spiritual modeling (the social learning of spiritual qualities), how various modes of meditation may foster spiritual modeling, and how spiritual modeling may be integrated into college education. He has led randomized trials of spiritual forms of meditation for college students and health professionals.

MICHELLE J. PEARCE, PhD, is an assistant clinical professor in the Duke University Medical Center, Department of Psychiatry and Behavioral Sciences. She is trained in clinical health psychology and helps medical patients cope with the stress and lifestyle changes of chronic illness.

ADI RAZ, BS, is a counseling psychology graduate student at the Institute of Transpersonal Psychology, Palo Alto, California.

T. ANNE RICHARDS, MA, is an interdisciplinary social scientist in anthropology and psychology. She retired from the University of California–San Francisco and –Berkeley and now continues working on special projects. She is a graduate of the advanced-studies program at the Yoga Room in Berkeley. Her publications include: "Spiritual Resources Following a Partner's Death from AIDS" in *Meaning Reconstruction and the Experience of Loss* and "The Effects of a Spiritually Based Intervention on Self-Management in the Workplace: A Qualitative Examination" in the *Journal of Advanced Nursing.*

SHAUNA L. SHAPIRO, PhD, is an associate professor of counseling psychology and author of numerous articles and chapters on mindfulness. Her recent book is *The Art and Science of Mindfulness* (American Psychological Association).

HUSTON SMITH, PhD, is Thomas J. Watson Professor of Religion and Distinguished Adjunct Professor of Philosophy, Emeritus, Syracuse University. For 15 years he was professor of philosophy at MIT and for a decade before that he taught at Washington University in St. Louis. Most recently he has served as visiting professor of religious studies, University of California–Berkeley. Holder of 12 honorary degrees, Smith's 14 books include *The World's Religions*, which has sold over 2.5 million copies, and *Why Religion Matters*, which won the Wilbur Award for the best book on religion published in 2001. In 1996 Bill Moyers devoted a five-part PBS special, *The Wisdom of Faith with Huston Smith*, to his life and work. His film documentaries on Hinduism, Tibetan Buddhism, and Sufism have all won international. awards, and the *Journal of Ethnomusicology* lauded his discovery of Tibetan multiphonic chanting, *Music of Tibet*, as "an important landmark in the study of music."

MARTHA E. STORTZ, PhD, is professor of historical theology and ethics at the Pacific Lutheran Theological Seminary at the Graduate Theological Union and a consultant. She is author of *A World According to God* (2004) and *Blessed to Follow* (2008).

SARITA TAMAYO-MORAGA, PhD, is a Zen priest in the Suzukiroshi lineage and a lecturer at Santa Clara University in the Religious Studies Department.

AMY B. WACHHOLTZ, PhD, MDiv, is an assistant professor of psychiatry at the University of Massachusetts Medical School, and the health psychologist on the Psychosomatic Medicine Consult Service at UMass Memorial Medical Center.

ZARI WEISS focuses on bringing spiritual direction to the Jewish community and has written a number of articles on the subject. She is currently the chair of the Committee on Rabbinic Spirituality, a past member of the Spiritual Leadership Task Force and the Wellness Committee of the CCAR, and past copresident of the Women's Rabbinic Network.